Praise for Apela Colorado and
WOMAN BETWEEN THE WORLDS

"This book offers readers a rare view into the journey of how a Native American woman became a shaman. As Apela reveals her life story, it becomes obvious she was meant to live in two worlds this lifetime."

CAROLINE MYSS,
AUTHOR OF *INTIMATE CONVERSATIONS WITH THE DIVINE*

*"This book is alive,
and it will continue to grow by the reader.
There are many two worlds in this world, and they exist at the same time.
They look like mirrors, but they are slightly different because the
phenomena that occur in one tribe are connected to the phenomena
of other tribes, and evolve while influencing each other.
Apela is an important spiritual messenger who told me that.
And her journey and my (your) journey will continue to
grow throughout the world, linking through this book."*

EIICHI, INDIGENOUS SPIRITUALITY OF JAPAN RESEARCHER

*"Nothing is more essential for the future of the planet than an
honoring and integration of indigenous wisdom in every realm. In this
brilliant, poignant, profound, superbly written book, Apela Colorado
offers us the treasures of a lifetime of shamanic passion and practice
as well as a practical template for all of us to start our journeys home
to celebrating and protecting the creation and ourselves. This essential
book should be in the backpack of every seeker, every policy maker, and
all those passionately concerned for the birth of a new humanity."*

ANDREW HARVEY, AUTHOR OF THE HOPE: A GUIDE TO SACRED ACTIVISM

*"I know Apela Colorado as a special human who possesses the power of
Umai Ene [goddess of creation], and knows the secrets of the Universe,
Nature, and Humanity that turn her into a magic box which keeps
these mysteries alive. She is a child of snow leopards, a prophet of the
golden age, a limitless human whom I deeply admire and respect."*

MURATALIEVA ELMIR, KYRGYZ CLAIRVOYANT

"What a Life! What a Story! What a Heroine's Journey! This is a book that takes us far beyond the general ignorance of our culture in relation to the existence of subtle levels of reality. In brilliantly vivid imagery, it tells the story of the initiation of a modern woman of mixed heritage (both Indigenous and French) into the depths of shamanic experience and wisdom. This led her to many different countries and the encounter with modern shamans of ancient Indigenous cultures— ultimately to the recognition of her supremely important mission in relation to them. Her courage in the face of enormous challenges is formidable. The way her path opens out, stage by stage, as if guided by invisible hands, and how she learns to trust it, is both moving and inspiring. A rare book that is both a treasure and a wise guide for the soul."

ANNE BARING, AUTHOR OF THE DREAM OF THE COSMOS

"I have been on this sacred path for over twenty years, and have become one family with you since—like all indigenous people are. We met at Arashan for the first time when I was fifty, and since then, for the past ten years, we have been collaborating on spreading the indigenous science around the world and lighting the sacred fire Uluu Ot in different countries. Your idea of lighting the sacred fire became a huge endeavor that took us traveling to 13 different countries as we called for protectors to light a fire. The snow leopard descended, and we prayed for the well-being of all humanity, for its prosperity, and world peace. Soon I am launching a new project about the snow leopard to work with youth and spread the indigenous knowledge about it further. Thank you for helping me to find my mission in life. You are an amazing anthropologist, scientist, and shaman. And thank you to deceased Gengish ata and Sonunbubu apa for helping us!"

ZHAPARKUL RAIMBEKOV, KYRGYZ SHAMAN

"We are living in a time, when we are no longer believing and trusting in the strength of ancestry, which is why each time we are becoming without roots, without foundations, mere robots guided by cell phones. We need to reconnect with the true source of our being. We need to meet again. When we meet, we meet everyone around us, and everyone finds us, because our essence is pure light. Apela's vision of seeing the world and seeing the spiritual path, makes us feel confident that we are not alone in our spiritual journey. From here in my little corner in the Amazon rain forest, I can feel the echo of this strength, and I come to express my management and gratitude for the hard work that she has developed with the indigenous wisdom around the world, and now she can share with the world through this book."

TASHKA YAWANAWA, CHIEF OF THE YAWANAWA PEOPLE OF YAWANAWA TERRITORY IN THE STATE OF ACRE, IN THE BRAZILIAN AMAZON RAIN FOREST

"Apela Colorado has written a masterful book on her journey from indigenous roots to contemporary society and back again. She profoundly differentiates between the worlds she has experienced, and dynamically unites them into her being in a way that illumines both ancient and modern, sacred and secular, tribal and cosmopolitan. She is a true elder for our time, pointing the way to the human future."

JIM GARRISON, PRESIDENT, UBIQUITY UNIVERSITY; CONVENER, HUMANITY RISING SUMMIT

"I met Apela for the first time on a mountaintop of Arashan, a sacred site in the west of Kyrgyzstan. She said that she had been working on a project to unite indigenous people all over the world. With other two Kyrgyz elders, Gengish ata and Sonunbubu apa (both now deceased), I gave her my blessing to light the Sacred fire (Uluu Ot) to help indigenous people remember their past and that they were one. Apela has been on her task for the past 10 years, and I have been helping her. We traveled together to 13 different countries and connected Elders of Occitan, Buratian, Kyrgyz, Native American, African, Mongolian, Altai, and Hawaiian people, and prayed together for world peace and reconnection of the people with nature. I am currently working with youth and children to carry on my work and the legacy of the snow leopard, which blessed us for this work that first time in Arashan, when we lit our first fire to remember. May we never forget again, and may Apela live long and prosper in her life and work. May she become a Light Mother for the whole world, may she escape the bad things, and may good things shower on her as pouring rain, her path be open and wide. May the creator help us to stay astray from bad things, and follow good things in life. May we serve humanity and help the return of whales into oceans, and snow leopards to our mountain tops. And may the spirit of whales and snow leopard return to us."

NARGIZA RYSKULOVA, JOURNALIST, BBC RUSSIA

"I took some time to translate the beautiful text that is
the chapter called 'The Caves' in your book.
A beautiful story, great memories, beautiful writing.
Two things particularly moved me—the first is your approach to fight
against claustrophobia and the way you conquered it and overcame your fear.
The second is your receptivity in these caves,
witnesses of the spirituality of our ancestors.
First the perfect 'communion' with this underground world and
then these perfect exchanges between you and the spirits represented
by all these paintings, witnesses of the great artistic mastery of the
Paleolithic shamans, but above all, still messengers of their spirituality
and their wisdom, of their perfect understanding of this world
where we are only small elements to respect life in all its forms.
Another aspect awakened in me fond memories—the sound,
the songs, the xylophones, the growling of the felines.
And then your modesty—because it is thanks to you that several
people were able to see and participate in these caves, not in
visits, but in real communion with this Paleolithic world.
Of course, I am thinking in particular of those shamans
and medicine men who had the chance to see and
participate in these great moments, thanks to you.
So, in summary, bravo for your book, memory of time, witness of
experiences, which, like the paintings in the caves, will be there for
a long time, will survive you, and will allow others who will not
have the chance to come to this 'land of sacred caves' to experience
great moments thanks to your emotions and your literature."

PASCAL RAUX, AUTHOR AND PALEONTOLOGIST

"Apela Colorado has brilliantly illuminated the depths of Indigenous
knowing through stories she tells with honesty and humor in a
register wrestled back from the wreckage of colonial history. She
speaks of relationships and journeys that have shaped her life, with
powerful messages on how humans are to be. Woman Between
the Worlds is a gift to a world at a precipice. A bringer of hope."

GRACE NONO, PH.D., AUTHOR OF SONG OF THE BABAYLAN: LIVING VOICES,
MEDICINES, SPIRITUALITIES OF PHILIPPINE RITUALIST-ORALIST-HEALERS

WOMAN
BETWEEN THE
WORLDS

WOMAN

BETWEEN THE

WORLDS

A Call to Your Ancestral and Indigenous Wisdom

APELA COLORADO, Ph.D.

HAY HOUSE

Carlsbad, California • New York City
London • Sydney • New Delhi

Published in the United Kingdom by:
Hay House UK Ltd, The Sixth Floor, Watson House,
54 Baker Street, London W1U 7BU
Tel: +44 (0)20 3927 7290; Fax: +44 (0)20 3927 7291
www.hayhouse.co.uk

Published in the United States of America by:
Hay House Inc., PO Box 5100, Carlsbad, CA 92018-5100
Tel: (1) 760 431 7695 or (800) 654 5126
Fax: (1) 760 431 6948 or (800) 650 5115; www.hayhouse.com

Published in Australia by:
Hay House Australia Pty Ltd, 18/36 Ralph St, Alexandria NSW 2015
Tel: (61) 2 9669 4299; Fax: (61) 2 9669 4144; www.hayhouse.com.au

Published in India by:
Hay House Publishers India, Muskaan Complex,
Plot No.3, B-2, Vasant Kunj, New Delhi 110 070
Tel: (91) 11 4176 1620; Fax: (91) 11 4176 1630; www.hayhouse.co.in

A catalogue record for this book is available from the British Library.

Tradepaper ISBN: 978-1-78817-567-8
E-book ISBN: 978-1-78817-571-5
Audiobook ISBN: 978-1-78817-609-5

Printed and bound by CPI Group (UK) Ltd, Croydon CR0 4YY

To Merle Patnode
1899–1962

I Remember.

CONTENTS

PREFACE

Dene practitioners like Hanson Ashley tell us that Mother Earth is between worlds, meaning that the Earth is going through a great shake-up that will ultimately restore the life-support systems of the world. Since the 1980s, the United Nations and other venerable global organizations have recognized Indigenous Peoples as the last reservoir of knowledge for sustainability and admonished us to learn from this wisdom. But who knows how to do so?

Dorothy Ninham, Cultural Practitioner, immersed me in my Oneida heritage. She not only brought me back to myself but also provided a ceremonial template and process that helped me find my way home to French Gaul indigenosity, to ceremonies within the Paleolithic painted caves of southern France and to the Occitan People who, despite two thousand years of oppression, still keep the Ancestral fires burning.

In this moment of monumental, terrifying planetary change, we are compelled to choose: to align with the forces of nature or perish as a species. I was lost to both of my genealogies, Oneida and French Gaul. *Woman Between the Worlds* traces my journey back in time to reclaim a Creation Story for the future. Stories of my experiences are selected and presented to emulate the ceremony and to provide a template and guide for readers, or as the Oneida Creation Story says, "for those who move about on the face of the earth."

Chapter 1

Map of Remembrance

Iroquois Creation Story

Before the Earth's crust was formed, there existed a Sky World. A luminous tree so high that no one could see its top, so holy that fruit and fragrant blossoms ceaselessly nourished and blessed the People. Some say that the Chief of this world received a vision to cut down the tree; others attribute the destruction to the actions of Sky Woman. Either way, the sacrifice of the tree set earthly creation in motion.

Sky Woman was pregnant and craved a certain plant, which only grew at the base of a sacred tree. She made her way there and, against prevailing sanctions, began to dig at the roots to gather what she needed. It was then she noticed something odd: a hole had broken through among the roots. She leaned over for a closer look. Far, far below, she could make out another world, one that was in total darkness and covered with water. Curious, she leaned farther, still trying to get a better view. She suddenly lost her balance and fell off the edge. Frantically, she grasped at the soil of the Sky World, trying to hold on. As she did, small particles of seed caught beneath her nails, but nothing she did could stop her downward momentum.

Something in the heavens, a nearly indiscernible shift, caught the eye of the birds and water animals who already existed in the world below. Within seconds, the pinprick of light blazed into an electric blue-white fire, becoming more brilliant and enormous with each passing second. Sky Woman was coming to Earth. The animals knew it, and as they traced her trajectory through the heavens, they began to think how to protect and receive her. Something needed to slow her descent, and she would need a place upon which to stand.

A massive sea turtle rose and said, "She can stand on my back."

The animals considered this and responded, "Large as you are, she may rest on you temporarily, but even you are not big enough for her to walk on. We will need some earth."

They could say this with confidence because they knew there was earth far beneath the water, but they were unsure of how to get it. One by one, the animals volunteered, but the depth was too much. One by one, they died in the effort. The blue-white light grew closer. Time was running out.

"I will try," said the muskrat, the smallest and least likely to succeed.

The other animals looked upon the muskrat silently. Down he went, farther and farther, until his little lungs felt like bursting. Just when he could no longer continue his descent, his paw touched and grasped a small amount of earth. He turned and began the long ascent toward the light, but nearing the surface his need for breath grew too strong. He inhaled and passed from this world. His small body bobbed to the surface.

At the same time, the swans flew upward. Creating a sort of blanket with their wings, they caught Sky Woman, slowed her descent, and lowered her gently to the turtle's back. She stood for a moment, then bent over to open the muskrat's paw and remove the soil, which she smoothed on the turtle's back, all the while dancing in a counterclockwise direction and singing a song of power, of thanksgiving and honor for the animals that helped her. The turtle grew and grew and grew, finally becoming the landmass we now know as North America. Because the muskrat and other small creatures had given their lives for her, she promised to remember and to honor them. In recognition of the turtle's gift, she marked its carapace with 13 sections in the middle of the shell and 28 around the edge, thus creating the lunar calendar to remind us of the cycles of life and of our origins.

With the seeds beneath her nails, Sky Woman gifted us with our sacred plants of heart-shaped strawberries, the first fruit of spring whose fragrance is said to lead us back to the spirit world. She also gifted us with tobacco, whose leaves we burn when we want to communicate with the Creator.

Sky Woman's daughter, pregnant by the West Wind, gave birth to twin boys. "Right-handed" boy was good and was born naturally. "Left-handed" boy was so bad he refused to be born naturally and killed his mother. The good twin went about creating beauty on Earth, sweet-smelling flowers, gentle brooks, and rolling hills. However, everything he did in love, the bad twin ruined or destroyed. If the first boy created a flower, the evil one put thorns on it. And so it went, until one fateful day, the bad twin taunted the good twin into a fight. On and on they fought until, finally realizing that neither could ever win, they divided life, dark from light, which is the way it has remained ever since.

Sky Woman buried her daughter who became Earth Mother. Sacred plants of corn, bean, and squash grew from her burial mound.

Upon her death, Sky Woman's body became the sun, the moon—shining light in darkness—and the stars, her helpers.

Chapter 2

THE EARLY YEARS

*"When you're out of balance, you need to go back to the
Creation Story of your people. At that place of Creation
Emergence, you put yourself in balance and from that place
of Creation, tell your story in a new balanced way."*

HANSON ASHLEY, M.A., NAVAJO HEALER

How do we find our indigenous Creation Story and our place in it today? How did we lose it in the first place? And how do we find and complete our relationships with all of life and reconnect, especially if we've been cut off from our culture and ceremonial ways for generations?

In order for people to lose their identity, a lot has to happen. Repeated and ongoing trauma, war, genocide, expropriation, substance dependencies, and intergenerational losses at every level block the transmission of life-renewing ceremonies. But the holistic mind of our Indigenous Ancestors holds a secret. When all time is present, we can perceive and retrieve wisdom embedded in the great cycles of time.

The trick is learning how to let go of our fabulously elevated, rational, dissociative mind. It's not easy. Recovering our Indigenous Mind and the powers that come with it requires that we remember our stories both personal and collective. We must look into the darkness of our forgotten origins and histories, often without the benefit of an extant body of ceremonies to guide us. Those of us with European ancestry are doubly challenged as we carry histories of both victims who have been stripped of our indigenosity and perpetrators who have been part of colonizing indigenous tribes. Since the arrival of Europeans to North America, Indigenous People have been asking, "Who are you?" When we can answer this, our Creation Story reignites.

Looking back, I can see that I was not the first to lose track of my place in creation. Thousands of years ago, maybe 15 or 20 Iroquoian People separated from an earlier people in what is today's northern Mexico, and possibly from still farther south. We migrated up the Mississippi Delta, lending a hand to create the earthen animal effigy and pyramidal mounds that dot the eastern woodlands, including the Great Serpent Mound in Ohio. However, something went wrong, and the people we helped tried to enslave us, to force us to work, so we separated again and moved on, ultimately arriving in today's homeland of Upstate New York and Southeastern Ontario.

Leaving behind our would-be oppressors did not free us from strife. Instead, upon arriving in our new homeland, we dissipated into nearly 500 years of war with people who were there before us and then into internecine warfare. Life was hell in the Great Lakes region, until grace, in the form of a vision, visited a man we refer to as Peacemaker. We know but do not say his real name—that is how much we treasure his gift.

It was a waterfall, essence of Divine Feminine, that instilled in him a vision of spiritual democracy, a way out of our evil and torment into peace. Peacemaker traveled around the multitude of small agrarian communities to discuss and generate support for his dream. Everyone wanted an end to the unrelenting strife and readily agreed to the plan. The only opposition was one terrifyingly dangerous, powerful man called Tadadaho, a person so evil that snakes grew in his hair. His diet of choice was other human beings. All the tribes that make up the Iroquois Confederacy, Mohawk, Seneca, Oneida, Onondaga, and Cayuga wanted to see the Great Law of Peace instituted, but it was impossible to do so as long as Snake Head remained at large. The Peacemaker was undaunted and did what all smart men do: he sought counsel from a wise old woman who laid out the only possible way to confront Tadadaho. It was also very risky.

Peacemaker moved silently through the forest, coming at last to the wood's edge and Tadadaho's compound. Smoke rose from the vent of the longhouse's roof. Tadadaho was home. Skirting the compound cautiously and trying to remain concealed, Peacemaker ever so slowly made his way around the edge of the clearing to the back of the house. Still partially hidden among the trees, he peered carefully about, satisfied he had not been seen, and knowing Tadadaho would never expect someone to come near his home, Peacemaker stepped into the clearing and quickly crossed the grassy periphery to the exterior wall of the longhouse. With extreme caution, he climbed soundlessly to the roof. At the eave, he flattened his body and silently sidled along the roof's curvature to the smoke hole. Ear to the roof, he listened intently. Nothing. Then, seeking the whereabouts of Tadadaho, he leaned over the aperture to take a look.

It was mealtime. Tadadaho had put a large crown-topped clay pot to boil over his wood fire. He was hungry and had some lovely human parts to cook up, so he walked over to see if the water was hot. Just as he leaned over to look at the water, the Peacemaker looked down from the roof. What Tadadaho saw was not his normal hideous image, but the Peacemaker's reflection. With one glance, he fell in love with what he took to be his own image.

The story doesn't tell us exactly the workings of Tadadaho's interior experience, but whatever it was, the transformation was so complete that the Peacemaker was able to come down off the roof and converse with him. In the end and after much work, Tadadaho at last agreed to put aside his violence and cruelty and to become a part of the Great Law of Peace. In exchange and in recognition of the enormous power Tadadaho had, he became the Keeper of the Fire for all five, and later, six nations. Even today, the position is called Tadadaho.

For the truth to be real, it must be lived. I didn't grow up knowing my Creation Story but the story knew me, and I was about to discover what that meant.

Like a thread through a needle, we drive in and out of the deep North Woods. The varied vista displays lakes, moraines, kettles, and gentle hills on the 35-mile drive to my grandparents'. We got a late start because my dad had worked an extra-long day, but daylight still holds long enough that early fall afternoon for me to see my favorite stretch of the road, the Lac du Flambeau Indian Reservation. There is something magical about this part of the land. Even at age three, I can feel it. Nearing the reservation, I stand up in the footwell of the blue, 1950 Plymouth and press my face to the back window.

The log cabins, clustered about a grassy clearing, come into view. Little kids, my age and younger, run about, playing in their underwear or without any clothes at all. Afternoon sun dapples through the dark spiky spruce and the bushy maples and shines off brown glass bottles scattered across the lawn. Adults lie here and there, face down in the grass. I don't have to ask why. I've already seen enough of alcohol to grasp the meaning. Quickly, I look away from the passed-out adults and move to the children. Sunlight shines off the tiny brown bodies skipping and playing among the post-drunk debris. I'm captivated. There is a way out of the misery.

Just then, my father glances in the rearview mirror and, seeing my rapt attention, says, "If you don't behave yourself, we're going to leave you here with the other Indians."

"I'm not an Indian!" I retort, frightened at the aspect of being abandoned.

"Yep, you are. Ask your mother," he says.

"Bill, don't say that."

"Well, it's the truth. You are Indian. Tell her, Gerry."

My mom sighs. "You don't have to tell her that way." Then, turning around in the passenger seat, she meets my eyes and says, "Yes, you are Indian and other things too."

I slump back into my seat; the happy feeling is gone, and the familiar emptiness returns. My parents light their umpteenth cigarettes, filling the car with noxious smoke.

"Please open the window, I can't breathe," I plead.

My mother opens her window a crack. I lie down on the back seat, trying to get beneath the smoke, trying to find a way to be with what I've just been told.

Sometime later, I wake. It's dark. We've made it to Gramma and Grampa's. The buzz and flicker of fluorescent lighting welcomes me to the newly renovated kitchen of their two-story, white-framed farmhouse.

Merle, my grandfather's name, is French for "raven" or "blackbird." He has a dark side: a quick temper that burns hot. But he's also the one openhearted connection I have. Even now, all these years later, I can see him squatting down on his heels to be at my height and catch me as I come running and tumbling into his arms.

This night is no different. Grampa leans over and sweeps me up in his arms, and in a surprising departure from his normal greeting, he does something odd. Instead of showing off his new cabinetry or latest project, or bidding me good night and turning me back over to my parents, he turns and walks us over to the window. He jerks on the tangled cord hanging at one side of the venetian blinds. The blinds scrape up, but just on one side.

"Look," he says, pointing out the window. "See the moon?"

Everyone rushes over, excited. I don't understand what they are talking about, and Grampa senses this.

"Look, Apela, see the moon?" he repeats, gesturing with the side of his hand.

I can feel his excitement, but all I see is our reflection in the glass.

"See, see what's happening? It's getting dark. Nearly a full lunar eclipse," he says a bit breathlessly. "It's happening right now!"

He takes one more look at my confused face, turns, and rushes us out the kitchen door, taking the porch steps at a jog. Once we clear the porch light at the bottom, we slide into the darkness of the backyard, moments from the eclipse's culmination. Grampa turns us ninety degrees south to face the eclipse directly. He shifts me from his right side to his left, then points up with his right arm, and with the side of his hand, he traces the movement of the Earth's shadow as it creeps across the moon.

"Look, Apela, see?"

An enormous black mist slides silently, minute by minute, from the leading edge of the moon toward totality. At last, only the thinnest silver slice remains. A second, deeper night falls around us; hundreds of stars appear in the formerly moonlit sky, silhouetting the nearby chicken coop and duck pen. All sounds in the surrounding woodland stop, and in the eerie darkness, my head drops into sleep on Grampa's warm, Pendleton-wool-covered shoulder.

～～～

I'm only putting a half effort into hoeing. It's late afternoon, and Gramma wants to get to the weeds before they do serious damage to the corn, beans, and other vegetables. School's out for the summer, and I have a week's stay with my grandparents. Gramma always has something going on, including very small-scale businesses. She's a rep for Watkins, a line of herbs, spices, and vitamins she delivers to customers' doors along with eggs, fresh from her chickens. I get to candle the eggs to be sure none have been fertilized. I also get to pluck the pullets—a job I hate. Driving around Oneida County, making deliveries, and getting treats along the way is fun. Hoeing the garden is not fun, as evening comes on and mosquitoes begin swarming.

"We'll just finish this row," Gramma says, straightening up from her hoeing.

I barely hear her, as I'm too busy eating baby peas fresh from the pod. Lifting her head and stretching it from side to side, she notices a car stopped on the highway, about a third of a mile from us. As we watch, the driver gets out of his car and motions to us tentatively. Gramma waves back, saying she doesn't think she knows him. The man moves to the back of the car, opens the trunk, and begins rummaging around.

"He must have a flat tire. Oh, look, there's another car. They can probably help him," she says.

The second car pulls up behind the first. Another man gets out and waves at us. This time we don't respond. For sure we don't recognize the second vehicle.

When a third car slows and someone rolls down the window, Gramma simply ignores them and gets back to her hoeing. Knowing the only way out of the chore is to finish it, I pick up my hoe and join her. In a few minutes, we finish the row.

"OK, that's it for today; it's getting too dark to see. We've done enough, and the mosquitoes are getting worse."

Resting our hoes on our shoulders, we walk to the farmhouse. As soon as we get there, the first car that had stopped turns into our driveway.

The stranger bursts out of his vehicle, clearly agitated. "You are so lucky! Didn't you see it? The whole time you were hoeing, there was a big black bear standing right behind you. The thing was huge! When I first stopped, he was about 15 or 20 feet away from you, right there by that clearing."

He points to the distant path into the forest.

"Then he came closer and closer. I was trying to warn you; that's why I was waving; I went to my trunk to see if I had a shotgun, but I didn't. The other cars saw it, too, but none of them had guns either. We were afraid to make a move toward you; afraid we might startle the bear and make him aggressive. He got within a few feet of you. He stood right there behind you two, watching you work. Funny, the bear didn't do anything; he just watched, and when you came back to the house, he slipped into the woods."

~~~

It's one of those rare North Woods summer days when the sun shines, and a slight south wind dispels the swarms of mosquitoes that dominate the low-lying kettle and lake moraine landscape of Vilas County. Our white sheer kitchen-window curtains puff out and then draw back into their screens like the house itself is catching a breather. In the softness of the day, my younger brother and sisters are napping. Seeing a chance to read her magazine, my mom looks at her watch, glances my way, and says, "It's a bit early, but the mail should be here by now." This is her way of saying, Apela, go get it, and give me some time to myself.

Mail! I hate this daily chore. The mailbox is on the highway; a three-quarters-of-a-mile bike ride. It's not that far, but the road is made of loose gravel, and my steel bike is heavy with thick-gauge rubber tires.

I go out the back door and up the walk, looking longingly down the hill to the lake. It's so pretty—bright blue with a white birch periphery that shimmers in happy celebration with the sparkle of the waves. *I'm swimming when I get back*, I promise myself, and then I turn to face the old bike leaning against the garage. I stand it upright, hop on, and take the first heart-stopping pedals into the daunting journey. I've one thing going for me: even with a small frame, I'm strong, determined, and competitive. Off I race, down the hill leading from the house. I veer around the corner, skirting the swamp with its algae, frogs, and rare Jack-in-the-pulpit flowers. Gaining a bit of momentum on the straightaway, I settle back on the seat, tiptoes touching the pedals. The handlebars are jiggling and shaking, sending shock waves of vibration through my small brown hands as I struggle for control on the gravel.

Tracing the road is the single electric line to the house. Raspberries flourish in the disturbed area beneath it. I discovered the hard way that wasps and bees were also there. After the bushes come the open meadows, a safe, friendly spot in the trip. At night, deer feast on the lush grasses and enjoy a salt lick my dad has put up to attract them. We kids love that salt lick, not only because it draws the deer, but also because we like to eat it. Any sharp stone will do as a chisel, and we can knock off a piece. We all agree the very best parts are where the lick is worn smooth from the deer tongues.

I'm pedaling hard because the worst challenge is still ahead. The third hill. I've never yet made it to the top without stopping. I've tried everything; approaching with speed, taking it steady, but somehow I always run out of steam and have to walk my bike to the crest. Determined to break my record, I stand on the pedals and give it my all—thrusting and pushing first one leg then another against the heavy rubber pedals. I lean all my 80 pounds forward, but two-thirds of the way up, the bike slows, and then lurches to a stop. Gripping the pitted steel handlebars, I lower my head and try to run the monster up the hill.

Sweating and gasping for breath, I steal a quick glance upward to assess my progress. I stop dead in my tracks. Growing up in the woods, I've learned to pay attention to feelings. Bears, and occasionally wolves, still frequent the area. I glance about with soft eyes and almost no movement. There's nothing ahead, nothing to the right or back of me. The feeling grows more intense. I turn left and stifle a scream. A few feet away, on a small rise at the forest edge stands an enormous 12-point buck. I freeze; the buck is twice my size with dangerous horns and hooves.

What is a deer doing out in broad daylight, exposed? Something is way off. My heart pounds in my ears. Minutes tick by. A rivulet of sweat runs down my back. I don't move a muscle, and the deer holds his ground. Standing at a slight angle, he takes me in as if he knows me. I don't look directly back, hoping to avoid any perceived challenge. But I can sense that I am being observed. Riding back down the hill is out of the question. To turn the bike around, I'd have to expose my back to the animal; the movement might incite him, and I wouldn't be able to see if he was charging.

Finally, unable to bear the stress, I raise my eyes to meet my fate. The sounds of the forest fall silent. My shaking, sweaty body suddenly cools. Seconds—maybe an eternity—pass. The mist clears from my mind, and I perceive my own reflection looking back at me in the huge, soft, black eyes of the deer. A feeling comes over me, gentle but so strong; a feeling that will stay with me a lifetime as will the question of what this encounter means in my life.

Then, I'm back in myself. The deer remains motionless, watching me, but the moment is complete. I'm no longer afraid, but shy. I turn away and push the clunker bike a few steps to the crest of the hill where I seize the mail. I hop back on and pedal away for all my worth, not once looking back.

~~~

There's a black-and-white photo with old-fashioned serrated edges that captures the moment when everything began to change, right before we moved to the city and my grandfather's alcoholism became active and took him away. Pook, my long-haired black-and-white tomcat and devoted friend, is looking over my shoulder from his perch atop the upright half of a massive, vertically split tree trunk. I'm standing on the base, which is nearly three feet across, and I'm gazing at the rust-red heartwood, so old the pith is powdery to the touch.

The White Pine had stood guard at the isthmus of the mouth of our small bay for over two hundred years. It was the sole old-growth forest survivor of a logging boom at the turn of the century. Being the last of its kind, it held, in precious memory, all the bioenergetics of what had been a vast primal, boreal forest. This sole survivor, angled at thirty degrees over the shoreline, formed a canopy reflected in the blue water of the shore.

It wasn't until you beheld this tree that you understood what old-growth forest meant—what the loss meant. While all the other pines were about 10–12 inches in diameter, this one was nearly three feet in width, and it towered above all the others. Because of its height, it caught even the upper currents of wind. No matter how sleepless or heartbroken I was, the sound of wind moving through the tree's lofty needled branches put me to sleep.

Late one summer night, a storm came up. Although sound asleep, I woke with a start. From outside came a great deep, twisting groan, followed by an enormous crack. Then silence. At breakfast the next morning, my dad broke the news that the old tree had been struck down. I gulped down my breakfast cereal and ran to the backyard shoreline, fear thudding in my heart. Surely just a branch or part of the tree had broken off; the tree couldn't be gone. It had lived through so much worse—thunderstorms, lightning strikes, and bitter, freezing winters had not felled it. How could a wind destroy it? Clearing the end of the house, I stopped abruptly and stared in utter disbelief. Where the ancient pine had stood was a jagged, five-foot-high stump. Shards of gray bark clung from the stump to an edge of the stem, as if trying to make it stand. Most of its 60-foot length was submerged in the clear blue water. Small fish were already darting in and out of the piney canopy. The wind had twisted the trunk and cracked it open along one side; it looked like an open book. I felt so bad, I wanted to run away and cry, but something drew me forward.

I stepped up onto the lateral half of the split trunk. The golden rust-colored interior exuded a pure and clean fragrance. I leaned over and pressed my face against the exposed heartwood. The pith was still warm and seemed to draw me in closer. I knelt down, knees sinking in the soft wood, and pressed my entire torso against the trunk. Imperceptibly at first and then in gathering force, a radiant energy like the best hug imaginable filled me.

I stayed huddled on that ancient tree for a long time, losing track of everything but the wonderful feeling. Then Pook suddenly appeared. He padded along the top edge of the trunk, leaned down, rubbed his head against my sad face, and purred. Someone, I don't remember who, snapped the picture.

Soon after that photograph was taken, the entire extended family left the North Woods and moved to Milwaukee, a city that proudly proclaimed itself the beer-producing capital of the world.

A high school of 3,000 students replaced my one-room school in the woods. Even in this conservative midwestern city, my style of dress and hair were hopelessly dated, my Canadian-border pattern of speech invited ridicule and exclusion.

The wild, uncontrollable weekend drinking parties of my parents and relatives continued. They filled me with disgust for my family and for myself, but also fired my determination to never drink, to make something of myself. And there was that strange stillness and feeling that presenced itself around the table when the word *Indian* was uttered. In the blackness of this time, the phone rang. Grampa, my connection to love, to feeling, had just passed away.

At night, with neon light spilling into my room, I put my face in the pillow and wept with loneliness for the woods and for myself. I threw myself into my schoolwork, studying science, math, and Latin—things the church said a person needed to get into a university. I even signed up for summer school sessions to add to my resume. No one I knew had ever been to university, and I didn't even know there was one in my city. But over the years, my grandfather had repeatedly said, "When Apela grows up, she is going to university." Whenever he said this, the extended family looked at me and seemed almost to step back in awe—I was the one who would bring honor and respect to the family. I was determined to make advanced education happen.

ʕ•ᴥ•ʔ

Chapter 3

PROVING GROUND

*"Remember you will only have the Pathway
for the sign to remember."*

SKY WOMAN

Milwaukee, Wisconsin, 1962–1975

My late teens and early twenties were the beginning of my
awakening; the years I finished school, the years I had my children
and married. They were years of loss and of discovery, and the
beginning of an ongoing pilgrimage into my identity. I was mixed-
blood, half-breed. Sometimes, this was good. I did not have to
suffer many of the indignities and hardships of dark-skinned,
full-blood Indians. I did not have to live on a reservation during
a time when the US government required permits to leave. I did
not have to go to boarding or residential schools—institutions
dedicated to providing a trade, while missionizing, assimilating,
and exterminating the original cultures of America. I stood on
the margin, neither completely French nor completely Indian,
an edgy, dangerous place with undiscovered potency and many,
many questions.

After six years of completing my bachelor's degree at the University of Wisconsin, I enrolled in the master's degree program for social work and soon became part of the movement to regain American Indian culture and spirituality. Community meetings provided a transitional platform for the recovery of identity. If you walked into one of these gatherings, you would have seen beautiful young people steaming mad and dressed to kill in "nouveau tradition"— brilliantly colored ribbon shirts, beadwork, and turquoise. Power to the people! Right on!

We had to react; the struggle of Indian people required it. Beneath the youthful bravado was deep-rooted fear that remembering our culture, regaining our power, was impossible. Were we too assimilated or just not deserving of our identity and ceremonies? Had we become the White Man? There was an ever-present undercurrent of sorrow and distress. What if we did get it back, and the US government took it away again? The law was not on our side. Native ceremonial ways, even something as simple as burning cedar, were still illegal and would remain so until the passage of the American Indian Religious Freedom Act in 1978.

One day, in a particularly heated venting, Rufus Kills Crow Indians, a visiting Lakota Elder, cleared his throat. We took the cultural cue and instantly fell silent—the wisdom of the Ancestors was about to become manifest. Taking a step forward, Rufus said quietly, "The power's not lost; you are." And then he leaned back against the wall.

Shocked disbelief filled the room; resistance hung thick in the air, and although I'm sure he felt it, none of us voiced what we were thinking. *Who let him in here?*

But the truth is I *was* lost. Rufus had named it.

Being with another Oneida was the most precious thing to me. In the company of Native People, I felt as if I'd found my grandfather's love again. I cherished who I could be in this community, and I tried my best to fit in, to suppress my "otherness." But I was different—my family's connection to the tribe had been severed. Besides, I looked half-and-half. The more I tried to fit in, the more deeply alienated I became, for I'd left half of myself at the door. I performed daily tasks with a detachment bordering on numbness. I was surviving, but always looking over my shoulder, expecting to get thrown out. It was during this time that I started to meet the people who would shine light on the path my grandfather had so long ago laid out for me.

Ever the true Iroquoian matriarch, Dorothy Ninham had raised six children and dealt with an alcoholic husband by creating the country's first Indian alcohol intervention program. She had the awesome power of always "knowing" and usually having the last word. One day my friend Kimmy rode with me to the airport to meet Dorothy. She had heard me talk about Dorothy in such positive terms that she wanted to meet her.

On the way, Kimmy asked a good question. "What do you say when people tell you, 'It doesn't matter what my tribe is, I'm American now,'?"

"Well," I replied, "I might come up with a lot of answers, but who you really need to ask is Dorothy. She always has a snappy answer, and it's right too."

"She's that good, huh?"

"Yes, and this will be a good test. She'll be tired from the flight, so we'll see what she can do."

The baggage carousel groaned into life. Dorothy came up to me for a quick hug, and I introduced her to Kimmy.

"Dorothy," I said, "Kimmy has a question she wants to ask you."

Dorothy raised an eyebrow.

"Go ahead," I urged Kimmy.

"Well," Kimmy said, "I work with a lot of people who say, 'It doesn't matter what tribe my Ancestors come from, I'm American now.' What do you say to them?"

As quickly as I could turn my head from Kim to Dorothy, I heard the answer.

"You tell them, if you love this land, wait until you see your own."

This was a different view—a view that showed us a way back home. Dorothy had co-founded the American Indian Movement and single-handedly brought spiritual practices back to our community. She had compassion for all, including a lost mixed-blood like me. She often invited me to traditional ceremonies to help me in my struggle, but I always found a reason to turn her down. Finally, she stood in front of me one day, insistent.

"Apela, you're comin' into this ceremony if I have to drag you kickin' and screamin'!"

Dorothy was clued in, aware of my precarious single-parent life. My little girl was a toddler. One day, while dressing her, it hit me. *What do I have to offer her about who she is and where to stand in life?*

A week later, I found myself sitting up in a tepee for a nightlong peyote ceremony. I was fuming. The last thing I needed was another drug in my life. After all, I was working on a master's degree in the hope that I could help heal my family from the effects of alcoholism. In principle and in my research, I argued for the return of traditional ceremonies to heal our communities, *but* this peyote ceremony was new to our people. Originally performed in southwestern native cultures, the peyote ceremony had spread north with the Pan-Indian movement. I was suspicious. The popularization of marijuana, amphetamines, and other mind-altering drugs, which gurus like Harvard professor Timothy Leary promoted as doorways to expanded consciousness, did not bother me. I saved my apprehension for my culture.

The pale-green mason jar of dried peyote was accompanied by an eagle feather staff, water drum, and prayer song. Slowly, the jar was passed from person to person. How bad could this be? I wondered. Then, with a soft thud, it landed in front of me. I took the spoon standing in the gray powdery mix, scooped out a modest amount, and paused. I was tempted just to pass the jar to the next person, except I could feel Dorothy's black eyes watching me. God, she could be a pain. Resigned, I lifted the spoon to my mouth. The stuff tasted like a combination of aspirin and dirt. Worse, since it was a fungus, when it mixed with my saliva, it began expanding in my mouth. Dismayed, I realized I had to swallow quickly or I might not get it down at all! It felt like fire and tasted revolting. (Most Native medicine has a foul taste, which is one of the reasons we have few hypochondriacs in our cultures.)

I was instantly hit with an intense gag reflex. My body heaved as I struggled to keep the peyote down. *I'll get her for this*, I promised myself, too busy to even glare at Dorothy. When I finally got the medicine down and passed the jar, I looked up and took heart; I was not alone in my misery. Our ceremonial leader, Leonard

Crow Dog, a young, brilliant, and exceedingly handsome Sioux with straight, blue-black, waist-length hair, was having problems of his own. Against strict interdictions, he had been drinking and partying the night before, and the spirit of the medicine was having none of it. Shaking his head and rolling his shoulders forward in a clockwise direction, he fought off the waves of nausea and lost.

Out came the empty three-pound coffee cans. The "door man" had a nice supply of such cans ready for moments when the medicine purges the body of illness. The way it looked, Crow Dog was going to need all of them. He was being put through his paces. In fact, the medicine was sort of mopping the ground with him. His vomiting went on and on, in direct correlation to the level of his partying. Each time he lifted his head from the can, he ritualistically shook and then rolled his shoulders forward.

A few hours into this with no sign of let-up, Dorothy, aware of the Ancestors' presence and definitely not wanting to transfer the symptoms to herself, whispered, "Leonard, you might want to try rolling your shoulders in the opposite direction!"

Meanwhile, his uncle Rufus High Hawk brought the jar of medicine back, plunked it down in front of Crow Dog and said, "Eat more."

Having had personal experience with recreational drugs, I sat in my part of the circle, waiting for the rush, that feeling of a drug moving through the veins and mind. Suddenly, I found myself standing in utter darkness. Just as terror was about to set in, right in front of me, a blind lifted to radiant gossamer, white light. The instant I beheld it, it poured over me, so pure, so full, and so alive. Utter joy and peace infused me. The thought came like this: *The drugs I believed were recreational and transformative were utter darkness, and the medicine I thought was a drug is* life. *I have touched the face of God.* Then I was back into the circle, listening to the chants. Now, I could hear the voice of an unseen spirit woman harmonizing with the voices of the drummer and singer. It was powerful and overwhelmingly beautiful.

The morning after the ceremony, I made the 20-mile drive back to my parents' house to collect my young daughter who had spent the night with them. My entire body, mind, and soul were at peace. I'd barely gotten out of the car when our family dog trotted up and pressed the full weight of her body against my legs. She just wanted to feel the spirit coming off me. It was a short-lived moment. My dad came barreling out of the house and ran right up to me. His body trembled with anger. Somehow, he'd heard about the ceremony. Shaking his finger at my face, he hissed, "Your mother and I worked all our lives to get out of the poverty, and in one generation, you want to go right back to the blanket!"★

Months after the peyote ceremony, I dreamed about Grampa burying a black pipe in the earthen wall of the root cellar beneath his farmhouse. A black pipe draws its strength from the thunder and lightning and is very powerful. I had to know if my dream was true. If it were, it meant a direct connection to the essence of indigenous spirituality. Aunties Inez and Alta, my grandfather's sisters, still lived. I had to talk with them. They were my only chance; there were no other people in our family who could help me. I struggled internally, thinking how to ask them what my heart longed to know—that we were spiritual, Indigenous Peoples. Surprisingly, when I asked my mom for help, she readily agreed. I was deliberately vague about my true purpose.

★   An indigenous way of life. A "blanket Indian" was a derogatory term used to denote an Indian who refused to assimilate.

I needn't have worried. Like Grampa, his sisters were warm, energetic, and open. I told them about my dream, careful not even to glance at my mother.

Inez, the older sister, spoke first. "Doesn't surprise me at all. We never saw him with a pipe, but I wouldn't be surprised if he had one. Your grampa helped build the house we lived in when we were young. As the house was being completed, we had a blanket curtain dividing the bedrooms from the main part of the house. We'd wake up, and Merle would be gone. No one would hear him leaving. He'd be off in the woods for four days at a time."

My heart leaped. Four is sacred to Indians; ceremonies happen in fours—vision fasts are four days, sweat lodges have four rounds, and the movement of seasons is in four. Aunt Inez, slender and dignified, rose from her chair. This was important; I leaned forward.

"One day, our father took us kids for a ride in his Model T. He said he had something to tell us. We figured it must be important if he was taking us for a ride to tell us. It was. I don't remember all that he said, but I do remember him telling us, 'You're not just French. You're also Indian, but don't worry, it's good; our family never did too much scalping or anything like that.'"

I would have laughed, but Aunt Inez was deadly serious, and her words, spoken from childhood memory, were so strong that they charged the air with energy.

Silence filled the room. My mother never denied her Indian heritage but also did not embrace it. I wondered if she regretted helping me. For a while no one spoke. Minutes ticked by. Aunt Alta, already ill with cancer, sat quietly. With a slight nod of her head, she indicated her agreement. Then Inez, hands raised to her chest, calmly lowered them, palms down to her lap. She looked directly at me and Alta and said the words that made me fall in love with her and myself, "I'm proud of every drop of Indian blood that flows through my veins."

Unlike many of the urban Indians I worked with, I'd grown up in the North Woods and knew my trees. I was so reverent of the ceremonies I was just learning about that I was afraid to gather and dry cedar to burn and pray with. Herb, our activist leader, was the best teacher you could hope for. He taught by example. Inadvertently, he, too, gave me the green light to begin living my culture. When he wasn't busy raising hell and pressing for needed social change, Herb liked to pass the time of day lecturing to young, usually attractive, women, who worked with him at the Indian Center. Although he would never admit it, he was also learning his culture, mostly from nearby tribes like the Lakota, who were more culturally intact.

One summer day, Herb walked out of his executive office into our secretarial pool. He sported his uniform—black shades, blue jeans, cowboy boots, and shirt bedecked with four-directions ribbons that shimmered and rippled when he moved. We jumped up from our chairs and stood when he approached, out of respect and because if you wanted to keep your job, you needed to provide an attentive audience. In his hand was a three-foot branch of extremely dry cedar. Fifteen minutes into his monologue, we were shifting from foot to foot. He warmed to his topic— the importance of knowing our sacred ways and how not just anybody could up and do these things. Then, to our horror and to illustrate his point, he struck a match. The flame barely brushed against the tip of the evergreen spray when it burst into an enormous fireball, roaring and dancing off the end of his arm. "Oh, oh," he said, backing up as if to get distance from his own hand. As we watched him dance backward, none of us showed any expression or made a sound, although if you looked, you could see shoulders shaking from pent-up laughter. "Go get a garbage can, quick!" he snarled. "See, this is what I was telling you. You gotta know what you're doing with these traditions."

He'd made his point—two of them. First, there's a learning curve with remembering sacred ways. Secondly, if he could do it, I knew for sure I could, and as Herb had demonstrated, reverence is important, and so is humor.

~~~

Before we are born, 10 grandmothers give us gifts. The first five are direct, such as our name or our language. The other five are parallel or mirrored—gifts a person would like to forget, even as they are being revealed.

Life always involves choices, and through these choices, our gifts become real or not. When we get stuck or life gets hard, there are the ceremonies, but to an Indian way of thinking, these ceremonies are not something you just *want* to do—quite the opposite. In the ceremony, you are going to look into what Aztecs call the Smoking Mirror, the shadowed, hidden recesses of life and mind, to see—and worse, to experience—the source of the imbalance. In so doing, you return to a state of harmony with the original instructions or Ancestral Grand Plan. Indians will always tell you, "Don't ask for power; just keep yourself low." The reason is simple—power means work, and lots of it. It is not just work you want to do, it's work in service of others and of life. Often, people won't even say thank-you, and you won't make any money. It's not allowed.

For a while, I went through something I call SLF, sweat lodge freak-out. Panic would hit me at unaccountable and unpredictable moments in a ceremony. The fear was so consuming that I would have to ask permission to leave. I worried that interrupting the ceremony would damage it, and my panic squeezed me hard. There was no choice but to suffer the ignominy and leave. A Medicine Man told me I "had gotten in the way of something" during an earlier ceremony, and this was causing my claustrophobic terrors. I remember, during the onset of one such moment, arguing with myself to try to calm down and regain control.

Apela, how long have Indians been doing Sweats?

Well, about 40,000 years, at least.

And how many Indians have died in them during this time?

Hesitantly, the response comes—*none*. I started to relax, to breathe, but just then, quick-like, the thought jumps up, *But if they died, they would not be around to tell about it!* And out the door I went, one more time.

In a sweat lodge, the rational mind has to surrender. First, for me at least, there's a hell of a fight before surrender; suffering ensues, and finally comes the dawn, the release, insight, and renewal. When you crawl out of the lodge on your hands and knees and stand before the fire beneath star-studded skies, fragrant cedar steam pours off your body, and you know you are one with Life. The purity of self is a beautiful experience.

~~~

My master's degree student placement was with the American Indian Council on Alcoholism and Drug Abuse, which was also the national headquarters of the American Indian Movement. It was there, only a week or so after I arrived, that Joe Colorado walked through the door. He had completed a 30-day treatment program for alcohol addiction and was now doing aftercare. He was 100 percent Apache with long black braided hair, swarthy red skin, soft black eyes, and a beautiful white smile; we took one look at each other and fell in love. He looked like all I wanted to be, all I longed for in my native identity. I was all he looked for in his search to find a place in the white world.

Joe was born at home in San Carlos, Arizona. He woke to the sounds of the desert and to the song of his grandfather welcoming the dawn. At six years of age, he was removed from his home and put in the Ignacio, Colorado, Bureau of Indian Affairs (BIA) boarding school. There he learned, through physical and psychological abuse, that his color, language, heritage, and even the ways of his family were detested by mainstream culture. He was not returned home until age nine. By this time, his father and grandparents had died. Struggling to feed her children, his mother, Morelia, agreed to a BIA relocation plan that promised a job and new start in a nearby city. She was given a small allowance and a bus ticket to Los Angeles—and that's the last she heard of the BIA and their plan.

Shortly after arriving in the newly forming Indian ghetto, she remarried. This made their lives worse. The man, Hispanic and consumed with machismo, pushed her and the children into migrant labor. Earning 25 cents per hour for backbreaking, soul-crushing work, they still might have improved their desperate circumstances except that he took their weekly wages, locked them in the apartment, and went drinking. At night, if Joe slept, it was with rats running over his body and in mortal fear of a rat bite or a beating. What he had to keep him going was his heritage, and in defiance of his stepfather's insults and abuse, he kept his black hair in long braids. The kids at school mocked him, calling him "Chief" or "Stupid Indian," and ganged up to beat him. He persisted, intensely proud of the little he knew of his culture.

After high school, he enlisted in the US Marine Corps, seeing it as a way to fight for his land. He discovered quite the opposite. It was the time of the Vietnam War; all branches of the military were desperate to recruit for the unpopular war. Minorities, including American Indians, were targeted. Although Joe grew up in a boarding school and in Los Angeles, because he was Apache, the Corps made him a scout, one of the most dangerous jobs imaginable.

At the end of his tour, Joe returned stateside. Protestors were at the airport, throwing things at the disembarking vets, screaming profanities at the "fucking pigs." There was no debriefing, no posttraumatic stress treatment, nor any support for transitioning back into society. In order to cope, Joe had a helper; he'd returned home with alcoholism and drug abuse. Due to this and a related car accident on base, the military gave him a dishonorable discharge.

Joe and I shared everything—our American Indian Movement activism, cultural research—and together, we succeeded in finding and participating in ancient ceremonies forbidden by government policy. From the ceremonies and our study of history, we saw the beauty, power, and potential of Native ways in contemporary society and wanted to do more, to be more effective in the struggle to secure the rights of our people, and to find, renew, and apply sacred ways of knowing and being to pressing problems.

~~~

It was a warm spring day at the University of Wisconsin. The soft, moist winds of Lake Michigan, redolent of fresh cut grass, caressed my dry winter skin. With just a few minutes between classes, I ran to the registrar's office to get a transcript of my course work, the last piece of information needed to secure my first professional job as a social worker. Taking the stairs two at a time, I made it to the door minutes before lunch break. "Registration temporarily located in the basement of Merrill Hall" read the sign on the door. Back down the stairs I went, cutting across sidewalks and around ornamental shrubs to get to Merrill Hall.

Halfway down to the basement, the stairs took a 90-degree turn. Pivoting on my left foot, about to take the last set of stairs, I was confronted full in the face by a rather stark gold poster with a sort of earthy-brown font: "American Indians, Alaska Natives, and Hawaiians—Ford Fellowship Program."

I froze in my tracks, confronted with the possibility of something in myself I didn't even know existed. A calling—no deeper than that, more like a knowing or a drive in the depths of my being— told me I was going for a doctor of philosophy. The thought was absurd. I was a single mother with student loans. I was eager to be done with education and keen to start my life and get out of debt. I'd have to be crazy to think of more schooling. Still, I stood there, riveted.

Is this possible? Can I qualify? With a doctorate, I could have the power to do something in life; maybe find a way to heal the alcoholism in my family and people. I could support my girl and myself. People would listen to me. I could make a difference. My life could really matter.

Then, catching myself in the daydream and remembering why I was in the building, and figuring a mixed-blood without deep cultural roots would never have a chance, I told myself, *I am sick of school and being broke. I'm getting my transcript, getting the hell out of here, and getting a job. I'm done with this.* I said this with a flourish of bravado and went down to the registrar.

However, the memory of that sign haunted me. A few weeks later, I returned to the stairwell of Merrill Hall, wondering if I would still get that strange, soft electric feeling when I read the words, "American Indians, Alaska Natives, and Hawaiians— Ford Fellowship Program." The sign was gone! I went up and down the stairs, thinking maybe I'd gotten the wrong floor. I felt a sense of panic. It made no sense at all except to make me realize: *This is crucial to my life.* I tore up the stairs and ran to the regular registrar's office. Bursting through the dark wooden, 1920s-style double doors, I made my way to the registrar. A sign hung on the door, "Closed." Damn! Stamping my foot, I wheeled around to leave, and there, right before me on the hallway wall, hung the relocated sign. Panting with emotion, I stood stock-still before the gold-and-brown sign, which was a bit dog-eared and pin-holed from the move. This time, I really took it in. I was going to apply. I knew it with every cell of my being. I reached out and took an application form from the cardboard container taped to the sign; there were just two left.

Still, I resisted filling it out. I was afraid to want it. I was afraid to risk claiming myself, believing that all Native people save me had a strong, intact sense of identity. I read the fine print over and over, but there wasn't anything I saw that would eliminate me from the competition. Deep down, a search had begun. "Where is the Indian within that says yes?" asked my soul. I wouldn't listen. Instead, I defaulted to the main skill I'd learned growing up in an alcoholic environment—hypervigilance. Scanning the ethers again and again, attempting to discern any flicker of movement or portent of danger, I couldn't make out any immediate threat. But you can never be sure. I hung back.

Days, then weeks, slipped by. Each day of avoidance added to the intense ball of anxiety growing inside. The night before the deadline, I found myself at O'Hare Airport, looking down at the application form. Either I filled it out now in longhand and mailed it to ensure it made the next day's post-date, or I lost my chance. With an hour to wait before my flight, I dug into my purse, pulled out a pen, and found a notebook. First question: "Why do you want to pursue an advanced degree program?" I'd read the questions so many times over the past few days, I actually didn't even need to reread them. Still, I froze, mind blank, unable to respond. With a sigh, more like a soft cry of utter frustration, I gave up, shuffled the papers together, and rose to toss the document into a nearby trash can.

Looking up, I saw my grampa standing by the woodstove. I ran to his arms, overjoyed to see him. He knelt down on one knee and opened his arms. Just like always, I could smell the tobacco from his pipe and felt the familiar scratch of his wool shirt against my cheek. With my eyes closed in delight, I heard him say as if from afar, "Apela is going to a university, even if I have to get a job!" Then he laughed and drew me closer. Every one of my huge French Indian family gathered around the woodstove smiled. My grampa was industrious, independent, and self-sufficient. There was no danger he would work for someone else. I knew it, too, and smiled.

Then, I was back in O'Hare Airport. The vision was gone, but a power was there, and, in its grip, I sat back down and wrote the vision as it had come to me. The next day, I dropped the application in the mail. In spite of all its flaws—not typed and posted at the last minute—it was accepted. Later, a member of the review committee told me that even though my application basically looked like crap and did not follow conventional format, the love between my grandfather and me was so evident and his dream of education for me so compelling, the review committee had decided to award me a full Ford Fellowship.

Holding that acceptance letter in my hand, I knew for the first time, through and through, that there was something more to life. There was more than the emptiness and terror of intergenerational addictions trauma. There was something wonderful, mysterious, soft, exciting, and powerful, and it had to do with identity. This much I knew; after all, I'd seen the sign.

Upon my acceptance into the doctoral program in Boston, Joe applied, and was admitted, to a master's program at nearby Goddard-Cambridge. We rented a U-Haul, hitched up the old Ford Skyline, and Joe, my five-year-old daughter, and I headed for the East Coast. There our family grew with the arrival of a boy and a girl. However, far removed from our families, cultures, and land, stresses begin to build.

Chapter 4

TRUTH MUST BE
LIVED TO BE REAL

Xinjiang Autonomous Region, China, 1978

We had been in Boston for one year when Joe met Chung, an economics major in one of his university classes, and brought him home to meet me. Chung came from Hong Kong where he had worked as a chef in a prestigious five-star restaurant, a milieu in which workers were cruelly exploited. Through his intelligence and sheer backbreaking labor, he had raised funds and landed a scholarship to Goddard. His master's degree research focused on the social revolution in the People's Republic of China. Dynastical enslavement, in place for thousands of years, had been abolished. People had food to eat and single-room homes to live in. Free education and health care was becoming available for the masses. Chung told us China was instituting policies and forming relationships with Indigenous Peoples we couldn't even dream of in our own Land. A quarter of the Earth's population was emerging from hell into the bright dream of a Communist state where everything was shared and there were no hierarchical rulers. His message was riveting.

For Indigenous People, truth must be lived to be real. Joe and I wanted to experience China. If even a fraction of what Chung believed was true, it could be a key to healing the relationship between American Indians and the dominant culture. Looking for a way to get us to the PRC, Chung introduced us to the US–China Peoples Friendship Association (USCPFA), an organization dedicated to the normalizing of political relations between the USA and China. In less than a year, USCPFA gave us scholarships for a monthlong study tour. Even though we were with a group of non-Native people and did not visit tribal areas, Joe and I were so inspired that we wanted to share what we had learned. We believed that, if other Native people—especially Cultural Practitioners and young people—could see this miracle of social change, we would have the power to transform the life of our People.

It was a big dream. Getting a group of Native people to China wasn't an easy thing to pull off. Studies, part-time jobs, and parenting young children meant Joe and I could barely keep up with daily chores, much less care for our relationship. But we decided, no matter what it took, that we would do all we could to make this exchange happen. It took mountains of paperwork, but two years later, in 1980, the official invitation arrived. The US–China People's Friendship Organization was dedicated to fostering relations with the United States, thus our small, politically inconsequential group, the American Indian Trip to China, was not only welcome, but would be hosted by the nation and allowed to visit the autonomous cultural regions. All in-country costs would be covered, and a team of guides and translators would be provided.

We were going to make history, and we knew it.

~~~

Beijing guides—young, bright university grads—met us on arrival and stayed with us day and night. They also maintained a jam-packed schedule that ran like clockwork. Each day, we discussed history, Communist philosophy, development issues, and government relationships with cultural minorities. Our guides even knew an important, albeit obscure, historical link between American Indians and the Chinese. Knowledge of the Iroquoian democracy inspired revolutionary socialist Friedrich Engels to write the seminal treatise, *The Origin of the Family, Private Property and the State*, based on the notes left by Karl Marx. We were not happy with Engels's assertion that "tribal" was a primitive stepping-stone on the way to socialist utopia, but Engels had created common ground for our exchange visit. We were touched that our hosts had taken the time to learn about an obscure historical tie, something that rarely if ever happened in our own country.

As we traveled around, however, we began to see the dark shadow of China's brilliant success. Mao's 1950s Five-Year Plan, based in a gradual development approach, was succeeding. But radical party members wanted more, so Mao launched the Great Leap Forward, a plan and ideology to make the working people—China's greatest resource—work faster, better, and cheaper to overcome the lag in industrialization and mechanization. They waged intense propaganda campaigns, instituted agricultural collectivization, and communes, but their extreme, coercive push created a schism. Urban areas prospered at the expense of rural lands, a lag that our hosts acknowledged. What was not readily admitted was the suffering the "contradiction" caused Indigenous People.

Inner Mongolia and the Muslim Xinjiang Autonomous Region were cases in point. Mongolian and Uyghur people didn't want to relinquish their lands or their culture, and resisted collectivization. The promise of health care and schools for their young was not persuasive. Traditional healing and educational systems worked fine.

Two weeks into the trip, the glow of socialism/communism was beginning to fade. We appreciated the political briefings and discussions, but we were an indigenous group—we needed time alone, in nature, in ceremonies; we wanted to meet local Indigenous Peoples outside of structured meetings. Fortunately, three loose camels on a plateau in Mongolia unwittingly came to our aid.

The first mistake those shaggy-necked, two-humped Bactrian camels made was complacency. Overcast, pleasantly cool weather, and grass—thick, green, and delicious—added to their joy of finding themselves free on the pasturelands. Life was good. The second mistake the threesome made was curiosity. Our small bus barreling across the vast Inner Mongolian pasturelands captivated their attention as they looked on from a hilltop vantage point. They stopped for a look. The third mistake was severely underestimating us. Even as Indians and Mongolians came spilling out over the landscape, the camels did not understand the pent-up power of two geographically diverse tribes who have just discovered their shared nomadic, herding heritage.

Moments before the camels appeared on the distant rise, our Mongolian driver mentioned to the guides his need for a break. The three hours of intense focus required to speed across the nonexistent road, a grassland highway, had taken its toll. A second Mongolian had stood in the bus's stepwell, scouting out holes, rocks, or any obstruction. Periodically, in the middle of nowhere, he'd call for a stop to get out and look around. He would get his bearings through what seemed a featureless landscape, hop back in the bus, dip his right hand in a direction, and off we'd go. As Indians, we appreciated this.

"Look," Collins Horse Looking, Lakota traveler, suddenly yelled. "Camels! Stop!"

"Yes, yes," a choir of us responded. "Please stop."

The driver did. We looked up the hill; the camels looked down. Inspiration was born. Without discussion, the driver opened the door, and the Mongolian guides and Plains Indians took off up the hill to catch a camel. Our Chinese guides, who had made room up front for the Mongolian navigators, were still dozing in the rear of the bus. When they awoke, it was to shock—their charges had taken off and left them behind. Hurriedly and loudly, they consulted, apparently concluding that if they couldn't stop it, they'd join it, and ran to catch up.

The lag time between when the camels saw the men spill out and the realization that they were targets was impressive, especially for the nearest camel. When he figured out he should run, he turned to discover his buddies had already taken off. Thrown into a sort of paralysis, he allowed the bus people to encircle him, but no one had a rope or bridle. Then in a brilliant stroke of indigenous genius, one of the Mongolians sped down the hill and ran up to a young girl who had, unfortunately for her, chosen to hitch a ride with us. Excitedly, he pointed to the beautiful fluorescent-pink sash wrapped about her green traditional tunic. She stepped back. Words were exchanged, and then, even from the hilltop distance, we observed the slow, reluctant way she unwrapped and surrendered the long tie. Back up the hill, sash in hand, the Mongolian raced, reentered the circle, and cautiously approached the camel. Slowly, he fashioned a bridle around the head of the long-eyelashed, cud-chewing gargantuan.

Turned out the camel was a pleasant sort of fellow. He gave each of us a nice little walk around the bus and patiently stood still for the photo op. When we released him, he trotted back up the hill in search of his traitorous friends. That is how American Indians and Mongolians bonded in the land of Genghis Khan. The world's first Mongolian-Indian camel roundup brought us together as nothing else had. After that, even without a shared language, there was no more distance between us. The bus filled with the sound of laughter, and we traveled on.

~~~

Collins Horse Looking had been one of the last people to join the China trip. He wasn't particularly interested in the travel. But the Medicine Men from the reservation had prayerfully considered and determined that of them, Collins must go, find the right place, and pray with the Pipe. To me, this was the single most important thing we could do. Every day, I'd ask Collins if this was the place. No, he'd shake his head. I was anxious. We were running out of time and, unbelievably, given the size of China, we were running out of places. I feared that Collins might also be running out of energy for the job. Early into the second week, he'd looked sick, and now it was worse; he was gray-faced and sweating. It was then I discovered that he had scarcely eaten over the past two weeks because he didn't care for Chinese food. But it went beyond that.

Some of our delegation, Collins included, had never used chopsticks. Unfortunately, there was no cutlery in the People's Republic of China. One day, on a long bus ride, we decided to really get into the chopstick realm, and to laugh at ourselves. We discussed which were the best for what purpose, wooden versus lacquered, blunt versus pointy—the ones you never wanted to use if you wished to avoid embarrassment—the best kind to start off with, and so on. The guides jumped to the topic with zeal. A true chopstick master, they said, had to be able to pick up a slippery black cloche-top mushroom afloat in gravy sauce without dropping it or getting gravy on their clothes. Some of us, sporting stains on our rumpled travel wear, knew exactly what they meant.

Lakota are known for their sense of humor, yet Collins had not participated in the chopstick talk; he didn't even crack a smile, which was odd. Into our fifth course at the banquet that night, a waiter noticed that Collins wasn't eating, and asked if there was something wrong with the food.

Quickly Collins responded. "No, I'm just waiting for the camel," he said, and laughed.

A half hour later, the waiter reappeared, carrying a silver-lidded dish. Dramatically, almost reverentially, he placed the dish before Collins, lifted the lid, and announced, "Sweet-and-sour camel hump." Even worse for Collins, the server had somehow, in the middle of Mongolia, found a fork. Besides humor, Lakota are also known for their courage and respect. Without a word of complaint, the stunned Medicine Man managed to eat and hold down a decent-sized helping. Maybe it was this sacrifice that opened the way for Collins.

Late the next afternoon, looking about the verdant grasslands of the Tien Shan Mountains, Collins walked up to me and announced, "This is the place." Then he walked off. Out of nowhere, one of our guides came running.

"Where is he going?"

"To meditate." I hastened to add, "For US and China peoples' friendship."

I didn't know Collins's exact intentions, and it wasn't my business.

"He cannot go alone; there are dogs, and many things can happen," the agitated guide exclaimed.

"Look," I said, "this is important culturally. He must do this; it's one of the purposes of our trip."

A cloud of worry and uncertainty passed over the guide's face, but after three weeks of American Indian unpredictability, he sighed and relented. "OK, but I must go with him."

"All right," I agreed. "But when he finds the place to meditate, you must leave him alone."

He agreed and ran to catch up. About an hour later, the two of them came off that lush green hill as best friends.

~~~

It was noon when we stepped off the grueling, two-day train ride from rainy, cool Inner Mongolia into the desert inferno of Turpan. It was in the Xinjiang Autonomous Region, China's westernmost province and home to the Muslim Uyghur Indigenous People. We were dressed too warmly. We hadn't known the weather would be so different from the cool, overcast climate of Mongolia.

By now, we had all surrendered any notion that we would connect culturally with China's tribal people. Our itinerary was so busy, and we were so tightly managed, it hadn't been possible. All we could think about was getting to our hotel for a shower and a nap before resuming our packed schedule. But the minute we stepped off the train, we were hit with an uncomfortable feeling. Something was off; you could sense the tension. There were no local politico-greeters to meet our train, and there were no buses awaiting us, even though the train was on time. Our guides, clearly in a panic, left our group standing under intense overhead sun while they tried to sort things out.

A half hour later, to pinch-hit, they returned with a few local politicians who knew nothing about our group. They were cordial and delivered a smashing, impromptu, de rigueur, socialist welcome, including a description of how the region was developing and lives improving under the Chinese. An hour later, as the speeches drew to a close, and we were ready to faint from heat and thirst, the buses arrived. In a jumble, we piled on, and in minutes were in air-conditioned bliss on our way to the local Friendship Hotel where still more unpleasant surprises awaited.

A big group had just left, and our rooms were not ready. "Would you like some lunch?" the guides inquired.

"Yes, we would."

After climbing up to the second floor of an old building, we walked into a huge dining room dotted with round tables covered in dirty, food-stained tablecloths. Exhausted-looking staff, too few for the number of tables, had no food to offer except what was left over from breakfast. The socialist dream of equal shares of resources for all people was clearly not happening in this outlying region, contrary to what Chinese officials had proudly proclaimed in our cross-country trip briefings. The hotel workers, indigenous Uyghur cultural minority, looked beat-up, demoralized, and as coerced as American Indians. We had traveled so far and with such hope just to confront the same circumstances as home. Slumping into our seats, we tried to make the best of it. Yet another hour later, the rooms still were not ready, and the perpetually chipper guides urged us back on the buses. We were going to visit an ancient historic site, not on any foreign visitors' itinerary. We grumbled at the prospect of more travel, but the guides assured us it was a short drive and that it would fill the time creatively until the rooms opened up.

Ten kilometers from Turpan, we arrived at Jiaohe, an ancient Silk Road caravan city.

"Welcome to Jiaohe," our guide called out optimistically.

God, don't these guys ever rest? I mused, ruefully. As a coleader of the trip, I tried to find a scrap of motivation to support the guides and make the best of our situation, but I just could not get myself to leave the comfort of the Mercedes bus seat. With a sigh, I glanced out the window. The site—drab earthen ruins—didn't look too promising, but at least it was a change from the surfeit of cavernous, colorless, cheaply constructed Soviet-style buildings that we'd been in.

"This way, this way, this way," the guide said, urging us off the bus and waving toward some unimpressive adobe walls.

Even being in the front seat, I was among the last to exit. Joe shared my malaise. His foot had barely touched the earth when he turned, mumbled something, and ducked back in the bus. I watched as the group wended its way to a break in the walls and assembled around our Beijing guides who, surprisingly, had not noticed my and Joe's absence. Even from the bus, the high-pitched whine and buzz of the lecturer's microphone could be heard.

"Jiaohe is more than 2,000 years old. It is an ancient city along the Silk Road. It means 'two rivers,' because it is situated on a plateau between two rivers." The guide laughed. "There's a saying—where two rivers meet, there is bound to be intelligence." He pressed on. "Unlike other ancient cities, Jiaohe has no city walls, possibly because the town is surrounded on three sides by mountains, including Flaming Mountain in the north and the Tien Shan mountains in the west. None of the houses faced the street, so we think, maybe, they were worried about security. Jiaohe houses were not made in a usual way. People dug downward into the earth to create them. Also"— he paused as if considering whether to mention it—"recently, graves have been discovered. The desert is an ideal place to preserve artifacts and bodies, so we know they were Caucasian." He added hastily, "That doesn't mean they were not Chinese. Different people met and exchanged ideas in cities along the Silk Road. We see this in the murals of the time that are infused with foreign elements in the pigments, style, and religious symbolism."

The metallic voice faded in the background as I shifted my attention to my husband, who had now stepped off the bus and was quietly, almost imperceptibly, dissolving into the desert.

Despite the Bureau of Indian Affairs' assimilative and genocidal policies and practices aimed at eradicating everything Apache, they had failed to eradicate Joe's tie with his land. Learning to know, love, and merge with the desert had been an essential part of his upbringing. Each day in early childhood, Joe's grandfather took him out in the desert, hoping to show him how to find his way around. Joe was young and easily distracted. When they returned home to the camp, his grandmother would look up, and his grandfather would shake his head gently. "We would have been lost today." One day, Joe got it, and *he* led the way and walked his grandfather out of the desert. That was right before he turned five and the government grabbed him. Even then, his traditional training continued. In the summer, when he was returned home, his uncle showed up, and despite his mother's protests, he took Joe off into the desert for weeks at a time. Once, they were gone for two full months.

For most of us, the word *desert* conjures up images of a lifeless, empty, silent, and forbidden wasteland. This view is one of its best mirages. In reality, the desert biome is passionately alive, a primordial shapeshifter. Sands move, form, dissolve, and form again in fantastic elaborations that spell out the mystery of the wind.

The expression begins when clouds—heavy with rain—confront mountains too high to surmount and release their life-giving moisture. This causes arid conditions on the opposite side of the mountains, but frees the wind for all it is meant to do.

Sand also has a peculiar power; it self-accumulates. Even in totally flat plains, rather than spreading out uniformly, sand has the tendency to heap itself up. Paradoxically, desert sand that looks dead is so nutrient rich, it only needs water to create life. Its dryness contains almost no organic nutrients. Instead, it is composed mainly of crystalline quartzite particles ranging in size from infinitesimal, powdery grains to minute but slightly larger particles.

It is a precise act of creation. Winds coming in over the peaks must blow from 10–20 miles per hour to catch the right weight of sand particles. The movement is complex, not just a push. Coarse particles are picked up and given a forward momentum, but their weight pulls them back to the surface, where they bounce back up into the air again. It is more like a circular movement within a forward thrust. Fine particulate will not bounce, but will bury itself instead, causing a second grain to be ejected and blown downward. When this happens, a state of fluidity is achieved.

When conditions are just right, you can see this in a low-flying cloud traveling downwind.

In an active desert system, strong winds build height on a dune and gentle winds extend its length; in either case, the wind and dune strive to achieve a 35-degree angle of repose, exquisitely edged in fine particles of dust. This gives rise to another of the desert's powers—it speaks. Heavier sand builds up from behind the wave, pushes the light edge grains down the slip face, whose curvature amplifies the movement into sounds ranging from a soft hiss to a roaring thunder. The fortunate traveler may hear distant music, drums, and voices. For a select few, for reasons known only to the sands, a distinct message may be given.

Joe was good at slipping away, but this time, I caught him. Something made me want to tag along. It was late afternoon. Clouds had moved in to blanket the sky and caused the temperatures to plunge dramatically. In silence, we angled over the hardpan earth, tracking around exposed rocks and spiny tufts of scrub. Heading east, toward the ruins, the path veered out, then looped back around to the west. At the entry to what must have been an old street, our faces aglow in the last rays of the setting sun, the desert grew strangely quiet. Earth, worn smooth by wind and age, created silken shadows that stretched and lengthened like fingers. The shadow fingers took shape and cupped, like hands lifted in prayer, hands holding us as if we were a votive offering, more one person than two.

Down the passageway, unseen, powdery particles of sand began to hiss and move. Forward, backward, swirling softly, advancing, retreating, coalescing, consolidating, collapsing, only to sweep and surge until a sound more like a feeling arose. Shhhhh, then an alternating rhythm like breathing. The winds buffeted our ears. Eddies of sand gathered into vortexes, larger and larger, spinning toward us and, in passing, anointing us in a smoky citrine dust.

Music. Laughter. Clapping hands. Stamping feet. Undulating circular skirts over tapered, silk trousers, ecstatic whirling in throbbing tambour time. Hearth fire blazing, filling the earthen surround in warm, apricot haze, and silhouetting an arm raised in toast. A long-sleeved arm of Silk Road antiquity draws a wife close, resting his head on her bosom, and smiles. A caravan has returned. A family reunited.

"Did you just hear something?" I asked, shaking dust from my cotton skirt.

A puzzled look crossed Joe's face. He glanced at his watch; several minutes had elapsed. "We'd better get back to the group," he said.

~~~

The late morning drive was hypnotic. We'd been on dusty roads under a sun so hot that heat waves prevented our driver from seeing ahead more than a short distance. Under such intense heat, the air conditioning was failing, creating a steamy greenhouse of our bus. It was a great relief to turn onto a larger, graded gravel road lined on either side with enormous, leafy shade trees. To our astonishment, a rush of glacial water coursed its way down a narrow canal on one side of the banked road. Children waded and played at the water's edge.

It was clear the driver was a bit lost; we'd sped up and slowed down a number of times as he sought direction. Spotting an old Uyghur man crouched in front of a high, whitewashed adobe wall and playing a kazoo-sounding flute, the driver stopped the bus, opened the door, and went to speak with the musician. We didn't wait for an invite. Our group of 20-some overheated people rose as one and surged out of the bus into a sea of loud, ethnic music pouring from behind the wall and into the canal of fresh, cool water.

Water in the desert is heaven. We splashed our faces and necks, and then, throwing convention to the winds, we hoisted up skirts and pants and waded in. The children retreated, but curiosity drew them back, and within a couple of moments, we were splashing water, gesturing, and laughing together.

Too soon, the driver reappeared, but he did so with a surprise. The music, he said, was from a traditional Uyghur wedding celebration, and we were invited. At first, we declined, wanting to respect the people's privacy, but the more we said no, the more Uyghurs appeared, urging us to join in. We did, and captured some great images to show for it: Oscar, in his Apache clothing, one arm extended in Central Asian traditional dance, the other holding a bunch of grapes over his open mouth. A little Uyghur girl in fluorescent-pink and burgundy cultural attire watched and laughed. Plates and trays of raisins, dates, and peanuts piled high and offered to us. In every photo, Uyghurs and Indians are pressing closely around each other in joy. Later that night, the bride would step across a fire and into her new life.

~~~

On the final leg of the trip, we had to let people know about a change in schedule.

Joe and I went up and down the train, knocking on compartment doors to spread the news. Joe knocked at the last door. No one answered, but since it was ajar, he poked his head in and instantly wished he had not. He had just caught two people in a most compromising situation. He quickly closed the door, but not before they had seen him; the damage was done. They were politically prominent conference Indians who had pressured to come on the trip at the last minute. They could not know that neither Joe nor I would gossip, but they had to be sure.

"We're going to have trouble when we get home," he said. And we did. The line of attack revolved around the trip's no alcohol policy.

The USCPFA had alerted us to the popular Chinese custom of toasting. Alcohol is not a part of American Indian spirituality, and because it was historically used against American Indians—the way opium had been used against the Chinese—and we also had recovering alcoholics on the trip, we had prearranged with our hosts that this would a no alcohol trip. We figured our hosts would eagerly support us in a show of solidarity. Some did, but most officials, accustomed to toasting as a mainstay of political socializing, were puzzled and clearly uninformed as to the workings of addiction. Some Chinese officials suggested things very dangerous to a recovering alcoholic, like having just one drink or drinking beer instead of the fiery, locally fermented *baiju*. Not drinking seemed rude; our hosts were at a loss for any alternative. To get past the impasse in etiquette, we drank water to join the Chinese toasts, but it was a bit awkward.

The Healers, activists, young people, and, of course, recovering alcoholics on the trip were in full support of the no drinking policy, but the conference Indians were angered, arguing that the policy made them look like children who couldn't handle alcohol.

A few weeks after the trip was over, they took their revenge. They began a smear campaign, maligning Joe and me both to funders of the trip and to the indigenous professional community. When I returned to my summer teaching job in native studies, the director, a friend, called me in to warn me that I had made some powerful enemies. He'd received a call advising him not to work with me. Some of my friends said I should fight back, but I didn't; my heart was broken, and not just because of the professional fall-out.

Shortly after the trip ended, Joe's alcoholism became active again. Our small student apartment was like a powder keg as he fought the desire to drink. He fought hard because he faced death; he had cirrhosis of the liver. Always impeccable, he rose one morning, put on clean jeans and ribbon shirt, his favorite high-top mocs, braided his hair, and went to the door.

I thought he was going to work, but instead, he turned and looked at me, hand on the doorknob, and said, "I'm going to drink. It's better I leave you and the kids alone."

That was it. We never saw him again.

Abruptly, I was alone with three children to support and a doctoral program to complete. Memories of the Silk Road ruin and that special wind faded, but the desert holds more than artifacts—it also holds gifts. A few years later, word came of Joe's death. Sorting through the last of his things, I came across his master's degree application. In it he had written: "From Madison to Halsted Street [Chicago Indian ghetto] I have witnessed the real horror of family breakup and seeing young Indian men and women end up on skid row or in prisons."

Gripped by grief and loss, a strange feeling came over me. Again, I beheld the magic moment in the desert—the reuniting caravan family—and wondered, *What if I had looked more carefully and chanced a glance at the face of the man holding his wife close, might it have been Joe? Might it have been me?*

Chapter 5

COPPER MOUNTAIN

"It will not be like before. You have no authority over your people. You are there to serve them, and this means you will always have fewer possessions than the rest of the people."

SKY WOMAN

Ketchikan, Alaska, 1982

The single-engine pontoon plane bumped, dropped, rose, and slammed its way through the windy Southeast Alaskan archipelago. Scores of dark green cedar islands rimmed in dark basalt dotted the gray-green Pacific. I used my jacket sleeve to wipe condensation from the tiny window and concentrated on the wild beauty zipping by beneath me—a boreal rain forest, the first pristine ecosystem I'd ever seen. God, it was so beautiful. As if the sky were thinking with me, a silver rainsquall suddenly wrapped around the tiny aircraft. For a few minutes, we were lost in the mist—no above, no below, motionless. Then, we felt a bump as the plane nosed through the outer edge of the cloud and directly confronted a massive, snow-covered peak—Copper Mountain. One of the oldest mountains in North America, it is filled with combinations of minerals and gems that exist nowhere else on earth that, together, work to create a powerful geomagnetic field.

I knew the mountain the instant I beheld its majesty. I had never been here, yet I had seen it in a vision in a peyote ceremony six years earlier. I'd driven over a thousand miles with small children from Boston to Wisconsin. I was desperate. I'd been stuck in my doctoral writing for more than a year, and my scholarship was at risk—and so was our survival. I needed help and looked to this ceremony to provide insight and practical direction. About five hours into the peyote ceremony, my back was hurting and so was my heart. As hard as I prayed, all I could see were some rocks floating in space. Dumb. Too much Disney. Try harder. But try as I might, there were no insights; there was nothing. I curled my head into my chest and cried.

The crackling fire grew silent. A soft darkness seeped in the tipi. I looked up, and I was standing in a lustrous, featureless world, so holy I averted my eyes in reverence. I looked up again; a massive brown eagle, talons outstretched, dropped down and ripped my spirit from my body. Blackness ensued. Then, I was on its back, speeding through cloud cover. Fierce winds tangled my long hair and whipped wet, dark strands about my face. Ecstasy replaced fright, and the clouds opened. Far below was a mountaintop covered in ice and snow. Instinctively, I pulled back. I could not survive in such a place. Instantly, we were back to the starting place, soaring swiftly in the dimensionless purity. Again the clouds parted. Now the mountain crown was wet, fresh, and green. Floodwaters had retreated. Voices, thousands of soaring birds, animals, deer, bear, and people moved, ebbed, and flowed together in celebration. Rafts, canoes, all manner of floating devices, lay anchored on this mountaintop. A new cycle had begun. Softly the vision began to fade when a new image flashed and dissolved. A woman dressed in white buckskin emerged from the mountain. To my shock, she had my face. Then I was back in the tipi and back to myself.

Now, unbelievably, I found myself flying over the very mountain I had seen in my vision. I was even approaching it from the same direction as then. I turned to the passenger next to me, a local Native man, and asked him what he knew about the mountain before us. "Copper Mountain," he said, and motioned toward it with his head. "It's sacred. Our people came here as the ice was retreating, but it was too cold, so they turned around and went back. The climate got warmer, so they came again and stayed. Time passed, a great flood came; it was bad. Almost everyone died. The people who made it to rafts and canoes had to fight off big animals trying to mount the rafts. The top of this mountain was the first land to show. Those that made it to land faced starvation and violence in the struggle to survive. There are still dragline anchors scattered around the peak, and one big oval one with a hole in it and fossilized rope on it. When the waters receded, it was the bear who led the people back down to land. There's even a chant about it." He paused, looking down at the white tide line edging the base of the mountain, then added, "Those old people carved messages on the rocks down there."

With that, he turned away. The conversation was over, but not for me. My heart and mind buzzed with excitement. For the first time in my life, a vision had become manifest, and I'd become conscious in it. A profound sense of belonging, a sense of place, enveloped me. I was on the threshold of a spiritual mystery and knew it with every fiber of my being. An ecstatic energy, like fire, coursed through my veins as habitual boundaries of separation, individualism, and isolation crumbled. A creative pulse began to stir in me, to move out of its own potentiality, and propelled me into a totally different world, one of holism of eternity—the Indigenous Mind. What could the encoded messages possibly reveal that would explain the magnitude, the majesty of this experience? I had to see the rocks.

Within a few months, I packed my belongings and moved my children and myself to a remote Native village near Copper Mountain. The move made sense. We could live decently and affordably, and we would have the chance to strengthen our indigenous identity by living in a pristine ecosystem with Native people who still lived a semi-subsistence lifestyle. Additionally, I could finish writing my doctoral dissertation in a place where ancient people had written their messages. Understanding the message of the petroglyphs became a passionate desire.

I applied for and received a modest research grant to pull together a small team of indigenous Cultural Practitioners and scientists, including Hanson Ashley, who had just finished his bachelor's degree in psychology and had also been initiated into his role as traditional Healer. There was one problem—the petroglyph site was remote. It was a half hour from the nearest village and across some of the most dangerous, frigid, fast-moving water in the Gulf of Alaska. We didn't have nearly enough funding to provide for a boat. We had to scrounge for transportation—usually persuading a local to take us. It was worth the effort.

Bowed over the side of the launch, I flung my legs, first one then the other, over the side. Sheets of icy water snaked around my feet and tumbled stones on the beach—a murmured prayer. Mist rose like breath from needle-shaped cedar trees that edged their way up to the snowcapped peak of Copper Mountain. I cast a glance over the tide line. Hundreds of boulders scored with messages from the ancients lay before me—a *locus sanctus*, a focus for ceremony and intimate interaction with the unseen world. I stood present to an intensely liminal visual world.

Filled with awe, I stood immobilized for several minutes before Hanson, speaking in Navajo, a language historically related to the local tribes, offered corn pollen and asked the mountain spirits permission to enter the site and to help us understand the symbolic messages of the petroglyphs. For an instant, everything went still, banners of mist swirled, dissolved, and formed about the pinnacle; then, as if a door had opened, we were granted entry, and all the normal sounds returned. Hanson nodded, OK.

We fanned out to document as many of the rocks as we could in the brief window of time we had. I took a couple of wobbly steps and stopped dead in my tracks. From a four-foot triangular basalt rock, a huge bear face peered directly at and, it seemed, through me. Quickly I noted its location, snapped a photo, gave thanks, and moved on to a nearby tear-shaped boulder. Its yard-wide diameter presented deeply engraved eyes, one spiraled, the other, three concentric rings. A line connected the eyes, which were outlined in a ruffle of adjoined lumpy circles. A face with rays, maybe the sun, peered out from the apex of the stone. But it was the next image that touched my heart—a bird with a stick in its beak and mischief in its eye. No doubt about it—Raven, the trickster creative spirit. I smiled in recognition. I knew this bird, always up to no good, the seven deadly sins all in one black feathery package. Elders loved to share traditional stories of his misadventures that led to terrible consequences for him but brought good to humanity. He always lived to see another day because he's sacred and cannot die.

What I came to next quickly wiped the smile from my face.

A monolithic being, intractably powerful, swept me into its force field faster than I could identify it—an enormous lizard-like being with a mouthful of razor-sharp teeth that held a human head between its massive jaws! My aversion to the graphic horror was instant before I'd even taken in the rest of the image, I'd rationalized that it symbolized a *rites de passage*. The primordial reptile covered the tabletop surface of a gigantic capsule-shaped rock and dominated the site. Two horizontal *Y* shapes bracketed a spiral in its gut; the body ended in a segmented tail. Its claws gripped an equally huge bird face, and stuck on its dorsal fin was a behemoth—maybe a whale or shark. Off to one side and above it were three nested and parallel *S* lines. Its two-ringed eye seized my attention, but before I could consider the meaning, I heard an urgent call from Hanson. Reluctantly, I turned, picked my way over the unstable beach stones, and came alongside him. A small red granite tablet-shaped rock in front of Hanson commanded our attention. It featured a heavily eroded image of what looked like a skeletal man, legs pulled up to his sides and bony arms folded straight up from the elbows.

"It's the Medicine Man," Hanson said quietly.

"Hurry, we've got to go! Now!" the captain shouted from the boat, alarm in his voice.

I looked out on the inlet. In just minutes, waves had kicked up; winds chased flecks of sea-foam from the peaks of the dark, mounting seas. I ran for the launch, mindless of the rocky pummeling my ankles took. Just shy of the boat, a strange thing happened. At full stride, I glanced down and caught a small face looking at me from a fist-sized triangular rock. In the split second we connected, the visage burned into my mind. It was aberrant, decidedly unfriendly, and looking toward the mountain with its back to the sea, something no oceangoing person would ever do. In my haste to escape, I forgot about it. I should not have.

The team, all six of us, scrambled into the rowboat and paddled furiously to the research vessel. The last of us had barely clambered on when the captain hit the engines hard forward. The vessel lurched into a huge oncoming wave. The bow pitched violently and engines stalled until we dropped down the backside of the wave. Again and again, we slammed into the waves until we made it into open waters. It was then we noticed that in our hurry to get underway, we had failed to pull anchor. At full speed, it was hydroplaning and skipping on its rope behind us. We were lucky no one was killed.

~~~

Two months later, I had to admit I'd gotten nowhere and wondered if the Ancestors had chosen the right person for this job. For the thousandth time, I thumbed through my field notes and mindlessly shuffled through the petroglyph photos scattered across the table. I thought about my lines of evidence, documentation, photos, and oral history.

I turned to science and sifted through our field journal. The main points were that 15,000 years earlier, twin retreating glaciers carried the boulders from the top of Copper Mountain and deposited them at the base in an east-west line. The complexity and perfection of the designs and the uniform grooves throughout the curvilinear swirls would have taken time to carve, so could not have been done in the rapid and dramatic fluctuations of modern-day tides. As the glaciers melted, seas rose and submerged the rocks for millennia. Later, glacial rebound raised the rocks from the sea. Randy, the Tlingit team geologist, reasoned that the rocks were most likely to have been inscribed shortly after they resurfaced and before the tidal actions we are familiar with today established themselves. His assessment encouraged me, because the timeline of the oral flood history and geology overlapped. One of the richest streams of knowledge came from traditional stories shared by Northwest Coast Elders who confirmed the bird with the stick was Raven bringing light and consciousness to the world. The Great Lizard they said was the water spirit, an ambivalent Creation Being. Hanson's rock was indeed a shaman. No one was sure about the design with the two eyes.

So, where did this leave me in my search to unravel the message?

Our interdisciplinary team had also worked out an intriguing possibility—the bank of petroglyphs function as a tidal clock and generator of narratives, telling us when and how to move to keep balance in life. The etchings are made visible when retreating tides leave water standing in the grooves. Varying tides highlight different images and composite stories. Because the information is so critical, the rocks are always placed at the site of environmental catastrophe to show what knowledge they are about. The "authors" of the petroglyphs had to devise symbols that could communicate across thousands of years to descendants who might not even speak the same language. Knowledge of local oral history can expedite the understanding, but the symbols themselves are so powerful that they impact the psyche and reveal truths through dreams, intuition, and chance encounter.

But I didn't have either timing or narrative; I was confused and stuck. I still didn't know how I fit into the mystery or what the "ancient printout" was.

In many Native languages, the words for petroglyphs mean "they give direction," pragmatically pointing to water or food, or history; metaphysically they give direction inter-dimensionally. Petroglyph images are precise and powerful; just one glance can imprint on our minds and in our hearts to draw us closer to life. There is an indigenous understanding that rocks carry the Story (of life) because life began with the rocks. Oneida, my tribe, means "people of the long-living or everlasting rock."

Dreams came. Night after night, the visages moved before me. I was awaking in an Ancestral embrace. Imperceptibly, my Western analytical mind was being rewired. I was already in the ceremony I was looking for but didn't know it. I worried and pushed for answers outside myself and the ancient initiation I had entered.

A few weeks later, the weather began its seasonal change. Approaching winter seas would be too dangerous for site visits. I desperately wanted to make one more trip to Copper Mountain, so did the only thing I could do. I lit my cedar, cleansed in the smoke, burned some tobacco, and asked the Ancestors for help. The second I finished, there was a knock at the door. I opened it and looked directly into the bright, blue eyes of Bill Lawton, a marine biologist who worked for an exclusive fishing resort up the coast. He wanted to know about local petroglyphs, particularly any that had to do with whales. He'd been on a fruitless search throughout summer, and in just a couple of weeks, the season and his employment would be ending; he wanted a strong finish. Bill had heard I might be able to give him the help he needed. He had a powerful, 20-foot, twin-engine vessel—exactly what I needed. We quickly agreed to team up. He'd take me to the rock site in exchange for cultural information on whales.

The next day we were bouncing and pounding on rolling, slate-colored waves. When we got to the site, we could not land. In the 40 minutes it took to make the journey, tides, rapid and chaotic, had moved in, alternately covering and revealing the stones. Just a scattering of incised boulders hugging close to the cliff face were above water. I was crestfallen; Bill was determined and gunned the engines. "We'll go around the point, climb over the back, and drop down on the site," he yelled above the sound of the wind, waves, and roar of the motors. I argued against it, feeling the danger, but he prevailed. Within ten minutes, we landed and began the difficult climb up the backside of a wet, slimy, tree-fallen, boreal rain forest hill. The closer we got to the crest, the creepier it felt; later, I would learn from Elders the peninsula was called Graveyard Point in recognition of a terrible intertribal battle that happened there. So many died that they were buried in situ. But there was no turning back. The fear of going back on my own was more terrifying than going forward. Besides, Bill was waving at me. He had just charged through the tree line and was standing on the cliff edge that looked down on the petroglyphs. I caught up with him. From where we stood, it was a 12-foot drop straight down to the rocks. I was young and strong but didn't see how I could get down. The cliff had only tiny, scattered outcroppings, and I was wearing oversized rubber boots.

A rock climber will tell you to avoid descending a site because accidents are more likely on the way down. Bill was undeterred. Stretching his six-foot height enabled him to cling to the top of the cliff, while the toes of his soggy sneakers sought and found tiny angled ridges that brought him down to the beach. "Hurry," he commanded. The tide was devouring the tiny strip of land still above water. I knew better, but the urgency and authority in his voice made me move. I turned my body, back to the sea, to crab walk down the cliff as Bill had done. But my foot never found purchase. My body torqued; I was falling backward, speeding to the rocks below. In the still, time-stopping milieu of shock, I had space to perceive death's approach and my hubris that called it to me. Sorrow and acceptance touched my heart just as a cushion of air, like invisible arms, cuddled me and, as soft as an eagle plume, lowered me to the ground. "Apela, my God, are you all right?" Bill shouted, running toward me. To my surprise, I nodded yes, I was. Helping me to my feet, we looked at each other and knew— time to get the hell out of there.

~~~

Winter rains and swells socked us in. Months passed. Still I persisted in my fruitless search to understand the meaning of the petroglyphs. Finally, I decided I needed to consult with an Elder from a strong cultural tribe, one that still maintained the ability to "read" the rocks. A Lakota friend from my doctoral program arranged for me to meet with Emory, an esteemed Medicine Man, the following summer.

I'd heard Emory speak a few years earlier during Indian Studies week at the University of California. In his presentation, he mentioned the importance of knowing our ancient writing systems and symbols. He was the first Elder I'd heard of who retained the ability to interpret petroglyphs from a coherent and unbroken indigenous science framework.

His was a warrior culture, distinctly patriarchal, so on arrival at the Ogalala Reservation, I sat with the women in the kitchen, waiting until one of Emory's helpers came to get me. Entering the small prefab living room, I was careful to slow myself to show respect as I approached the old man seated on a beat-up, threadbare reservation armchair. Emory lived the life of an ascetic, not because tradition required it but as a result of the heartbreaking poverty and living conditions of his people.

Thin, dressed in a faded plaid shirt and worn slacks, Emory spoke about the way he lived, in a shack with a broken window, and often with little food to eat even in the fierce cold of high plains winters. This was his way of letting me know how he held his powers—the humility and sacrifice underlying what I was asking him to share and the need for me to respect it. I knelt before him, looked down when he spoke to show respect and to take in all of what he was saying, then offered tobacco along with a fistful of photographs, and asked him to interpret the meaning of 30,000-year-old Ancestral messages. He held the photos for a minute as if considering something, then satisfied, glanced up at me. To Native people, rock images are mystical conduits, and therefore not normally photographed. I explained that local Elders had permitted me to take the pictures, because the rocks, numbering nearly one hundred, were being stolen from their remote, tide-line repository at the base of a sacred mountain. Due to the outcome of genocide, the people had lost the memory of how to read them. When they learned of my experience and saw my interest, the Elders had encouraged me to visit Healers from other tribes. Emory nodded his assent and began to shuffle slowly through the pictures. He stopped at the one I was most curious about. Seconds, then minutes ticked by in utter silence as he studied the image. Then he said, "This is the Great Lizard; where the lizard touches its face to the earth, there is water. According to our Stories, when the Great Lizard comes, people will be filled with fear; the Lizard strikes terror in human hearts. He is a soul searcher who sees from both front and back. He is continually searching for truth and seeks people who cannot control their fear—people who do not yet know truth. If people do not know how to deal with fear, they could be killed or turned into stone. The Sioux Story teaches the importance of staring fear in the face."

I wanted to ask questions, but could feel it wasn't allowed. I could also sense a tension, an edginess in the room, that I assumed came from my presence as a woman. I was on borrowed time, but the Sioux are fierce in their values and, even though they might not like a strange, mixed-blood, woman professor to have immediate access to their preeminent Healer, tribal values dictated respect for visitors and, above all, sharing even in the face of desperate poverty.

Determined in my purpose, I did not run, although I wanted to. I tried to make myself small, to take as little time and energy as possible. Silently, I pointed at other important photos. In response, Emory shook his head no, or spoke a few words in English or in his language, interpreted by an intense young Sioux man. About twenty minutes into it, I began to feel weird—weak and dizzy. Kneeling at the coffee table, photos arrayed before me, I shook my head slightly and caught a strange sight. Around his left arm, bent at the elbow, Emory was yarding up a luminous blue thread—thread that was being pulled out of me! He didn't expect a mixed-blood like me to see in a sacred way, and before this moment, I wouldn't have thought so either. Caught in the act, Emory jammed his left arm behind his back. Rage blazed through me. This was spiritual rape. In one move, I stood up, swept the photos into a plastic bag, and made for my car. I never looked back.

The next day I called Kaulaity, my Kiowa friend and Healer. I told him what had happened, what I'd felt and seen, and asked his counsel.

"Hmm." he said. The line grew quiet for a few seconds. "The man is getting old, losing his powers. He doesn't want to let go, so he thought he'd help himself to some of yours."

"But how long would Emory have continued if I hadn't caught him? Would he have killed me?"

"Yes," Kaulaity responded. "Not right away, he'd have done it so you'd get down the road, and then something would have happened; nobody would know. By the way," he said, just before hanging up, "when you fell at that rock site, did you notice something?"

I'd forgotten I'd mentioned the incident to him, but the moment he asked the question, I flashed back to the instant I became conscious, lying there on the beach. Head turned toward the water, I'd opened my eyes, and there he was, the evil little triangle-faced rock I'd seen during my first visit to the site with Hanson.

I hung up the phone, strode into my office, whipped out the petroglyph photo box, seized that triangle-head image, shredded it, burned it, and then burned the ashes. And that's how I learned the limits of my rational mind.

Chapter 6

CHIEF DAANAWÁA<u>K</u>

Juneau, Alaska, 1981–1985

I survived my brush with bad medicine and, with my research grant coming to an end, moved to Juneau, Alaska's state capital, hoping to find a job. Naive of the professional world, I had never questioned the belief that, if I managed to graduate, I would be sought after. In reality, no provisions had been made to help this first generation of advanced-degreed Indigenous People transition into the high-level jobs such training should afford.

I was frustrated and worried. My rigorous training had given me razor-sharp analytical skills. I could analyze my individual situation deeply and place it within the social, political, cultural, and economic underpinning of the American Indian struggle. Indeed, my professors had taught me to seek the root of injustice at its innermost source, the hidden confines of capitalistic and patriarchal institutions.

I could see all this, yet could not change my circumstances even in Juneau. I took every short-term, low-paying contract I could find, but couldn't pay all my bills, adequately support my children, or even afford health care. My anger and hurt grew. Every day the rain came; the gray, low-hanging clouds of the boreal rain forest darkened my mood further and honed the pain. As weeks, then months, rolled by, a sense of failure wrapped around me like a shroud. Crazed with worry, I found a practice that helped. When the stress got too much, I'd run across the road to edge and slip my way down the eroded, hardpan banks of the nearby river.

Lemon Creek should have been beautiful. Nestled between massive seaside mountains, the creek and its valley are headed by a glacier. The glacier's movement had fractured into magnificent crystalline structures that refracted polarized sunlight into fuzzy white, greens, grays, and blues. At night, the shadow of the ice edge came alive in the shimmering, leaping, and spinning fluorescence of the *aurora borealis*. There it ended.

The local government had decided to build a correctional institute at the head of the river. Heavy earth-moving equipment roared in and clear-cut the dense old-growth forest. Eagle habitats, salmonberries, salal, blueberries, huckleberries, and the ancient healing plant—Devil's club, a brittle thorny scrub that gives the rain forest its sour-minty fragrance—had all been destroyed. Exposed fragile topsoil was completely washed away in the 62.5 inches of Juneau's annual rainfall. Nothing was left except hardpan and rivulets of rain. But sometimes, in the early morning mists, I'd hear a soft "chuck, chuck, chuck" raven comfort sound and catch a glimmer of blue-black in the secondary-growth alder shrubs.

Chief Daanawáak, also known by his English name, Austin Hammond, was a traditional Storyteller who lived in Juneau during the time I was there. A member of the Tlingit tribe, he possessed the corpus of Raven stories. He could convene the spirit for telling them and knew the complete genealogies of both Raven and Eagle Clans from the beginning of time to the present. This striking intellectual achievement was offset by the fact that he should not have had to care for the Eagle lineage. Forces that few people beyond the tribe knew—the bombing of Native villages by the United States Navy, Western-introduced epidemics, the onslaught of virulent assimilative missionary practices, the subsequent genocide, and government-run boarding schools—meant there was no Eagle Clan person left to carry the genealogy. There was no one to report the loss to, no overarching framework of authority, except that of the heart—and in this case, the broken heart.

Seeing the destruction of his culture and people, Austin did what people of his generation did; he tried to fit in. He became a commercially successful fisherman and an active member, along with his wife, in the local fundamentalist Christian church in Juneau. He was a recognized leader in the assimilative journey of Tlingit people. That is, until the Ancestors knocked at the door of his Tlingit reality. Returning from a fishing trip, a few miles out from the dock, pain gripped his chest, sweat poured off his body, and darkness took him. When he came to, he was so weak he could scarcely lift his arm.

How can I make it in, how can I tie up the boat? he anguished.

Then a second attack hit, and maybe, he thought later, a third. As he lay unconscious on the deck, the spirit of his grandfather appeared to him. "Grandson, those stories I gave to you—don't die with them; pass them on."

When the Great Spirit gives us a vision, we are also given a power. Thus, Austin regained consciousness and, with excruciating effort, returned to the dock a new man—a man with a vision, determined to bring his Tlingit culture back to help future generations and to help life renew. In short order, he called together his people, government representatives, and Native Corporation leaders in a ceremony at Deer Rock. The Deer is a messenger of peace, and this sacred site was peace manifest. During the ritual, he announced his plan to create a culture camp on ancient traditional lands, which the state and a Native Corporation claimed title to under Western law. He emptied his bank account and put his life savings into the creation of a Raven Clan House and a youth camp situated on the Chilkoot, a swift-moving glacial river running at the base of Southeast Alaska's Coast Mountains.

This was not going to be a popular move, for the land held vast acreages of old-growth timber and mountains full of precious metals. However, because of the ceremony and the respect for Chief Daanawáak, both government and business looked the other way. His stature made people want to be like that—good. But the resurgence of culture cost him, and not just money. His wife divorced him, he was thrown out of his church, and became subject to community ridicule. When I met Chief Daanawáak, he lived outside his community with a local non-native family. They not only loved him, but, with law and education degrees between them, Richard and Julie Folta also helped move his work through the intense conflicts between old and new cultural forms.

The clan house was a 15-minute drive into Juneau and up the side of the hill into "old town." It was here I learned about the stories, the old ones that take you to a different place and time, that make you feel your creative life force and your place in it. They change you forever. They have the power to do this because they are not just stories the way we think of them in modern times, but they are spirits; they are alive. To "hear" them, we must purify ourselves and ask permission to enter.

For hundreds of years, entering a traditional longhouse has marked the symbolic journey to receive the stories. Imagine walking through bone-chilling, rainy Southeast Alaskan winds until you reach the front of a cedar longhouse. In the exact center of the exterior face stands an elaborately carved totem pole depicting the history and genealogy of the clan. Near the bottom, a small oval opening, raised about knee height from the ground, serves as an entryway. Stooping to crawl through, you are born into and continue the story depicted on the pole. It is more than a symbolic act; there's a certain force field in place, an interaction between the cedar, the geometry, and the rituals that put the pole in place. Something happens; a sixth sense or awareness kicks in to tell you Ancestral spirits are close. After entering the house on all fours, you stand up, and are embraced by the warmth of the central fire and enveloped in a simmering mist of minty and slightly sour-smelling Devil's Club. The name misleads. Like hands, the palmate-shaped green leaves grow spirally up a three- to five-foot brittle spiny stem; their fragrance purifies, protects, and carries you deep inside an ancient forest, inside yourself.

On this particular evening, I stepped out of sideways-blowing boreal forest rains and into Raven House. Hanson Ashley accompanied me. He was a cultural person fluent in his Navajo language, even in the secret, sacred ceremonial variant, and so was Chief Daanawáa<u>k</u>. I was eager for the two to meet, cherishing the possibility of remembering and renewing forgotten ancestry, overcoming historical destructions, and sensing that whatever happened was going to be wonderful.

Chief Daanawáa<u>k</u>'s clan house had been modernized. It had a small, carved wood raven image above a modern door. A wood stove replaced the fire pit. Standing in the mudroom, Hanson and I stamped our feet loudly. Julie heard our coastal door knock, opened the door, and with a smile and handshake, welcomed us in. Seated next to the woodstove, in his beat-up, overstuffed chair, Chief Daanawáa<u>k</u> nodded his head in recognition and motioned for us to pull up chairs in a semicircle around the radiant, warm stove. He was dignified and impeccable in every sense, a real feat in blustery rain forest conditions. A bolo tie with a silver raven design encircled the neck of his soft, garnet-and-olive plaid wool shirt, highlighting the luster of his white brush-cut hair and contrasting powerfully with his ruddy, weathered complexion.

Relaxing, I stretched my legs closer to the fire. My hair, sopping wet against my sweater, was a frizzy mess. My feet were icy cold, and my sneakers were speckled with gray glacial till and splotchy raindrops. My esteem for Daanawáak was great, and I wished I could have looked more presentable.

Daanawáak shook Hanson's hand, holding it between his big, rough fisherman's hands and smiled softly. Hanson introduced himself, his tribe, clan, and name, and expressed his pleasure in meeting a beloved Elder. Beyond this, I wasn't so sure about the communication. English was a distant second language for the chief, and despite wanting to speak of complex cultural, spiritual ideas, neither Hanson nor I spoke Tlingit. But Daanawáak's nonstandard English often evidenced a startling advantage—he could speak "Indian in English."

We sat in silence for a few minutes, long enough to take in the genealogies, both Raven and Eagle, covering the opposite wall floor-to-ceiling, and we fell into deep repose with the crackle and uplifting fragrance of the cedar fire intermingled with the smoky smell of hard dried salmon, stored for winter. I had a warm, wonderful, secure feeling of being with Daanawáak and being at the numinous story threshold.

Clearing his throat several times, he began, "This is the first story ever told. There are no stories before this. This story begins at a time before the Earth's crust was firm."

So the story of the Fog Hat began. White Raven spirit and Black Raven, the trickster whose only interest is to get things moving, are in a boat, jigging for halibut. Black Raven begins to challenge White Raven, saying, "I'm older than you." He does so three times despite White Raven's warning to stop. Finally, White Raven reacts. He puts on a hat and invokes a fog so thick you cannot see land or even your hand in front of your face. Now, Black Raven gets scared and admits, "You're older than me." With that, White Raven removes his hat and the fog dissipates. The lesson of the story is fundamental to Indigenous People: Never put yourself above another. Keep yourself low.

On it went. When Daanawáak finished a story, Hanson began one of his own, and then Daanawáak picked it up with a new story. More and more, the varying stories alluded to trees, but I couldn't see where the topic was going, especially since it wasn't even clear they understood each other's English. On the drive over, I had allowed for a leisurely hour or so of visiting, but as hour three approached, I was getting nervous. In fewer than ten minutes, I needed to pick up my four-year-old girl from Indian Head Start. However, Daanawáak was deep into a story. I didn't dare interrupt. Traditional story protocols are very clear on this point: if you stop a story, you cut your life short. But school was closing, and there was no one to watch my little girl.

What should I do? How can I make this right? I fretted, furtively glancing at my wristwatch. Finally, I had to go, no matter what the consequences. But before I could interject, Hanson did.

"Excuse me," he said quietly.

I was shocked. What was happening? For Hanson to break the story, it had to be very important. Glancing his way, I could gauge his Navajo excitement by the way he folded one hand over the other and got extra still.

"What were those words you just said?" Hanson asked.

Daanawáak repeated the ancient words in Tlingit that Bear uttered while raising a Dog Fish to the heavens. He did so to give honor and thanks for the fish that stayed behind the other spawning fish and sacrificed itself so that the bears had food. The words are catalytic. Through the agency of the prayer, the sunlight filtering through the dark spruce forest falls on the body of the plain gray fish and imbues it with the vivid green, rust, and yellow colors we know it by today.

Hanson smiled broadly and shook his head in amazement. "You know, those words are exactly the same in the old Navajo ceremonial language. Not many people know it anymore."

The room grew still, then filled with a thick presence of love. The men looked at each other and laughed quietly; they had found their relationship, never mind that it was thousands of years ago, and who knows in what part of North America that the Tlingit and Navajo tribes were last one people. But the language knew and seemed happy to remind us.

Then Hanson said what seemed to be a non sequitur, "We know about that sacred tree, too, and I would like you to come visit us in Navajo land soon."

To my utter amazement, Daanawáak nodded his head in agreement and, without further discussion, said, "Well, I'll be coming to see you soon, maybe before Christmas."

I was able to pick up my daughter on time that day. In the days that followed, as I considered the trip to Arizona, the stress between how I thought I should live and the pull of my heart was never sharper. Logically, the trip made no sense. Christmas was just a week away, and given the frequent fog-driven airport closures, there was a good chance I wouldn't make it back in time to celebrate with my children. Was this really Ancestral imperative, or thinly disguised selfishness? Even the night before, I still couldn't figure out why I was risking so much. I had borrowed the money for the trip without knowing how I'd pay it back.

However, Native ceremonies have a strange quality to them; they start long before you know you are in them. With all the distress, I didn't think about the larger, central meaning; the confrontation and separation was a gift, the Blessing Way of Navajo life had just opened up to me. This tearing, this internal bifurcation of the old and new, is a common pre-ceremonial experience. Healers understand it and will say, "Spirit has us." African friends put it more directly, "Ancestors are riding us." Traditionally, American Indians have viewed this as normal.

~~~

Think about dawn. In the east, a silvery, liquid morning star clears the horizon, and something remarkable happens. The night, like a shadow, removes in a slight almost imperceptible breeze, dropping the temperature to the coldest, purest moment of the day. It is the time of the Ancestors, a time when the veil between the worlds is thin. The atmosphere quickens, night sounds grow still, and all life pauses for just a second. Then, the soft song of a wide-eyed bird reaches out, stirs up, and sweeps in the voices of smaller and smaller birds—an amorous synchronizing with the shifting colors of the sky. In a swirling crescendo of song, the sun rises with soft fingerlike rays to caress Mother Earth, who sighs in life-giving morning dew. Creation renews.

The morning star doesn't doubt whether or not she should appear. But in the between-worlds moments, in the dark, I get scared and want to bolt. I suppose I return to the danger of childhood, of sleeping too heavily and not being aware of alcoholics returning and lurking about my bedroom. And, unlike the morning star shimmering on the horizon, I do not see the light of spirit touching my soul or feel the divine breath that puts all into motion. I am consumed with an urgency, a need to move. It's about trust, but it's not all bad; sometimes the fears keep me from making a bad choice or make me strong and clear about choices I do make. Other times, it's just crazy displacement activities. It can be hard to tell the difference, and that's where the Stories come in.

One day I had asked our Mohawk Elder, Rarihokwats, about the moment of creative suspension between the dark and the light. He was quiet for a few moments, discerning my sincerity and looking for the dimension, the point in reality, where we would meet. When he found that, he'd know the story that pertained and, through it, would bring the worlds together. In a while, he began, "Toward the end of the late hours of night when there is darkness, and the night spirits are active, a change takes place that recreates the history of the Earth. If you are sitting in the forest, listening to the night sounds in the darkness, you notice a purpleness begin to displace the darkness. As you watch, that dark purple becomes lighter and gradually changes into a deep red. The red mixes with oranges and then yellows. Soon, a light that is gray, and rapidly lightening brighter and brighter, appears until the sun rises. The shifts of colors represent the colors of each of the five suns or epochs to arrive at today's. Each represents change within ourselves as we emerge from darkness figuratively and literally, as we are reborn from the sweat lodge."

Rarihokwats paused and then, seemingly out of nowhere, he began a new story.

"I will tell you a spark story. Saw it happen. Elder Ernie Benedict was demonstrating the old technique of starting a fire with a bowstring. The string is wrapped around the shaft so that, as the bow is moved back and forth, the shaft spins and spins in a small depression in a piece of wood. The friction heats the wood enough that the punk wood starts to smoke and then turns to ember and then bursts into flame. Back and forth, back and forth, back and forth, back and forth, Ernie went. And finally, after much effort, the smoke, then the spark! And at that moment, Ernie, perspiring from all the effort, watched a bead of sweat run down his nose and, with dead accuracy, put out the spark."

Finishing his story, Rarihokwats glanced at me. Our eyes met in a split second of silence, and then we laughed and laughed, at the perversity of life, at our all too human and ineffectual attempts to be holy, and we laughed in celebration of our Indigenous Way. Again, this is a way that advises, "Keep yourself low, never try to be too holy, put yourself above another, or take yourself too seriously." There's another part to it—laughter. Laughter equalizes intensity, restores harmony, and places us in accord with life. It brings the worlds together.

Rarihokwats's story touched on the innermost nature of dawn; when the sacred is exposed, we must cover it back up before taking our leave. Our laughter did that and simultaneously attested to the profundity of what we experienced. There are ways—rituals for respecting and potentiating the life force, its male and female aspects—even in language. If Rarihokwats had told me only about the power of dawn as he saw it, I might look to him as a guru, as someone above me. But in the indigenous view of life, there are no teachers. The best connection is the direct connection, and no one should ever come between a person and their Creator. Ever. Elders advise that the best thing we can do is share our stories with each other and possibly keep another person from hurting themselves or save them time on their journey to self-discovery.

We cannot say exactly how these Stories came into being or how old they are, but we know they are ancient because they often contain archaic terms, and because the people telling them have been selected and trained to tell them in exactly the same way, generation after generation. They are so central to life that they were, until recent times, whispered into a baby's ears. Thus, as a child encountered life situations, it was like turning pages in a well-known book. A person knew where they fit, could see likely outcomes of a situation, and knew what direction to go in and where to look for help when necessary.

When the Stories stop, when we no longer know them, violence and rigidity begin; we get stuck and become easily manipulated. The healing is remembering; restoring the sacred feminine or creative principle. Through this, we bring forgiveness, redemption, and wholeness to our lives.

~~~

As I winged my way to Arizona with Chief Daanawáak, I had no idea of the Story that pertained to my situation, or that I was indeed in search of one, the very one I was living. I reflected the world at large, fractured in relationship to my indigenous Creation Story, not seeing its relevance, or why and how I'd became separated from the original instructions of my People. In a way, I was worse off than most people. I knew my Oneida Creation Story, but understood it in a Western dissociative way, as metaphor—and a rather dull, lifeless one at that. Worse, I had no sense at all that a French Creation Story might be out there waiting for me.

Chapter 7

WASCO

Arizona, December 1984

Getting to the remote Navajo Reservation was a full day of travel. Then, we had a day of waiting to go to an all-night ceremony before making our way back to Phoenix airport to return home to Juneau for Christmas Eve—all this in a mere four days. Trust the Ancestors, I told myself; it will work out. I did not feel it. It was the first time I had ever accompanied an Elder on a journey, much less a man of such standing as Chief Daanawáak. I was nervous and uncertain of how to behave in a cultural way. I prayed for the approval of this esteemed Cultural Practitioner who personified warmth, self-acceptance, belonging, identity, and a world of wisdom my heart longed for. I listened and observed with every fiber of my being, Indigenous and Western.

Daanawáak was Raven Chief, and I had been adopted into the Ravens. Maybe that's how all the mischief ensued—Raven. Our journey had started well enough, the weather had lifted, and our Alaska Airlines flight made it out of Juneau. Hanson met us at Phoenix airport, and Daanawáak and Flora, Hanson's wife, caught up as we waited, eyes on the baggage carousel. This get-together was more than it appeared on the surface. It was rare, even in the 1980s, for Native people to connect from such a distance, and even harder for cultural people. Only the Indian bureaucrats working for the various branches of the government were well traveled, so much so, they actually earned a name, Conference Indians. But this wasn't us, and if you looked at the American Indian stats for the time, you'd see why. Average life expectancy for Indians was 47 years compared to about 70 for non-Natives; infant mortality was twice the national average. The average annual income for a family of four was $1,500 versus $20,000 for mainstream citizens. Native people didn't have many chances. Hanson, Daanawáak, and I were blessed to have opportunities others didn't—still, money was a hard one.

With the last pieces of luggage collected, the steel belt of the carousel now whizzed around its track, glimmering in the fluorescent light of Phoenix airport. Daanawáak's bag was missing.

"I'll go check," Hanson said, and walked off to find the lost luggage claim.

Flora, Daanawáak, and I stood there in a small semicircle. Silent. Even in the desert and the deep of Monument Valley, you can hear a pin drop from miles away. Navajo conversation is like that. When it's at its best, it's still. Ten minutes or so of such silence transpired—an eternity to my postdoc mind—when Flora said softly, "I'll go find out what's going on."

The moment she was out of earshot, Daanawáak cleared his throat, a Tlingit "call to order." I snapped to; he wasn't the type to impose, this had to be important. It was and what he said was chilling. He'd left home early and had forgotten to take his heart medicine. He'd also forgotten to put it in his carry-on. It was something he needed to take every day, and he'd already been feeling poorly for several hours. I did a quick mental inventory. Lost bag? Check. Lost medications? Check. There was no way to fix the problem from where we stood.

"Do you think Julie is home?" I asked.

He looked at his watch. "Yes," he said, "she should be by now."

Anxious to find a payphone, but not wanting to show it, I walked with apparent calmness toward the airport interior. Once out of Daanawáak's sight, I broke into a full run through the vast, empty terminal. When I finally found a phone, I realized I'd have to call collect; long distance to Alaska would require at least five or six dollars in change that I didn't have, and there were no shops or kiosks to exchange dollars for coins.

The phone rang a couple of times, then Julie picked up. Unfazed, she accepted the reverse charges. When she said hello, I instantly burst into the story. She interrupted to say, "If I get off the phone now, I think I can just catch the pharmacy here before it closes. Give me your number and stay put. I'll call you right back."

As I stood staring at the phone, hoping against hope everything worked out, Hanson, Flora, and Daanawáak somehow materialized around me. Indians are like that. We might be a bit sketchy with linear time, but we can be darn impressive when it comes to whole-mind time.

Hanson confirmed the bag was lost, but the airline had promised to deliver it when they located it. Through several long-distance calls to Alaska, we arranged to pick up a replacement prescription at a Flagstaff pharmacy. There was nothing to do about Daanawáak's clothing. We left Phoenix with Daanawáak wearing the thin maroon golf sweater and small-brim fedora he'd worn for the flight.

An old Volkswagen roared past us on the opposite side of the road, covering us in a big black cloud of exhaust. As our van barreled through to the other side of the noxious nebula, Hanson remarked, "You know how the VW has that shovel-shaped hood and trunk that point down?"

Yes, we did.

"Well, to the Navajo, it looks like a nose. We call them Road Smellers."

We all chuckled, both at the joke and because it broke the tension of the big drive and even bigger worry about getting to the Flagstaff pharmacy and Daanawáak's replacement medications before something untoward happened.

"Well, it's a good name too. According to the Navajo, we are in the Fourth World, the smelly world, and coming to a between-worlds time. The car is like the time," Hanson said.

We leaned forward to hear more, but he had already turned his full attention to the road ahead.

Night had fallen by the time we hit Flagstaff; it was about two minutes before nine, and the drugstore closed on the hour. We quickly paid for the medicines, gave them to Daanawáak, and jumped back in the car and headed for our destination, Shonto. By the time we got to Hanson's house, the high desert environs had turned truly cold. Dry, powdery snow blew across the hardpan, swirled and seeped about the tufts of dried grass. Even in the house, drafts of bone-chilling cold gusted through the thin-walled Bureau of Indian Affairs construction. I worried about Daanawáak taking chill.

That's how I got to learn about making a sacred fire. Daanawáak looked over my shoulder as I chucked shavings, kindling, and pieces of mesquite into the stove. When he saw that I was about to light it, he stopped me and spoke about the meaning of the fire, about its warmth, light, and intelligence. How just seeing the sun makes our hearts open up. "Talk to it," he said. "Feed it, and tell it your love." I stopped, ashamed I'd not known to do this, and so grateful to be taught the right way to relate to it. To show him what his words meant, I kept that fire blazing throughout our four-day stay.

The next morning, the sun came out. We left the house and stepped into the dramatic vista of our Chimney Rock surroundings—enormous red fingers of earth pointed to the sky, and a soft bleating of a distant flock of sheep could be heard in the still desert air. Even with the sunshine, it was still cold, and when we spoke, our words hung in little clouds in the desert air.

Two hogans made of plywood stood adjacent to the house. On the second night, we entered one for an all-night peyote ceremony designed to heal Daanawáak's heart problems and to lift some of his sorrows. Chief among his worries was something he had not mentioned at the airport. The priceless heirloom Chilkat woven robe, belonging to his shaman grandfather, was also in the lost suitcase. I gasped as the three-fold nightmare consumed me. The robe had to be worth in excess of $100,000; if the airlines did ever find his case and open it, surely the robe would go missing. And finally, and most significantly for the ceremony, the designs on the robe carried the healing power of his sacred river, the spirit Daanawáak needed to align with.

Daanawáak's worries were palpable. About midnight, the Navajo Medicine Man, eyes black and full of spirit, looked over at him and said, "Don't worry, I saw your suitcase. It's OK. You'll get it back."

Daanawáak wasn't quite convinced and showed it. So the Medicine Man ate more medicine and prayed really hard, sweat streaming down his face from the intensity and fervor.

About a half hour into this, he said, "The spirits showed me your blanket." He began to describe in detail the curvilinear pattern of symbols and crests woven into the mustard, cream, and black mountain-goat fur and cedar-bark robe. "Don't worry," he said, "the Spirits showed me where it is. It will be returned tomorrow."

Then, as their eyes met, it seemed they both saw right through time and were enjoying a rich, warm conversation with Daanawáak's long-departed shaman grandfather who had used the blanket in healing rituals.

As they spoke, a strange anxiety, shadowlike, came over me. A liminal frisson marked the inter-zone. Terror flashed through me. I was no longer in the hogan, but stood suspended in deep, dark, dangerous, indigo waters. Then, moving with tremendous velocity, I was sucked swiftly toward a huge white luminous triangle. I tried to stop, to back away, to wake up, but nothing could stop or alter the progression of my movement or fear. Closing in on the glowing object, I knew viscerally that it was an enormous, single tooth, larger than me, in the jaw of some unimaginably sized leviathan. I must have asked, surely not consciously, what it was. Instantly, a petroglyph image of the dreaded sea monster, Wasco, flashed in my mind, and along with it, the embodied knowledge of its workings and powers. The dread was so intense, my reality split, and for a second, part of me was glancing down at my chest. I could see the calico fabric of my ribbon shirt visibly rising and falling with each throb of my heart. I couldn't speak or ask for help, because the second I saw my shirt, I was plunged back into the depths. The huge jaw opened; everything went black. Sometime later—maybe an instant, maybe an hour, maybe an eternity—I found myself in a huge bubble of air, floating upward to the surface. I had survived.

I had been initiated into the sacred mysteries of water, but I didn't know that. All I knew was that I'd been scared nearly to death. When I looked around, seeing in a normal way, I was back in the hogan, looking into the eyes of the Medicine Man. Sweat dripped from his exhausted face, and his hair was soaked with perspiration—or maybe sea water. He'd been with me all along.

By dawn, it was clear that Daanawáak's prayers had been answered and that he would have the health to complete his cultural work with young people. He wanted to express his thanks but found his English too limiting for the depth and complexity of what he felt, so he had me interpret for him. Later, I realized we had all been speaking English with Navajo or Tlingit inflections. None of us even questioned the translation process, but if we had, we might have heard a soft caw in the background.

The dying fire crackled and popped in the sacred quiet of ceremonial dawn.

The Medicine Man looked over at me and told me a story that related to my experience. It was about White Shell Changing Woman, and about how there was or would be a time when the Earth was dying. This was because of too much sun, too much fire, and, it was implied, too much distorted male energy. White Shell went to Fajada Butte to fast. She got the vision she was praying for. In accordance with the message, she gathered up her twin boys, and told them they had to go on a walk, a migration, to find the life-giving rains. She told them they must not eat anything on the way. They walked west to the ocean, but on the long journey across the desert, one son found and ate an egg.

When they reached the ocean, he told his mother, "I'm changing. Put me in the ocean."

She did, and he morphed into a gigantic sea monster. The People of the Coast appreciated her mission and agreed to take her by canoe to the "island farthest west." Her sea monster son swam alongside the canoe during the voyage. Before she had left, she promised the Navajo that when she arrived to the island she would send back rains. To this very day, when the clouds move in from the west, the Navajo say, "It's that sacred woman sending us the rain."

Then, in a closing remark, almost offhandedly, the Medicine Man looked at Chief Daanawáa<u>k</u> and me and said, "There are four sacred mountains. One of them, you know about and still respect in your Land. The other is deteriorating, and people are forgetting. The third is unknown, and one is beneath the waves. This one, beneath the waves, is rising and will be seen again. That White Raven that's been seen and that you've been talking about is from that mountain. He's a messenger sent to tell us, 'Change. The between-world's time is coming.'"

Just before we left Navajo land, the suitcase was delivered. We loaded it back in the car and headed for the airport.

Winging our way home to Juneau on a nearly empty Christmas Eve flight, we talked and laughed about lost medicines, dirty clothes, and lost bags. Daanawáa<u>k</u> leaned over and whispered conspiratorially, "When we get back home, you get off first. Take my hat and give it to Julie, who'll be picking me up, and tell her, 'We lost the medicines, we lost the bag, and we lost Mr. Hammond. This is all that is left.'"

The plane wheels hit the tarmac of the ice-fog enshrouded Juneau airport, and we were home.

In the days to come, whenever I thought about the experience, it came back as if it had just happened. New knowledge and responsibility were coming.

Chapter 8

RAVEN'S GIFT

Juneau, Alaska, 1985

A year later, Daanawáak and the Foltas had moved to Haines, leaving a huge hole in my life. I was still in Juneau, rent was due, and my car was low on gas. The pieces of my life, like a broken clay pot, were in shards. Hanging up on a call from a bill collector, heart full of fear, I gathered up my medicine bag and made for Lemon Creek. The day was like my mood—dull, gray clouds so rain soaked and low, it seemed they could bump the top of my head. In despair, I dropped to my knees on the cold, damp sand of the bank and sobbed.

A movement on the far side of the stream caught my attention. I looked up and into the glittery obsidian eye of a huge black raven. He cocked his head to one side as if considering something, and then began shouldering side-to-side, dancing in an up-to-the-minute raven rhythm. Diffused diamond light of the northern rain forest refracted the glimmer of blue, green, lavender, and gold in the movement of this dark-winged dancer. White Raven, a spiritual antecedent and twin to Black Raven, is known for purity and high-mindedness, while Black Raven is known as a trickster spirit, a demigod in his own right, but full of mischief and trouble. Traditional stories bring out his greed, gluttony, promiscuity, and cleverness. With Raven, it's always the case that wrong motivations and behaviors trigger confusion and disaster but eventuate in good luck with lots of chills, thrills, and laughter to anyone hearing the story. Just knowing a Raven story is in the offing makes you want, raven-like, to wiggle your butt, snuggle into a soft chair, and get ready. Often, this naughty Raven, victim of his own doing, brings a great good to life and humanity. Raven can never die.

In one of Chief Daanawáak's more laudatory Raven stories, Raven brings light to the world. At the time of the story, people exist but are living in darkness. A beautiful, young daughter of a chief has the daily habit of going down to the stream to get a drink of water. From on high, maybe from a tree, Raven is watching her. One day, he gets an idea. He transforms himself into a hemlock needle and floats on the water. When the chief's daughter takes a drink, she swallows the needle and becomes pregnant. When her condition becomes known, everyone is upset, for this girl has been protected and has never been with a man. How can this be? When it's time for the birth, the grandmother puts a bearskin down for the delivery, but the baby won't come. The grandmother has been around; she's not easily fooled. On a hunch, she removes the skin and puts down moss, which is one of Raven's nesting materials. Right away, the baby boy comes.

"I knew it," she says. "It's that Raven."

As the handsome, charming child grows, the grandfather comes to love him very much. The boy knows it. He also knows there are three big bentwood boxes in the longhouse, which are always kept closed. The child wants them, so he begins to cry and cry. Eventually, worn down and consumed with concern, the grandfather gives him the boxes, one at a time, and although the boy is not supposed to open them, he does. Out of the boxes come the moon, the stars, and the sun. Then, in deep trouble, the boy transforms into White Raven and escapes by flying up through the smoke hole. He gets stuck, and in the effort to get free, covers himself with soot. This is how white Raven becomes black, and how light is brought into the world. It's a very different story from that of religion or science. This story of life takes into account both light and dark.

In another story set in the time of darkness, Raven encounters people fishing for eulachon. He asks for some, and they say no. He asks again, and again people refuse to share. Finally, he threatens and says, "If you don't share, I'm going to break light on you."

They still won't share. So Raven breaks the light, and when he does, all the beings run for cover. Some go into the ocean and become whales, others run into the forest and become animals. The point is, unlike the religious views, people don't only revere light, they run from it, and Raven knows they will. Too much of anything will destroy. Too much clear fire, and the earth burns. Both dark and light are necessary for life. The ancient stories take this into account.

Sitting on the bank of Lemon Creek, I remembered Daanawáak's words that the Stories are like pages turning in a book, guiding us through life. "Isn't there a Raven who would help me?" I implored aloud.

The words had barely come from my mouth when a sound, like a tea towel being snapped, cracked behind me. Startled, I jumped to my feet just as the Raven hopped up from his side of the stream and took to the air. With extraordinary speed, he came right at me, actually at my inner eye. It happened so fast, and yet I could hear, as if in slow motion, each beat of his broad, black wings as he approached. *Fwap, fwap, fwap!* Somehow, the pulse slowed my mind and brought my spirit back into myself. Nothing existed except the moment. About three feet above me, he halted, midair. He hovered and fanned his wings downward to my upturned face. Instinctively, I raised my arms in prayer, nearly touching that blue-black, shining being. He was that close. Tears, unbidden, streamed down my face as overwhelming emotions coursed through my body.

He then dropped to chest level, about three feet out from me, and began a slow, sunwise circle around my body. A second Raven, who later I realized had been standing behind me from the beginning and whose wings snapping open had created the tea-towel sound, joined the first Raven. They circled my body, once, twice, three times in total aerial cacophony. Upside down, sideways, and right side up they flew. Then, apparently satisfied, they took off, one behind the other toward the Gastineau Channel.

I didn't want them to go and started to follow, but then stopped myself. *Enough is enough*, I said to myself, and stood there on that wet, sandy bank by myself, laughing, crying, and thanking Raven and anyone else who was listening.

I wanted to savor the experience, but eventually the late afternoon chill began to seep into my bones, and I reluctantly turned and walked back toward the house. The riverbed was as familiar to me as the back of my hand, but stalling for time, I looked down through the clear, cold water as if I had never seen it before and spotted something very different. There, in a shallow eddy, was an eight-inch-wide swirl of gold dust and pebbles. Gold! The answer to my prayers! This would cover my rent, phone, car payment, and maybe more. I had to act, but what to do? How to pan for gold? I needed a gold pan. *I'll run back to the house, find something to use—a colander? No, the gold will leak out along with the sand. A cake pan? What about that painted souvenir pan? Yes, that would work, but where was it?* I'd have to run back to the house, find it, and rush back. *No! That might take too long; the gold could be washed away by that time.* My mind raced. *What can I do? I can't leave; it might disappear any second. If I take my eyes off it, I might not find it again.*

I looked down at the gold again. Beautiful! My entire body was filled with desire. I wanted it so much. I could see all my problems disappearing right before my eyes, but as I felt my lust and struggled to figure out how to take the gold, something else moved inside. I looked at the stream, my dearest friend who had comforted me for so long. The gold rush in the 1890s and recent "development" had rendered it barren. To cash in the gold, I'd have to take it to an assayer and report where I found it. I could see a mini gold rush happening all over again, and this time, not to a pristine ecosystem but to this devastated, riverine landscape.

Finally, shaking with effort, I turned away from the gold and walked back to the house. The shadow of the experience, like the bird itself, walked along with me.

Over the years, I asked many people about that Raven story. Some said, "You should have taken the gold." Others said, "It's good you left it behind; you can't trust a Raven." Inside, I worried that I had refused a gift of Spirit—that I walked away from the gold because I didn't think I deserved it. Maybe my concern for the stream was just an affect to keep me from facing darker motivations, but I wasn't exactly sure, because the experience truly was so overwhelming. Apart from wishing I'd gotten the gold, just thinking about that day and those ravens always brings back some of the wonder and joy I'd felt. True, for a few desperate minutes, I did try to figure out how to pan for that gold dust and could not think of a way, but I also didn't care. I had spoken with ravens. What more was there?

~~~

Overnight, the winds had turned around and blew in from the north with such force they scraped the thick cloud cover clean from a stunning blue-gray sky. It was January, and the road to my waterfall destination hadn't been plowed. Trying to keep my lightweight Ford station wagon on frozen, earthen tracks, visible only where snow had melted or blown away, took total concentration. I gripped the wheel tightly. The farther into the woods I went, the deeper the snow was. My heart raced, and a thin film of sweat covered my body. I had one chance to do this. Tomorrow, I was leaving Southeastern Alaska, maybe for good.

The waterfall waited, resplendent in its roaring ice-mist power. It had been such a long time—since the coming of the tall ships—that the People's voice had fallen quiet and ceremonies all but stopped. The headwater's glacier continued to reflect and imbue glowing, zinging, overhead auroras; to receive rain, dew, snow, and all forms of moisture. Its fracturing inward weight and movement continued to crush all impurities from the waters. Seasons later, in a final act of devotion, the glacier still issued an endless rush of icy, pure waters surging toward the edge of the falls, crashing, hissing, and roaring into the waiting mouth of the lagoon.

Where did the invitation come from? I didn't know, but it had me and I was scared, knowing I was about to try something terrifyingly dangerous yet tantalizingly ecstatic if only I could make it through.

Maybe the glimmer of this invitation had begun on my first trip to Juneau. I was on a window seat of an Alaskan Airlines flight. As we circled for a final approach, I looked down on an ice field so massive, I realized it had to be a glacier, the first I'd ever seen. Huge jagged crystals of ice refracted the overcast sky into graduated shades of silver-gray, winter sea green, and indigo. Ice edge angularities and crevice shadows dramatized the sheer size of the river of ice. It had to be more than 20 miles long, and its terminus height at least 70 feet. The expanse of ice was so great that, for a moment, it seemed to suspend the plane, motionless, midair.

An odd feeling came over me. There was something in this sweeping view that made me ache with longing, like encountering an old love. I wanted to hold close the moment, the place, and I had an eerie sense that the feelings weren't just from me. It was as if I were being seen and welcomed, which made no sense. I was looking at ice, a glacier. But no matter how I tried to figure it out, I couldn't tear myself from the beauty.

Or maybe it was after I had relocated to Juneau, when my younger sister arrived for her first visit to the area. The Mendenhall Glacier is close to the airport—driving by could be an immediate, dramatic welcome. Heavy snows had closed the road for weeks, but now, with the thaw in the air, there was a chance it might be open. To my delight, it was. Our animated reunion chatter faded as we concentrated on the road ahead. Steam rose from the warming blacktop, but I proceeded slowly, wary of black ice. Barely a quarter of a mile into the stretch, I felt something strange. Veils of mist, an eerie winter sea green–gray color, hung so low that the tips of the spruces seemed to touch them.

I pulled over and parked the car at the entry to the parking lot. No one else was there. We stepped out and took a breath of cold, clear air. It was then we noticed the eagles, a pair of them on a dark, spiky branch just beyond the car. We noticed another pair off to the side. Behind the second set of eagles, there was another and another, and then scores—no, hundreds—of eagle pairs that snapped into relief. Like fractals, the more you looked, the deeper into it you went. Nothing moved, and then there was an awe-filled silence. No raven caws, no shrill eagle whistles—just absolute silence, so nameless and deep, it made you want to drop to your knees in reverence. A deer stood, stock-still in the snow-covered muskeg, looking directly ahead. Following its gaze, we looked up and gasped. The massive glacier face was a shocking blue, a hue so lustrous and intense it seized your soul. No, it was your soul, and took your breath in an ecstatic embrace. It was the face of God. They all knew.

Something in my sister and me knew too. We never said a word, but simultaneously, we got back into the car, softly closed the doors, and drove slowly out of the park. Some days later, I returned and left a tobacco offering.

Oddly, my sister and I never spoke of that moment for years.

Now, as I prepared for my farewell to Southeast Alaska. I knew the waterfall ritual I was going to do could kill me. Adding to the danger was that fact that I was going alone, without cultural support or protection. *Why didn't I think of this in the summer?* I anguished. *I can still back out*, I told myself, knowing I wouldn't.

Even in warm weather, my ankles would burn with cold and numbness seconds after stepping into the stream. Now it was deep winter and the water so cold, steam rose from it. Stepping to the water's edge, wearing only sneakers and a sweat suit over my swimsuit, I did some rapid mental calculations. *How far from the bank to the falls? How deep? Can I just walk in? If I have to swim, I'll never make it; I'll die of hypothermia first. How to do it?* Even in the few seconds it took to consider these questions, my body had started to shake with cold.

OK, I'll take off my sweatshirt and pants? No, that will take too long. I'll lose too much body heat. Better I take off my socks and shoes first and keep my sweats on. But that won't work—my feet will freeze to the ground. OK, slip off one sock, stand atop the shoe, then slip off the other one. OK, done.

I wobbled on my right shoe, but managed to slip off the left without my right foot slipping off the sneaker to the ground. Next, I took off the sweatpants and pulled my sweatshirt off. Shock! A split-second delay in reaction and an animalistic moan emanated from deep within my trembling, shivering body. I had thirteen minutes left to live, tops.

Will—sheer will—forced my right foot off the shoe platform toward the water. My toes entered the arctic currents, first one foot, then the other, and within seconds, my entire body erupted in convulsive, jerking death throes, lungs gasping raggedly, trying to pull back my essence. *Please*, my soul cried, *please help*—to whom I don't even know, but something, someone, seemed to hear, and a split second before I submerged to certain death, a gust of north wind ripped through the falls, gathered up moisture, and showered me, head to toe, in icy mist. No need to swim to the roaring falls; they had come to me. With chattering teeth and shaking legs, I jumped back on the bank.

Hands frozen like crab claws, I clumsily yanked the sweatshirt over my head, shoved my feet into the pant legs, and pulled them up with my wrists. I rammed my feet into the unlaced sneakers and dashed back to the car, socks stuffed under my arm. Thank God I'd left the engine and heater running. Warmth—ecstatic, delicious warmth—infused my icy tissues and lungs.

"Thank you, thank you," I said. And then? Realizing I'd actually done it, I gave a full-throated Iroquois whoop of joy!

Looking through the windshield at the waterfall, I shook my head in utter amazement. I felt so light, so serene, yet paradoxically alive with energy, and also sad. I would leave this land at dawn, and I did not know if or when I would ever return. Tears came. I needed something, maybe a feather, a stick, something to keep the moment strong in me. I dashed from the car to the stream and looked down. A shimmer of light moved beneath the waters. Reaching into the frigid waters, my hand settled on a small, flat ovoid piece of shale gleaming with blackness and sparkle like a Raven's eye, and I put it in my pocket.

"*Gunalchéesh* (thank you)," I said in the best Tlingit I could manage, and then I got back in my car and left.

> *I have gone to a waterfall*
> *A cold moving water*
> *I have stood beneath the water*
> *Clean!*
>
> *If there is hate in my heart*
> *If there is wrong doing*
> *I want that to wash out*
> *Wash out to the ocean*
> *And let it go…*

RICHARD DALTON, TLINGIT, RAVEN CLAN

Chapter 9

THE RISE OF THE FEMININE

*"You will be going back to the place you
first acquired thought and reason."*

SKY WOMAN

Alberta, Canada, 1986

For some time, I'd heard about a miracle in Alberta, Canada. Entire tribes were said to be recovering from alcoholism. My mind said it was impossible, but for something this central to my life, I had to see firsthand. Off we went, my children and I, on a reconnaissance trip that would last eight years. Barely had I arrived when, serendipitously, I was offered—and accepted—a full-time academic posting in social welfare, with an indigenous emphasis, at the University of Calgary, the heart of Indian Country. Three huge linguistic groups, Algonquin, Athabaskan, and Siouan, and nearly a dozen culturally strong tribes—Blackfeet, Cree, Dogrib, Slavey, Nakota, and Dene—populate the province and surround the city.

Shortly after my hire, I walked into my new office at the university and looked out the window toward the river gorge and the rolling prairies that enveloped it. In the distance, an Indian woman, dressed in pre-contact clothing, appeared at the top of a hill and walked toward me. I blinked my eyes in disbelief.

But what followed—a trip to the Louisiana Choctaw and the following dream—convinced me that She was real.

Something to my right catches my attention. My world is opalescent and silvery, filled with expectancy but lacking any defining feature; I'm on edge. From a distance, a small, dark shape approaches. Odd, how even from afar, in one instant I can make out the contours of his muscular chest and legs as if he were next to me; in the next, he's a dot on the horizon. Closer and closer he comes, the nearer, the more bizarre. His dark head is round and rough like a piece of lava, yet, like a child, his head is nearly as wide as his shoulders. He's focused on me. He approaches in a broad, arcing counterclockwise curve; I can feel his power and am scared. In a few effortless steps, he covers an impossible amount of ground and stops right in front of me and looks directly at and through me. Completely in his grip, I am seized with an intense sense of concentration. His head is a boulder, but in this mindset, I'm not thrown. Satisfied, he turns away and again appears in the distance. In a few seconds, he turns around and looks at me over his shoulder. When our eyes meet, he is in my face but also standing afar. A second, identical Being has arrived. Between them, they carry a three-foot-long capsule-shaped boulder. They stop before me, place the boulder at my feet, and look right at me. Intuitively, I know the rock is hollow and, like a drum, can be used to send vibratory messages. The first Being reaches into a nonexistent pocket on the side of his leg and produces a bundle of red-ocher painted sticks. Checking to see that I'm paying attention, he places the bundle on the rock. The message comes. "You must remember." Without touch or word, the Being directs my attention to the right. A number of rock-headed Beings have formed a ceremonial circle. From the periphery, I see in the center a beautiful, young Native woman, Western attired in long white modern dress and trendy shorn hair. Broken in spirit, she holds her head in her hands and weeps; she is unable to move. The Beings hold hands and, as they look at her, emit an inaudible, high-pitched vibration. Her body jerks and lurches. Dropping her hands, she lifts her head, and begins to dance, awkwardly at first, and then with fluidity.

~~~

For the truth to be real, it must be lived. *Oneida* means "the everlasting stone." In old times, when Oneida migrated, the sacred rock would levitate and travel with the People. For years, I had wished to know some of the secrets of that rock. But it remained silent. This dream changed everything. My Ancestors, the Rock Beings, had touched me. Waking, I found myself filled with spirit, energy, and anticipation.

A few weeks later, I traveled to Louisiana to consult with Jerry Jackson, chief of the Louisiana Choctaw. "Do you have a rock I can use?" I asked. I wanted to move our business conversation into something more intimate and to demonstrate a Talking Circle process we could use in the upcoming Youth Addictions Prevention Camp we were working on. Tactfully, he explained that few rocks exist in the Mississippi Delta. I found this odd. No rocks? He was brief; but still, my attention wandered, and his voice grew distant. The rock-headed Being flashed in my mind.

Jerry paused and looked at me questioningly.

"I had a strange dream the other night about a hollow rock," I offered in explanation.

"Hold on. Hold on right there. I'm not the one you need to talk to," Jerry said, raising his palm toward me. Turning, he called to his assistant. "Go get Aunt Mary. Tell her there's someone she's got to meet."

Pokni, Turtle grandmother, walked through the conference-room door. She looked just like the vision of the woman I'd seen from my office. Dark-skinned, dressed in a traditional maroon calico dress, gray hair in a single plait to her waist; just to look at her opened your heart. Mary Jones was love. Grandchildren walked on either side of her.

As I would learn, Mary was an Elder of few words. "It's surprising what you can see when you're quiet," she would say later, but she was quick to laugh, especially at the twists and turns of life.

Filled with reverence and wonder, I stood to greet her, introduced myself, and offered her tobacco in exchange for her counsel. She took a chair at the table and listened to my dream. As I spoke, she covered her mouth with her hands and shook her head.

"I don't believe it. I don't believe it. You just dreamed our rattle rock and Kwanokasha, the Little Person of the forest, who uses it to heal people. We haven't thought of them for a long time. My daddy used to tell us stories—how Choctaws would be walking in the woods and suddenly get hit on the head with one of those hollow stones." She chuckled. "That's the only way you can get them. The Little People got to give you one. They are Tricksters. They like to throw them at you." She shook her head again and smiled. So began a lifelong friendship.

A few days later, just before I left the youth camp, Mary called me for a ceremony. As she moved a small bundle through cedar smoke, she said, "Girl, the Spirits done gave you a ceremony. This will help."

I smudged and held out my hands to receive the gift. It felt heavy and made a slight sound. Lifting the clean yellow cloth, I beheld an earth-red spindle-shaped rock with a deep seam, as if a potter had overlapped a piece of thick clay.

"It's our rattle rock. Like seeds, it has all the colors of the directions inside, all the directions, all the colors of people on Earth. That's what makes the sound. Don't ever open it."

~~~

"It's the time for women to come forward; women must lead now." I'd heard Indigenous Healers say this for years. Finally, in a ceremony Blackfeet colleagues and I had organized at the Majorville Medicine Wheel in Alberta, I experienced the imperative firsthand. Forty Indigenous Healers and scientists from around the world piled out of the vans and trekked across the high prairie to the top of a small hill surmounted by a rock ring centered with a raised rock altar. As far as we knew, we might be the first ceremonial assemblage at this site since the colonization of the West. Today, New Age books and social media have commercialized and made a fetish of the Medicine Wheel; but it is sacred and powerful, and much of its knowledge kept secret by initiated Medicine Societies. At the time, we sought out Elders and Healers, but no one seemed to know the exact ceremony for the site. We did know that the wheel was traditionally a place for communities to gain collective vision and direction, and it was intimated that an ancient Healer might be buried in the central cairn. Our prayer was to find a way to bring the Western and Indigenous ways of knowing together without eliminating either.

Amethyst, my Blackfeet friend, and I had persuaded her traditional mother to take us seriously and to help us organize the ritual. We were young women, outgunned by powerful, mostly male Healers, with one or two indigenous grandmothers folded into the mix to keep heart in the matter. We were both scared and amazed that such an accomplished group had responded to our invitation, and we worried about our first ever role as ceremonial celebrants.

We reached the top of the hill and to begin the ceremony, in accordance with Amethyst's mom's instructions, women from different cultures—Australian Aboriginal, Jewish, and Native American—prepared to move, each onto a different direction of the Wheel. I was leading the way, but just at the entry, Hopi spokesperson Thomas Banyacya stopped me to give me directions on how to do the ceremony. I didn't know what to say or do. How could I disagree with such an esteemed Elder? The Hopi were one of the most intact Indian tribes in the country. I was awestruck by his presence, but the ceremonial action he prescribed contradicted what we'd planned.

I excused myself and ran quickly to Pokni. Breathlessly, I blurted out the situation. She took it all in and softly replied, "We're doing this just the way you girls planned it. Go tell him."

My fear mounted. Instead of finding a solution, I was in a double-barreled indigenous Elder conundrum. Surely, there had to be an answer more amenable to Thomas's direction, but one look in Gramma's eye told me that the conversation was over. Scared or not, I had to say no to the Hopi Elder. Walking with dread, in cadence with my pounding heart, I went to Thomas. Reserved and silent, dark eyes hazy with cataracts, he appraised me. I took a breath, trying to speak quietly like Mary. Instead, I heard a high-pitched, squeaky voice citing too quickly Blackfeet tradition, "The way we were told to do this is that women from different cultures must take their places on each of the directions and pray."

The winds gusted and roared in my ears as I waited for Thomas to respond.

"Yes," he said, "and when you are done, I'll bring the rest of them in."

I nearly collapsed with relief and didn't have to be told twice. North, east, and south directions were already covered when Amethyst and I, so afraid of failure that we combined forces, scurried to the west direction. When our turn to pray came, my hands shook so badly I couldn't get the matches to light, and when I did, the wind blew them out. Again and again we tried. Finally, foreheads beaded in sweat, running low on matches and dignity, we got one spark to take in the braid of fragrant sweet grass. We breathed a collective sigh of relief and, with tenderness and a sense of urgency, cupped the abalone shell holding the smoldering sweet grass.

As the smoke rose, a sense of peace overtook me. I heard myself praying for the Western and Indigenous minds to quit fighting, to meet, and to help the Earth and humanity heal. Looking up at the sky and not thinking anything, I noticed something odd. One puffy white cloud, alone in the vast blue sky, slid in over our heads.

In a moment of synchronicity, I heard a voice, "What you are praying for is already happening. The key is to restore the balance between male and female."

I was stunned, never having expected to hear a Spirit voice—and so quickly—but had no time to take it in, as Thomas, true to his word, brought the rest of the group onto the wheel.

Waving a small, slender branch, Mayan Elder Hunbatz Man looked up to the clear prairie sky and began to speak to the scattered cumulus clouds lying along the distant horizon. In no time at all, the clouds began to move toward his pointer stick. In they came, faster and faster, from all four directions. Then, as if according to plan, the clouds stopped, forming a perfect ring above our ceremonial circle.

One of the participants, a well-known physicist, abandoned both his English reserve and scientific objectivity, exclaiming, "Did you see that? Hunbatz waved a stick, and the clouds moved in from all four directions, some against the wind! It's impossible!"

I don't remember much after this. The ceremony flowed powerfully and swiftly to its conclusion. I returned to myself and normal consciousness as we moved sunwise and single file off the wheel. I was the last to leave. Stepping from the north direction, Thomas was there, inscrutable as ever, waiting. Considering what he might say, I felt the icy grip of trepidation softly squeezing my lungs.

Just then, Thomas leaned over and gave me a big hug, and for good measure, he turned and hugged Gramma too! "I've been on the road for the Hopi Nation since 1947," he exclaimed, "and everywhere I go, I have to do both parts of the ceremony, the man's and the woman's. The way you women did it today, the way you dressed, everything. I've been waiting to see this since then!"

Once back at the university, as we unpacked the vans and organized things for the next day, I thought back to the miracle of the clouds. "Amethyst, did you see what he did with those clouds?" I asked, still astonished.

"Yes." She snorted, unimpressed. "Him and that stick. Did you ever notice how men always have to have something to wave around? If a woman did it, she would just use her prayers!"

But a few days later, in my office, the euphoria I'd felt when I heard that small cloud's "answer" faded. Peering out the window, I hoped against hope that "She" would be there. Winds rippled through the prairie grass, and I heard myself whisper "But who knows how to restore the balance between male and female?"

~~~

A few months after the Medicine Wheel ceremony, Blackfeet friends, Narcisse and Betty, and I went to a conference in Ottawa. It ended early, and we found ourselves with a half day of free time. We decided to make use of our rental car and drive to see Bear Clan Mohawk Chief, Tom Porter, at his settlement in Upstate New York—the one "local" person we had all met and respected. None of us had been there before, but estimated the trip to be a two-hour scenic drive through the brilliant fall colors of Ontario forest. Indeed, the leaves were ablaze in a red, orange, and gold glow backlit by the setting sun. As we whizzed down the nearly empty road, the colors, shadow, and light swirled about as if we were engulfed in a gigantic kaleidoscope. There was a light feeling, too, as if we had been dislocated from the constraints of chronological time.

The drive took longer than we thought. We didn't mind, as it was an unexpected holiday. Besides, Blackfeet people love to laugh, so the miles zipped by almost unnoticed.

"This reminds me of driving," Narcisse, who was driving, offered in a deadpan voice.

But the humor faded with the end of the third hour. Night had fallen, and rain moved in. Wipers, like a maxed-out metronome, beat faster and faster, sloshing water back and forth across the windshield. Tension built like a thick ball of energy as we moved deeper into the forest. We were anxious, afraid we had missed a sign or turn.

"Look!" I exclaimed, "There it is, the sign! The turn off to Tom's place!"

Beneath the name of the town, the sign read, "Franklin County," the very place denoted on my family tree. My heart pounded, my throat went dry, icy fear slithered across my body, possessing me.

I'm five, running, just steps in front of my raging father. In the small house, the only place to hide is beneath my tiny clothes hanging from a pole. I slide beneath them and curl into the smallest shape I can, right side out, protecting vital organs. "Who do you think you are? You're nothing!" he roars. I cup my hands to the side of my head, trying to still the voice and protect myself from the blows. And then everything stops. Everything is quiet. My spirit has left my body.

I'd survive, traumatized, and unconscious of it, until this very moment.

Narcisse drove around the small settlement in search of a pay phone. He called Tom, who immediately invited us to meet him at the community center where he was teaching a class in culture to a group of young people. As we walked through the door, Clan Mothers, Chiefs, and community people stood in a line. Tom had quickly organized them in a traditional greeting ceremony. In the background, drummers and singers beat out a lively, ancient woodlands song as we visitors snaked our way past the receiving line. At the end of the line, we stopped before Tom and were asked to identify ourselves by tribe and to explain the purpose of our visit, ostensibly to pay respects, and for me silently, unknowingly, to retrieve my spirit, frozen since childhood.

We asked permission to come into the community and were warmly received with handshakes, smiles, and refreshments. Observing us throughout the ceremony, Tom must have seen something. He invited us to his home, a log cabin lit by kerosene lamps, situated on the edge of the woods.

Sitting at my Chief's table, I couldn't think how or where to begin. I was on a numinous threshold, the nexus of my childhood trauma. My fighter, survivor instinct kicked in, and from out of nowhere I heard myself pose an innocuous question. "My family says that we left this town to go to Wisconsin in 1823. But we're Oneida, and this is Mohawk land."

Outwardly, it was a banal inquiry; internally, it was terrifyingly risky: trusting a male authority figure to proclaim my reality, gambling that this cultural man truly embodied Skanagoah, the great tree of life, a northern pine, always green, and whose purifying fragrance and white roots constitute the Iroquois Great Law of Peace.

If I hadn't been so afraid, I might have recalled the traditional story I'd read about mistreated Iroquois children who escaped into the woods to do a mysterious dance so powerful that it elevated them into the heavens where they became the twinkling lights of the Pleiades. In the denouement, the spirit of one of the children returns to Earth, morphing into the White Pine. If I'd been able to think, I might have recalled my childhood, standing in the split-open, downed pine and known it was time for the child to emerge. But that hope—no, that prophecy—wasn't even an echo in the buzzing fear of my mind.

Tom cleared his throat. "After the American Revolution, life became a nightmare for our People. In opposition to the other four tribes of the Hodenosaunee or Iroquois, Oneida sided with the colonists, even taking food to George Washington's troops, who were starving in the deep winter on the Delaware River. The Americans were supposed to be long-standing friends. Benjamin Franklin and other founding fathers studied our Constitution, the Great Law of Peace, and democratic processes to help develop their own Articles of Confederation and later the US Constitution. But after the war, they forgot about our friendship and sent in mounted troops to raze and burn entire Iroquois communities, cornfields, and gardens. They starved us off our lands and then sent in missionaries to convert us and relocate us in the West. Many Oneida people fled their homes and came here for protection because the Mohawk were still strong."

The flame wavered in the kerosene lamp, a soft darkness, a feeling of love, filled the log house. Miraculously, I'd been brought through time and arrived at the exact place where my Oneida Ancestors, fleeing the horrors of genocide, had sought refuge. Skanagoah, sacred tree of peace. I met them here. And something more—in the clarity of trauma released, I remembered the moment my father was about to hit me, how I'd looked up, eyes full of fear, and met his. In that instant, his arms dropped to his sides, his eyes filled with tears, as if remembering a moment in his own childhood. He turned and walked away—and now, beneath the tree and with Tom's help, I forgave him. I love him.

Chapter 10

WAI'I'INI—THE
WATERS OF DESIRE

Hawaii, 1991

The DC-10, red-eye from Calgary to Honolulu slid into a slow curving drift. The change in flight pattern was subtle, but I felt it and awoke. It was 4 a.m. A full moon bathed the darkened, half-empty cabin in a bluish luster. In the arc of the turn, the sound of the engine disappeared; nothing or no one moved. Dream and reality came together in an edgy surrealistic moment. I looked out my window seat, trying to get my bearings. A deep indigo sky with glimmering stars merged seamlessly with the luminous crested waves of the darkened seas below. We seemed suspended in time and space. Coming out of the turn, a distant flash caught my eye and took my breath. A towering cumulonimbus thundercloud, beauteous and dangerous, hung in the void directly before us. Shaped like a monstrous moon jellyfish, its "tentacles" of lightning flashed from the medusa down to the sea. One instant the flattened cloud head was nearly black, the next, a brilliant haze of sheet lightning, then black again. An image of Wasco, potent water spirit petroglyph, seared through my consciousness, and I awoke a second time just as the jet engines throttled up to avoid the storm. I had almost forgotten about the petroglyphs. The move to Alberta, the distance from the petroglyph site, and my failure to decode the symbols had nudged them to the corner of my mind. Yet here at 35,000 feet, the whole experience returned with force. A frisson of excitement moved through me.

~~~

A few months earlier, off the coast of Africa, a wave, innocuous at first, had taken shape. Speeding west across the Atlantic and around South America, it made its way to the warm waters of the Pacific where it met an enormous, elongated, atmospheric trough of low pressure running north to south. Out of the resultant weathered curve appeared a large ragged eye. On August 2, 1991, Hurricane Fefa hit the Hawaiian Islands. Monster waves churned up, sending seawater spraying, and storm surges washed away layers of sand, exposing petroglyphs that had been hidden for hundreds of years.

The morning after the storm, Keoki, camera in hand, made his way down the beach. Working low-paying part-time jobs, his wealth was the beauty of his Hawaiian culture and island. Sporadic unemployment gave him time that day to check out storm damage and, although he could not have predicted it, experience an epiphany. Following the shoreline, wet beach sand squishing between his toes, Keoki was alert to changes.

It was the calm after the storm. Shallow tide-line water was still and crystal clear, the final expression of the African wave. He looked down; what he saw at first shocked, then thrilled him. A field of ancient symbols, messages from his Ancestors lay before him. In his entire life, nothing this momentous had ever happened to him. With tenderness and awe, he moved from image to image, clicking the shutter of his beat-up Kodak camera. Within two days, ocean swells carried in sand and re-covered the site. Except for the prints nestled in the plastic pockets of Keoki's three-ring binder, the transmission would have been lost.

~~~

During our descent into Honolulu, the verdant green Ko'olau Mountains of O'ahu seemed to reach out and hug our Canadian plane. In the final moments, our aircraft swooped through the arc of a glorious, deeply hued rainbow. A spontaneous round of applause and cheers erupted from the passengers when the wheels touched down.

I'd come to Hawaii for an environmental conference and to visit my oldest daughter, a University of Hawaii student. My two younger children were staying with their grandparents. This trip gave me, a single working mother, precious time when all I had to think about was myself. In less than an hour, a taxi took me to my hotel to drop off my luggage, then directly to the convention center for registration, and then I made a mad dash to the conference hall where the opening ceremony was underway. Just as I dropped into my theater seat, a chant burst forth, alternating between powerful rumbling and tremulous quavering, as if the voice of the sea itself—Kumu Hula John Lake, Cultural Practitioner, entered the auditorium. Dressed in a forest-green *kihei* (shoulder sarong) and fern head lei, he slowly made his way from left to right in front of us. As he chanted, images of life evolving from the sea to the mountains flashed on the massive floor-to-ceiling display screen behind him. The audience was spellbound. I was perplexed and ready to be pissed off. Why would the organizers use a science-based slide show on evolution to accompany, or maybe rationalize, his chant?

During the coffee break, I queued up with the crowd to meet Mr. Lake. His performance must have taken a lot of energy, but he greeted each of us as if we were the first. Kumu took my hand and cradled it in his massive Polynesian hands. I introduced myself and my tribe, thanked him, and asked what the slide show had to do with his chant. He looked at me for a moment, allowing for the ire beneath my words to dissipate. "I was chanting the Kumulipo, a creation chant. For Hawaiians, life begins in the sea and evolves. Science is a lot like it." What? A native cosmology that could ground science in the sacred? I wanted to know more but didn't want to keep others waiting. Releasing my hand, he added, "In our culture, everything is passed down from our *kupuna*, family Elders. My auntie, Alice Shaw Ka'ehukai, meaning "wind on the sea," taught me the chant I just offered." Nodding my appreciation, I turned and made for the coffee and might have forgotten the exchange except that I had had a gramma Alice whom I loved.

Making my way through a throng of people, I picked up a cup from the table, thrust it beneath the spigot of a silver samovar, and pressed down the lever. A gurgle of rich, dark, Kona coffee splashed and swirled into my demitasse, releasing a divine fragrance that assailed my senses. And the flavor! So soft and exotic, my knees nearly weakened. A colleague from Canada spotted me standing there in a stuporific caffeine reverie and beelined over to me. With him was a middle-aged Hawaiian man, deeply tanned, thin, and dressed in worn, well-washed surf shorts, rubber slippers, and a faded T-shirt. A three-ring binder, plastic pages sliding out at the corner, was tucked beneath his arm. "I'm so glad I found you!" my Chinook friend gushed. "Apela, this is Keoki. We met

Merle David Patnode (Grampa).

Grampa, me (back), and my cousins.

American Indian Movement Center; Herb Powless (left) and Dennis Banks (right), activist leaders.

The world's first Mongolian-American Indian camel roundup.

Taking a two-day train journey from Inner Mongolia to Turpan in China's Xinjiang Autonomous Region. Apela (center).

The ruins of Jiaohe, an ancient Silk Road caravan city, Xinjiang, China.

Hanson Ashley, M.A., traditional Navajo healer. Advisor for petroglyph research at Copper Mountain, Alaska.

Sketch of the Great Water Spirit petroglyph, Copper Mountain. Known as Moʻo in Hawaii. Sketch by Chyna Colorado.

Tlingit Chief Daanawáak, also known by his English name, Austin Hammond (center).

The Mendenhall Glacier, Juneau, Alaska. It's close to the airport and provides an immediate dramatic confrontation with life.

Thomas Banyacya, Hopi spokesperson (left) and Pokni Mary Jones, Elder of the Louisiana Choctaw (right).

The West Maui Mountains, whose traditional name is Mauna Kahalawai, "House of the Waters and Moon."

Dr. Erick Gbodossou,
a Vodun Healer from Benin.

Miwok Ceremonial hosts, Lanny (left) and Esther Pinola (center)
with Apela (right) in California.

Goree Island,
Senegal,
site of a
traditional
healing
conference.

Tsuno Daishi, the Horned Great Master
and indigenous Japanese healing spirit.

角大師

三千院門跡

Tendai Buddhists describe Tsuno
as a demon. Sanzen-in Temple,
Ohara, Kyoto, Japan.

Ancestral transmissions:
Grampa through me;
me through this book.

Striking the flint
to ignite Uluu
Ot, the Sacred
Fire of ancestral
remembrance and
renewal.

The first Uluu Ot ceremony, 2008.

Kyrgyz shaman Jaygylkan (left) and Hawaiian Elder
Auntie Maile Shaw (right) exchange breath of life
after a fire ceremony in Kyrgyzstan.

Walking to the ancient temple of Umai (Earth Mother), Kyrgyzstan.

at breakfast this morning. When I saw his rock pictures, I knew the two of you had to meet." With that, he took off for his next workshop.

Keoki cleared his throat and shifted nervously from foot to foot, obviously uncomfortable in the professional setting. Nearby, armchairs hidden beneath potted palms offered some privacy. Wordlessly, we hightailed over there and sat down. Without preliminaries, Keoki put the album on the coffee table before us and opened it. Antediluvian symbols swam before my eyes, an entire bank of them! Just as Alaskan Elders had said, they were inscribed before sea rise on the tide lines to give metaphysical and practical direction to ocean navigators. With riveted attention, I tried to make sense of them as quickly as I could. I could feel Keoki's desire to run.

Concentric rings, identical to the petroglyphs on the Northwest Coast recorded three great Earth cycles, numerous petroglyph men and women asserted the significance of genealogy, but abstract signs were beyond my comprehension, especially at the speed Keoki was turning through the pages. If only I could have copies, but I knew better than to ask. This meant too much to him. Abruptly he stood and closed the book; a brief smile moved across his face, and he looked me in the eye as if to say, "See, I told you so," and stepped back. We shook hands; I thanked him profusely, trying to connect. He wasn't the least bit interested. He was a humble man held in rapture. I, on the other hand, would be trying furiously to figure out the images for days. Rock messages are like that. Once you see them and they "see" you, you just can't get them out of your mind. Surrealist art deliberately exploits the uncanny sensation that the visual image means something, that it is familiar at a deep subconscious level. Because the messages of rock petroglyphs are never quite accessible, it keeps us returning to try and understand the mystery.

I never caught on that I might already be living the message.

~~~

A week into my Oʻahu holiday, the phone rang. It was Dorothy, my Haida artist friend, calling from Vancouver. She was coming to the islands and invited me to join her on Maui. As a special treat, we would visit a traditional Hawaiian carver, someone dear to her and her artist husband. Wanting to connect with cultural people of the islands, I leaped at the chance.

The *puu ewa*, or chicken skin feeling, began when we reached the *pali*, the rocky finger of land that juts out into the Pacific, marking the shift in the route south from the airport to the west side of the island. Mythologically, the road is more—much more. Situated at the base of Haleakala ("House of the Sun") Mountain, the Maui airport is in the storied dimension pertaining to light, expansion, and male energy. The west side, including the town of Lahaina, is about the moon, waters, and feminine powers. In fact, the traditional name of the West Maui Mountains is Mauna Kahalawai, "House of the Waters."

Strange feelings of hovering between two worlds grew more pronounced the closer we came to Lahaina. I was both here and in the Navajo ceremony in the high desert of Arizona six years prior. We drove into the small town, rounded a corner, and pulled into the carport of an A-frame version of a chief's traditional grasshouse. Dorothy turned off the engine. As we gathered up our things, the back door of the house opened. Keola stepped out, shot a glance at us, and trotted down the porch stairs to greet us. The hair on the back of my neck stood up as a visionary wave of remembrance washed over me. I looked hard; a trail of bubbles emanated from him as if he were breathing under water. *My God, it's the vision! The sea spirit, the Navajo ceremony come to life!*

"Aloha, welcome," Keola said as he stepped off the stairs and into my life—my future husband and home. I would not return to Canada, except to get my children.

Keola had designed and built—with his own hands—the small house, based on traditional Hawaiian grasshouse architecture. It was the only such place on all six islands. Three-dimensional images of the Hawaiian gods, bowls of light, and every manner of artifact, all carved by him, filled the house.

The nameplate on a canoe painting caught my eye. "What does this name, *Mo'olele*, mean?"

"The flying, probably more accurate to say quarking, lizard or dragon."

"What? What did you say?"

"The lizard is an animal that goes between physical and temporal dimensions. It can go into the water, but always comes back to land. That's why I gave the name to the canoe—so that it could always return safely."

He looked off for a moment, considering where to begin. "A *mo'o* (pronounced mow-oh) a giant 34-foot black lizard, lived in the old pond across the street. In Hawaiian, *mo'o* means "something iterative"; it represents your genealogy. Each vertebra of its spine is a generation. A favorite grandchild is a *mo'opuna*, and a *mo'olelo* is a genealogical chant. A *Kahuna*, sacred site guardian, took care of the pond and the ways. When we were growing up, they used to tell us that if we misbehaved the Moʻo would eat us. Even now, we don't kill little lizards or geckos because our *tutus* (grandparents) told us they are related to the Kihawahine, the lizard goddess."

I was a newcomer and a guest, so I tried to control my excitement as I hurriedly sketched out what had happened to me with the lizard, coming upon the Alaskan Wasco petroglyph on the rocks at Copper Mountain, and the terror of the "design" coming alive in the Navajo ceremony.

To my absolute wonder, Keola's Hawaiian Moʻo Story picked up where the Native American story ended. This was the island farthest west where White Shell Woman and her water spirit son had come for the life-giving waters to send back to Navajo land, which was dying of thirst. Until this moment, I had no idea that traditional stories comprised an interlocking global web of knowledge. It all fit together—and somehow my life in it.

"Here? The pond and lizard are right here?" I asked a little too loudly. "Can we go see it? Can I meet the sacred site guardian?'

"There's nothing to see now. The plantation dammed the headwaters and diverted the stream to irrigate their sugar cane. The pond became stagnant, began to stink and breed mosquitoes. In the early 1900s, the plantation provided a 'community service' by filling it with earth dredged out of the harbor, and… garbage." Keola looked off, struggling to control his emotion. "Mrs. Shaw died in 1956. They say Alice might have been the last Kahuna, the one that knows the secrets of the place. I knew her when I was a kid. She was my grandmother's friend. Like my gramma, she was part Hauʻoli, or European. Her grandfather came from Ireland. She knew something about the Moʻo—that's for sure. If you're around tomorrow, I'll take you to my sister's next door. Alice's granddaughter, Noni, is staying with her."

I looked out the kitchen window. Beyond the streetlight, a shadow hung low and close to the ground where the waters should have been. I was devastated. I'd come so close. I was nine when Mrs. Shaw died—young, but old enough to have known her. Alice Shaw was the embodiment of all I sought: a woman who moved between the worlds and knew the old ways of sacred power. She knew about the water spirit and could have helped me decipher the petroglyphs so I could understand my own relationship to the water spirit, maybe discover a sacred power of my own. My body trembled in anguish.

The next morning, I met up with Keola, who walked me over to his sister's house. Auntie Babe was busy watching her grandchildren but took time for a quick, friendly, introduction. Moving from the entryway into the living room, I saw a flaxen-haired, thirtyish woman, attired in an unassuming loose dress, sitting in a chair near the picture window. An instantaneous flash of energy, of love, flowed between us the minute our eyes met, and our embrace was that of long-lost friends. "Aloha," she said softly, "I'm Noni Shaw."

Keola hugged Noni and told her of my interest in the Mo'o, and because of the special feeling, the *mana*, that now filled the room and coursed through my body, I told her what had happened to me—about the Wasco petroglyph and the Navajo ceremony, how I'd been devoured and breathed out by a great lizard, and how that vision had turned my life upside down. I knew, instinctively, I would not be returning to Canada but didn't know what to do next.

The comfort, the *Aloha*, I felt in Noni's presence triggered a rush of words and emotion as I related my story. "I'm searching," I concluded, "to find out what this means. A Spirit's got me. I can't stop looking, and I want to! But none of it is making any sense."

Noni nodded her understanding. "My grandmother Alice Shaw was a caretaker to Mokuhinia Pond; the island in the pond, called Mokuʻula; and the Moʻo," she began—somewhat cautiously I thought. "She owned the land around the pond. Her house was just a half block away from here, on the ocean, next to the pond." Noni stopped as if testing if it were right to proceed. I sat on the edge of my chair for what seemed an eternity. "We think she was a Kahu, a spiritual practitioner."

Silence.

"Is anyone following in her footsteps?"

Noni gently shook her head. "No. It would probably be too hard to do it now."

I thanked her and rose to leave. Noni stepped forward to hug me. The Aloha, love, and warmth flowed between us, and we parted as family.

Keola and I walked through Lahaina's streets and its string of tourist shops until we reached the community park that now covered the site. In the weeks to come, I would learn that this site had been so sacred that only the Kahuna and monarchy were allowed on the ceremonial island. It was the essence of Hawaiian spirituality and of women's sacred powers. Kauʻaula, the red stream, a thinly disguised reference to menses, coursed its way down from the House of the Moon Mountains to the pond. Mokuʻula denoted a red island, a place of birth and rebirth. Two cemeteries were on the sacred site: one on the islet itself from prehistoric times, and the other, more recent, on the periphery of the pond. For hidden reasons, powerful cultural people, a veritable "who's who" of their time, chose interment here. With the Hawaiian Kingdom falling apart, the islet became a final retreat and refuge for King Kamehameha III and for traditional Hawaiian culture.

~~~

Moku'ula Island, 1838

On a moonlit night, a Kahuna, holder of the secret knowledge, approaches an altar at the edge of Moku'ula islet. The sheer gravitas of what is about to happen will establish the power and mystery of the site for all time. On this night, the deepest cultural practices will be employed while seeming to break with all tradition. Guests, sailors, and hundreds of people have turned out for the show and the beauty of Polynesian women. Boston missionaries arrive, excited by the chance to ferret out remaining heathens. Businessmen and politicians on the lookout for power—and threats to it—are there. Hawaiians with a focused intensity, and perhaps a few newcomers with a sense of curiosity or wonder, have all been invited to attend. Murmurs— speculative, derisive, and dismissive—rustle through the people arrayed on the banks of the 13-acre body of water. Small children allowed up past bedtime scurry through the crowd, playing tag and teasing each other.

The Kahuna, black eyes filled with passion, begins chanting in the unique, complex compositional processes of Polynesia, "*E iho ana o luna, e pi'i ana o lalo.* Bring down that which is above by means of the light. To ascend, take from darkness into light that which is below by means of light."

Her voice, rich with vibrato, seems to move both the chant and Kahuna ever so slowly toward the waterside altar. Heart-touching sounds, tonal patterns, and vibrations carry the same frequency as that being called.

"*E hui ana nā moku.* This will transform the spiritual energy as it flows from Source and integrates all of you, giving peace. This will affect you profoundly, change your life, bring illumination."

Silence falls over the crowd.

Aulima in hand, the priestess rubs the straight, chocolate-colored hardwood stick in its soft, lightwood *aunaki* base. Back and forth it goes, invoking a tender, powerful sensuality, quintessence of Aloha.

"*E kū ana ka paia,*" her voice breaks in.

"*I'i.* You will feel the delightful supreme fire."

Everyone feels it, but it's an ambivalent experience, for this is a time of strident Christianity. Men, accustomed to certitude, shift their weight from foot to foot. Women, cheeks flushed, make inconsequential adjustments to their clothing, and children stop dead in their tracks.

A spark flies from the aunaki to a prepared bed of dry moss cradled in a waxy green ti leaf. The priestess leans forward, cradles the leaf, and ever so gently blows until the spark takes hold. An orange glow smolders up and through strands of moss. Tenderly, she places this spark of life on waiting kindling and breathes life into it. Flames erupt, dance, and swirl with the rise and fall of her voice in prayer. Small fish school into a vesica piscis geometry, their transparent fins nearly motionless, float, stationary in the water, singly and collectively, facing the altar. The priestess nods to the fish and to her helpers who move in to *malama*, to cherish and care for the fire. It is time.

Why this Kahuna, the last of a generation trained in arcane spiritual practices of Hawaii, decided to share the deep occult practices of Mokuhinia, the pond, we may never know. Maybe it was the sacred site's centrality to conception and the continuity of life, or maybe she was just fed up with all the lies about betterment of the race, profit, and Christ in the face of so much destruction and death. Perhaps she had a premonition and invoked and put into motion something that would make a difference in the times to come. Whatever it was, it was so important that she risked exposing herself and the *huna*, the secret ways of connecting to unseen dimensions and beings. The ceremony was performed in a time of extreme cultural duress, surrounded by hatred and greed. To be certain the night would be remembered, Hawaiian historian Kamakau made a record of the event and the chant, which was actually a 100-year-old prophecy first uttered by Kipihe, a noted *kaula*, or orator, from Kona.

Walking to the water's edge, the Kahuna glances upward to the east and the notched mountain crest, the "vagina of the moon." Silver light quivers and dances between the tips like a flame catching on the wick of an oil lamp. Brighter, stronger, the lustrous fluid undulates. Suddenly, a brilliant ray of translucent light shoots out into the dark, starlit sky, followed by another and another. The rays fan back and forth, then dissolve as the outer arc of a magnificent full moon pushes itself up through the labia and ascends in the nighttime sky. Jettisoning Calvinistic reticence, the crowd gasps and surges forward to the water's edge, trying to get a better look.

Nearly overhead, the moon's light reflects on the still pond and begins to dance, skip, and move in strange ways, first stretching, then contracting, forming grooves and ridges in the water. The crowd hushes, and like the fish, totally intent, draws itself in and presses forward. There is a terrible commotion beneath the water's surface. The tone, resonance, and frequency of the Kahuna's ululation rise and intensify as the helpers join in. Faster and harder, the waves move, but just in one spot. Suddenly, a woman screams, and the crowd gasps; some run in terror while others freeze in place as the head of a 30-foot black Mo'o surfaces. Then, as if greeting a dear friend, the ceremonialist Kahuna leans over the edge of the pond toward the Mo'o. Calmly, she reaches down near the altar to pick up a gourd of the ritual drink, *awa*, and ever so slowly, she pours it into the water. The beige-colored drink billows out and floats in a cloud toward the waiting lizard that drinks deeply. In a few moments, it begins to roll back and forth in the water with delight. Dread transforms into reverence. The crowd falls silent. No one moves—no one wants to. An entire disparate community has entered *Manawa*, sacred time. Some fortunate ones merge into the time of creative darkness, the unfolding world of *Po*.

With the ceremonial realization achieved, the Mo'o slides back into the dark waters, the fire dims, and the chanting ends.

The moon's glissade carries time and consciousness west toward the ocean. Stillness, beauty, and peace shimmer in the air and, slowly, as if waking from a dream, people begin to stir, to collect themselves and make their way back home. Minutes, maybe hours, have passed.

Standing in the shadows of a nonendemic, false kamane tree, a plantation businessman, intent on damming and diverting the headwaters of Mokuhinia for sugar cane, turns to leave. Then, as if having a second thought, he stops. Taking in the moment, his eyes narrow, and his lips press into a thin line; he'll do all he can to stop this hocus-pocus bullshit.

Shortly after this ceremony in 1838, the conquest of the Hawaiian Islands neared culmination. Two-thirds of Indigenous People had died or were dying from European illnesses, or were "peaceably extinguished," as reported in a national newspaper of the time. A native monarchy supplanted tribal forms of governance. The spirituality of Aloha, the original nature-based ways, would be violently suppressed along with all forms of culture. As the people and culture perished, so did the islands and sea suffer.

One hundred years later, brought here by a vision, I stood, mixed-blood, perpetrator and victim, at the edge of the devastated sacred site. What was I being asked to do? What could I possibly have to offer?

Chapter 11

KANEWAIOLA—THE CRY THAT CATCHES IN THE THROAT

Maui, Hawaii, 1991

Polynesia runs 3,200 miles from the Tropic of Cancer to the Tropic of Capricorn, and is neatly bisected by the equator. The climate, currents, and characteristics of both hemispheres are identical and yet opposite: When it's summer in the north, it's winter in the south, water swirling one way in the south swirls opposite in the north, and so on.

The architecture of the Polynesian canoe represents this geography and underlying cosmology. In the chant known as the Kumulipo, Creation progresses through *wa* or units of time. *Wa'a* refers to the giant double-hulled oceangoing canoes of Polynesia. The design of the wa'a evinces cosmic lovemaking—twin hulls, one male, one female, are constructed and exist separately. A ceremony is held to join the *iako* (yoke pieces) and *pola* (platform) to the wa'a. *Pola* signifies the complex cycle of the planet Venus—as morning star, evening star, and then its disappearance. This mirrors the Hawaiian understanding of the phases and process of love.

Esteemed Hawaiian Elder Hale Makua put it this way: "The wa'a is actually an analogy for the very process of material creation. There is no output from a state of order (two separate hulls). When the hulls are joined (separations and divisions surface), chaos must ensue and invent its own pattern or connection, yin/ yang (male/female) will find their ecstatic balance and flow again, and creation will manifest at that still point just before the new flow begins—over and over again."

The passion of the Polynesian mind lies in its extraordinary ability to embrace and creatively use paradox. If the two hulls are joined at precisely the right distance, the canoe, at full sailing speed, will create its own wake to surf on—a perpetual motion machine. Similarly, in *Ho'oponopono*, the traditional conflict resolution process, the Cultural Practitioner helps create a network between the opposing viewpoints or habitual selves that allows dualistic consciousness to stand while becoming fully embodied by the ecstatic love of Aloha.

When I met Keola, found the pond, and learned about Alice Shaw, I knew I'd come to the right place. I fervently believed the ceremonies of the Mo'o would be restored and that I had been brought here to help make it happen. So did Keola.

One of the first things Keola and I did was to join forces with other friends and form an organization dedicated to restoring Mokuhinia Pond. For Hawaiians, the waters of the pond and the lizard in it—like the fetus in the womb—represent conception, the moment and exact point of the material and spiritual worlds meeting. Before the American sugar barons invaded, Mokuhinia was so holy that to raise one's voice or drop a piece of litter in its environs could be punishable by death. Common people were not even allowed access to the pond's ceremonial island. These sanctions kept the island and pond vibrant with fresh, clean water and life. Arriving Europeans described Lahaina as the Venice of the Pacific.

In contemporary times, the local government had constructed a tennis court and baseball fields over the site. Unknowingly, young people slid into home base over the graves of their Ancestors.

We were determined to reclaim and restore the indigenous sanctity of the place.

Once we proved the existence of burials on the former islet, federal law superseded local and state laws; the playing fields were moved, fences taken down, and the door opened for renewal. We rejoiced and set up a monument on the old island: a *Pohaku*, a large standing stone, guardian of the dark sacred time of creation. Now there was a focal point for culture-based ceremony and prayer. It also marked our promise to Mokuhinia to restore her waters.

New love equals new energy. Immediately following the monument installation, Keola and I jumped feet first into a massive three-year community project to build a 64-foot double-hulled traditional oceangoing canoe. Traditionally, the wood carver, *Kalai Wa'a*, holds a central and sacred role—without him there would be no canoe, and therefore no Polynesians. Keola, an expert carver, wanted to help heal historical wounds of colonization, sugar cane plantations, and exploitative tourism. For my part, having learned that the Hawaiian canoe embodies the Mo'o, or water spirit, I leaped at the chance to join in. My background in community organizing was a seamless fit for the project and for the deepening of our relationship.

Our first task was to find a work site. The land we found turned out to be Alice Shaw's former homesite. The project took off. Within a year, volunteers put in over 15,000 hours of work—unheard of on an island filled with vacationers and locals working two jobs at minimum wage. Every day we woke eager to get to work. It was as if our love had been writ large.

Just as we were about to connect the twin hulls, something foreboding happened.

A public ceremony, complete with local politicians, was being held at the site of the old pond. On the islands, it's customary to offer Hawaiian prayers at such events. Keola made his first traditional awa offering on our group's behalf. When he released the awa powder, a whirlwind appeared out of nowhere and spun the offering in a visible small tornado. He was shaken by the moment, and afterward said he felt an energy surge up from the ground through his feet and body. Two days later, an ancient, black rock mo'o appeared on a table in the canoe house. No one saw it come, and no one ever found out where it came from. Elders said they didn't know any more of these existed. Surely the pond would be restored, the ceremony and culture certain to rebound. We rejoiced. It was short-lived.

The next day, we joined the hulls, and all hell broke loose. At issue was ownership. Macho, heavy-breathing guys whose highest aspiration was to have the power of the *luna*, the sugar cane plantation overseer who had dominated their families for generations, said the canoe was theirs. Assimilated and unreflective, they physically threatened board members, including women; they rigged an election and took the project over. In the face of such hostility, public participation halted, even though visitors and other non-Hawaiian-descended people had done 90 percent of the work. We called on Hawaiian Elders to help. In the name of protecting their "cultural" rights, the thugs laughed in the face of the Elders. Over the course of the next year, they hired other designers and removed, sold, or destroyed the traditional Hawaiian, curvilinear, feminine design features and replaced them with Western, straight line canoe parts.

It was a bitter moment. The project had started out so well, so filled with love. In 20 years of indigenous community development work, I'd never seen anything like it. Why would the Ancestors allow this injustice, this boot stomp on a cultural, spiritual renaissance? Maybe there would never be a way to come to peace with the loss of the Americas and parallel destruction of my family. But this was the closest I'd come, and I wasn't doing it alone. I was furious to find myself lost again. I dug deep into myself, trying to make sense of it, but nothing, no truth, no explanation emanated. In the still moments of life, I blamed myself for daring to believe I had a place in the community or a role in our healing.

Keola and I stood at the doorway of darkness. It would take him three years to pull through severe depression, and I would soon confront catastrophic illness, but in the moment, I railed against the injustice to women, culture, and to the sacred site.

～～

During those early years on Maui, the story of the ravens and the gold persisted in my thoughts. There was something more to it, something I couldn't put my finger on. From time to time, when I met someone whom I thought might shed light on the experience, I'd mention what had happened that overcast fall day when I'd walked Lemon Creek. One day, I told the story to my Athabascan friends Adelheid and Kay who listened attentively.

This time I ended the story with a question, "Did I do the right thing, leaving the gold there, or should I have tried to take it?"

They looked at me and nodded their heads sympathetically, as if to say, "That's a Raven, all right." Being Indian, they might have left it right there, but Kay is an Elder and a Healer. She had a view into it.

Looking over her cup of coffee, she asked softly, "What happened next?"

"I... I never thought of that," I stammered.

The entire next year—this is a Raven story after all—I thought about her question a lot. Nothing came. I saw no connections, until one dawn as I lay in bed and listened to the song of tropical birds. The ones with the biggest eyes began, and with each added increment of light, smaller-eyed birds joined in, one species at a time. This went on until it was completely light, and the song reached crescendo. Half-awake, I found myself remembering a wealthy socialite party I had attended in New York City soon after I left Alaska.

I was there because a philanthropist, one of our university board members, wanted me to meet others who might support my work with Indigenous Wisdom. I'm a bit introverted, don't drink, and generally don't do well in that kind of social setting, so I was nervous. The first thing I noticed was the clothing. Although this was an informal party in the city's Meatpacking District, the way people dressed was an art in itself. Designer ensembles tastefully and seamlessly merged with personality and status. I looked at my own clothing. Wisely, I'd chosen an Indian tunic, full-length skirt, and high-top moccasins. I was in a category of my own, hopefully adding some welcomed "non-ensemble" diversity.

The room was filled with the quiet clink of glasses. Intelligent and stimulating conversation on topics and tangents I'd never considered swirled around me. I was supposed to be putting my best foot forward and promoting interest in my work; instead, I made for the bathroom to catch my breath and bearings. The heavy door shut with a soft thud behind me. The room was as big as my bedroom. I went to the sink and splashed cold water on my face; the towel was so thick it felt like a pillow to my face. I wanted to rest there until the party was over. Looking at myself in the mirror, I took a breath and reminded myself of all the good that could come from this gathering. I opened the door and plunged back into the crowd.

My timing was off; people had already aggregated into small, engaged conversations. I sat down on an overstuffed confidante, picked up a magazine, and idly leafed through it. My anxiety was building. I didn't know what to do or how to be.

Then my hostess appeared, leaned over, and said, "Come with me. I want to introduce you to someone."

We made our way past potted palms and floor-to-ceiling windows, through several large, noise-filled rooms to a couple of men seated face-to-face near the window of a small study. One man, wind tanned, eyes bright with intelligence and humor, rose to meet us. I found myself staring, eye level, at his necktie. Two things hit me at once; the name—he was a Rockefeller—and the design on the tie: scores of tiny, Northwest Coast–style black ravens! I laughed out loud. Raven, of course! The whole experience instantly made sense, the feeling of edginess amidst the beauty of the home, my Indigenous self set in great secular power. This is the kind of thing our special bird delights in. I found my footing. I belonged here.

David Rockefeller smiled. "You like my tie."

"Yes, I lived in Alaska for many years and was taken into the Raven Clan. That's why I recognize the design."

He replied in his warm, sonorous rumble of a voice, "That's very interesting. I was adopted into the Raven Clan in a ceremony given by a Tlingit Chief, a great orator and Storyteller. You may know of him—Daanawáa<u>k</u>, or in English, Austin Hammond."

"Yes!" I nearly shouted with relief. This was why I was at this gathering; it was for this meeting. "Chief Daanawáa<u>k</u>, Raven Clan Chief, was my mentor."

David smiled. "We have a lot to talk about," he said, gesturing to two empty plush chairs.

~~~

Ancestral messengers kept pouring into my life—philanthropists, foundation directors, program officers, and a steady stream of Indigenous Elders and Healers. Each had a strong Earth ethic and vision that connected with mine. The Kihawahine—freshwater lizard goddess, spirit of conception, of the love that unites the seen and unseen worlds—was on the move, but *still* I didn't see it. Since the pond was filled and there were no living Kahunas who knew the ceremonies, I unconsciously believed that the way—and maybe the spirit—had left.

I met William E. (Bill) Simon when he came to my home to buy artwork from Keola. Our rapport was immediate. A self-made man, Bill had risen from the working class, and was considered one of the founders of the modern conservative movement. He eventually served as the treasury secretary of the United States.

Ultimately, he emerged as one of the best financial minds of the 20th century. He made a lot of enemies on the way up, and was honest about it.

"Most people don't like me—think I'm an ass."

"Yes," I responded, "but a precious one." We laughed.

He had a sharp-witted, mercurial personality and was a ball of energy. Bill was also a man who loved his Catholic faith, donating millions to charity and serving as a Eucharistic minister. The church recognized his contribution and awarded him membership in the institutionally prestigious Knights of Saint John, a modern offshoot of the medieval Knights Templar. His passionate faith and place of prominence within the church eventually empowered me to confront my issues with it. With Bill as a friend, no one would dare lay a hand on me.

One Sunday, when Bill was on the island, I joined him for Mass. Our island churches are small, human-scale edifices. Holy Rosary in Paia was basically one large room. It had no transept; just a set of double doors placed before and on either side of the altar. The weather was sultry and uncomfortably hot, so both sets of doors had been opened. The Mass progressed. About halfway through, just before Communion, a stillness and sanctity took hold. At the same moment, the heavens opened up. Torrents of rain roared off the roof, shushed and splattered on the sidewalk, and streamed so intensely off the doorframes, it looked like beaded curtains. The moment was an exquisite blend of nature and religion.

Kneeling, deep in prayer with a rosary wrapped around one hand, Bill looked over at me. "Apela, we have done this through many iterations."

And because our connection was real, I responded, "I know, I just had the same thought."

The Mass ended. Father Gary stood at the foyer, shaking hands and visiting with congregants.

"He's a good priest," Bill said. He introduced us when we reached the head of the line, and I agreed. A few days later, I called to schedule what I hoped would be a ritual of reconciliation.

When I was a child, the rite of reconciliation was called confession, and it usually occurred in a dark, confined place. This was good for self-examination, but dangerous when pedophile priests roamed freely. Father Gary met me at the church door and led me to a pew in the front of the church.

"Let's sit here," he said quietly.

"Father," I said, "I want to make peace with the church."

He looked down for a moment to consider the matter. "I think it will be fine. Let's begin."

With that, I poured out my experiences—how at age nine, the glimpse of the gold chalice seen through an open church door had caught my attention, and how I begged my parents for permission to attend services. I spoke of how I loved my sky-blue catechism book, and how the weekly services became a refuge from the violence in my alcoholic home, how I studied for my Communion. The advances of a pedophile priest were shattering, a betrayal that led me to abandon an important place of refuge. When I finished, Father Gary asked me if there was anything more. I shook my head, too choked with emotion to speak.

"Normally, at this time, I give people prayers to say in atonement, but in your case, there is no need. You have suffered for years and missed out on the blessings of faith. So just say the closing prayer, an act of confession, and I will give you a blessing."

Ritual complete, he stood to go. I stood, too, in respect. He smiled and held out his arms. I stepped forward into his embrace.

"Welcome home," he said.

Chapter 12

THE SHADOWS

*"There will be those who will live among creation, and
there will be those who will try and control it."*

IROQUOIS CREATION STORY

The years of volunteer work on the Polynesian canoe project had burned through my modest Canadian university savings. I needed a job, and I needed one quickly—I had teenage children to care for. One day the phone rang, and out of the blue came an offer to help set up a fully accredited, advanced degree university program in San Francisco. Jurgen Kremer, psychologist, university department head at the California Institute of Integral Studies, who had extensive experience working with Indigenous People, was calling. He saw a need for diversity within the student body and the pedagogy of the institution. A mutual friend had recommended me.

I flew to California to meet with him. We connected on the spot and within hours came up with a daring plan. Conventional native studies programs objectified Native People and taught from a Western perspective. We would stand this model on end! Instead of Western pedagogy, we'd teach from an indigenous perspective, then selectively fold in the best, most appropriate knowledge of the West. We'd draw on colleagues from both worlds to teach. The approach would nudge academe toward inclusivity and nurture the reemergence of protocols for international indigenous unification. Periodicals like *Winds of Change* and the *American Indian Science and Engineering Journal* called it a "breakthrough in education." We believed it.

Within six months, we recruited and admitted students and found a perfect place to meet, a retreat center situated in the California redwoods. The site included guest cottages, a state-of-the-art theater, pool-room, and even a fire pit with a tipi. It was perfect for an indigenous-oriented program, and even though it was always cold and dark, every building featured a wood-burning fireplace. When cold, we could build a fire to warm up.

I didn't need a fire to warm me. As a mixed-heritage person, the chance to consciously bring the worlds together filled me with happiness and excitement. I was no longer alone, moving back and forth between disparate identities. Here was a place I could share both success and failure, and learn as well as teach. Looking back, I think how strange it was that we never really considered the implications of the Center's name, The Shadows.

A team of international Indigenous Healers—Choctaw, Mary Jones; our local hosts and Miwok Elders, Lanny and Esther Pinola; Hawaiian Elder, Hale Makua; a doctor and Vodun Healer from Benin, Erick Gbodossou—guided the development of the work. But the intertribal student body didn't necessarily share our international tribal perspective, and there were no models to draw from. They assumed they were entering a typical native studies program and preferred to stay within conventional tribal parameters. Navajo stayed with Navajo, Nez Perce with Nez Perce. Tensions escalated with everyone thrust together for 24 hours a day in a contained environment. In the hundreds of years since European contact, tribes have had to fight every day of life to assert boundaries, to protect Lands and People. Suddenly students were being asked to drop their walls, to risk vulnerability—and ultimately be graded for it—and intimacy with others, and to do so in a new, untested academic process. Classes felt more like a battleground than a place of learning.

Guest instructor Buddy Powless, a young Oneida Medicine Man I'd known since his childhood, caught me running through bushy baby redwoods on my way to the next class. Looking at me, pointedly, he observed, "I thought you said these were traditional people." His words pierced my heart. Despite our dream to attract and serve Cultural Practitioners, the fact was, only one student, Hanson Ashley, who'd worked with me on the Alaskan petroglyph project, was a Healer—and barely halfway through the first semester, he had decided to withdraw from the program. "This is not what I was looking for," he had said softly.

Our sole international participant, a woman from Southeast Asia who had experienced such cultural trauma that she only spoke in whispers, confronted me, saying, "If I knew it was going to be this bad, I would have stayed home. I thought this would be different."

If I lectured, assimilated students looked to Jurgen for approval. If Jurgen spoke, the more cultural students looked to me for affirmation. Like a striker on flint, tensions erupted into violence.

One day, a repetitive clicking sound, soft, then iteratively growing louder until it dominated the Talking Circle process, emanated from a male student with a stiletto knife in his hand, a Vietnam vet with plenty of unresolved anger.

The bifurcation triggered childhood memories of alcohol-fueled rage. I trembled with fear and silently prayed to the Ancestors for help. A movement outside the door caught my eye.

Esther and Lanny stood in the entryway. There had to be an emergency for them to show up unannounced. Jurgen looked at me, nodded, and took over the class. Stunned and relieved, I went to the door to meet them.

"We had to come," Esther said. "Are you all right? We were home when the feelings got so strong that we had to come and check up on you." She wrapped her arms around me and drew me close. "I thought so." She stood back. "Let's see what we can do."

An hour later a ceremonial fire blazed; students and faculty alike sang, prayed, danced, and shared stories; we concluded with a good meal. We were not alone in the horrors of a genocidal past or the immediate effects of internalized self-hatred and projection. Healers had come to help us through a narrow, frightening passage.

Shortly after her intervention at The Shadows, Esther decided to share and teach her ceremonial songs to all of us—a huge act of trust. But tragically, like the history of California Indian people, she never had the opportunity. The university downsized and terminated the program. Shortly after, Esther passed away.

The devastating news of termination also held a blessing. The hard fact was I did not have the strength to continue the work.

~~~

After my time at The Shadows and my sojourn in academic life, I returned to Maui both weaker and stronger. Weaker because my health was rapidly deteriorating—headaches, physical weakness, and weight loss had become "normal." My T-shirts hung loosely on my small frame. The inner strength I felt was thanks to Hanson. Before he had left the program, he offered this advice: "When you're out of balance, you need to go back to the Creation Story of your people. At that place of Creation Emergence, you put yourself in balance, and from that place of Creation, tell your story in a new balanced way."

Instinctively I knew this was the spiritual work before me. I would find my health and creativity by embodying my Creation Story. Abstract knowledge of it was not enough. What to do? Like a flash, I saw Chief Daanawáak, preeminent Storyteller, in my mind's eye. It had been almost 10 years since we'd seen each other, and almost that long since we'd spoken.

Filled with anticipation, I mentally hurried the impulses of my touchtone phone as it connected with Alaska. In a couple of rings, Betsy, a young student of his and friend of mine, picked up. Excited to reconnect, we repeatedly talked over and interrupted each other before dissolving into laughter. But when I asked about Chief Daanawáak, the line grew quiet. "I guess you didn't hear. Austin passed away." I crumbled inside, devastated by his loss and because now I saw no way forward in my healing.

A few weeks later, I joined David Rockefeller in Alaska, and we made a pilgrimage to pay our respects to Daanawáak. Our treaded boots crunched on the frozen gravel of the cemetery entryway. Piercing north winds roared off the glacier-covered Chilkat Mountains and cut through my blue jeans and parkas as if I wore nothing.

"Over there," David said, and pointed toward an enormous spruce tree just inside the fence. Swirled in freezing winds, thin dusts of snow rose up against tombstones and, just as quickly, subsided. Beneath the tree, desiccated earth, gray, dead grass, and translucent sheets of icy snow marked the area we were looking for. I clenched my teeth, willing myself forward and noting the empty feeling inside. I don't know what I expected, but surely something, some sign that the Stories Daanawáak had lived for, the formulae of Creation, would somehow be evident. I wore three parkas and still trembled with cold and weakness. *Death is stalking me*, I thought.

David stopped. I did too. Together we looked down at the final resting place of Austin Hammond, beloved Tlingit Chief.

~~~

Diana Stone, sparkly, intelligent, woman of wealth, was fiercely determined to instill spirituality in the US government. It was her exploration of the Iroquois Great Law of Peace, Native North America's oldest living democracy, that brought us together. However, over the last few days, her focus was on organizing a dinner meeting with her friend Jean, a Jungian psychologist, feminist, and medical doctor.

"What's up?" I asked.

She shrugged her shoulders with an indifference belying an inborn clairvoyance, laughed, and responded, "What do I know? It just seems important the two of you meet."

Coordinating three busy schedules was real work, but Diana's grit catalyzed the meeting at the last possible moment. I'd just finished two weeks of teaching, fund-raising, and meetings and had one free day to enjoy our friendship and the redwoods before I flew to Maui. I was a bit ambivalent, until I saw the menu, a light, healthy version of authentic Italian food. Despite my recent loss of appetite and continued battle with headaches, I savored the tangy marinara, *insalata mista* with its exquisite balance of sweet and sour balsamic dressing, and heavenly soft, warm, olive oil–brushed salty bread sticks.

The conversation was just as good, but the ability to taste, to have an appetite, reassured me that my symptoms were fleeting. Then, near the end of the meal, the all too familiar bone-deep exhaustion and tremulousness returned with a vengeance. I craved rest but did not want to risk being rude. Diane and Jean were enjoying after-dinner coffees and relishing a conversation about coming from a Western mind into a holistic spiritual life and the crazy, upside-down, inside-out chaos that comes with this big change. Jean's anecdotes were lively and informative, spiced with health metaphors derived from her medical background. Perhaps this is what enabled—no, necessitated—my meeting her.

Setting her coffee back down in its saucer, Jean leaned slightly forward, resting her forearms against the edge of the table, and said the words that changed my life.

"About this initiation into women's spirituality—it's not like cancer, and you have it. In that case, there's a course of action, a treatment plan, and it works or it doesn't." Her black eyes glanced my way as she continued her story.

From that moment, I was in another, surreal world. Her message— "cancer, and you have it"—echoed over and over in my mind. I broke out in a cold, clammy sweat, my chest constricted, and I panted for breath. I'd always had lumpy, fibroid-prone breasts, but recently, I'd noticed a small lump, the width of half of a pencil eraser. Since that discovery, I'd drank more water, avoided caffeine, and employed traditional Hawaiian remedies—ti leaf poultice, an herbal tea, and I'd been blessed at a *heiau*, a sacred site dedicated to health. But the tiny rock-hard lump had stubbornly remained in place.

At last, dinner ended. The minute the waiter returned with our receipt, I shot from my chair, filled with a sense of urgency. By the time we reached our car, I'd formulated a plan. It was Wednesday. If I could change my ticket to arrive on Maui by noon Friday, I could get into the clinic before its weekend closing. I called the airlines as soon as we got back to the house. Amazingly, the ticket change went smoothly.

My plan was underway, but I was still scared. Sleep would not come. Instead, as the night wore on, images of "what if" devoured my mind.

My God, I have cancer. No, I don't. I can't. I'm dying. Chemotherapy. Radiation. Oh God, what will happen to me? No, I'm OK. I'm sure I'm OK. On and on it went. I have it, I don't. I can't have it, I do. No, I don't. Someone help me; hold me. Tell me I will live.

At 4:30, I quit trying to sleep, got up, dressed, and tried to pray but could not calm the deepening sense of foreboding and distress. I considered my options and saw only one—going to Mass at the local church. Diana was asleep, so the only way to town was a three-quarter-mile walk. Normally I loved it, but I felt so weak I didn't know if I could make it. I decided to try; if it was too hard, I could turn around and come back.

Carefully shutting off the alarm system, I opened the door and stepped into the overcast, foggy morning. A Raven's *chuk-chuk* call could be heard in the distance, followed by the trill of a Stellar's jay. Closing the door behind me, I made my way down the twisting drive to the road. This much was easy, downhill all the way. The path was another matter. There was no sidewalk, just a shallow roadside rut carpeted with an acrid layer of little sword-shaped sequoia needles.

Apart from their gigantic size and antiquity, coastal redwoods are distinguished in some remarkable ways. They stump sprout, and even if fire razes a forest, they can promptly resprout. Seedlings can receive nutrition from other related canopy trees; they can regenerate even in the deep shade of their cover. Some redwoods have no chlorophyll of their own and survive because they are completely supported by the root connection with other trees.

I stopped, picked a needle from the ground, and looked up, following the taper of the tree from the buttressed base to its canopy more than 300 feet above me. Choking back tears, I whispered to the trees, "Maybe I will never see you again. I am sick and so very tired. Thank you for allowing me to be with you, for all the ceremonies and good memories we've shared."

I heard myself draw a deep breath of cool, clean air, pungent with earthy undertones, and right there on the side of the road, peace came over me.

"Thank you, thank you." I repeated. This time saying it with a sense of being loved.

Our Lady of Mount Carmel Catholic Church stands on a hill in Mill Valley. I'd been there many times, and always felt comfort—a home away from home. Despite the early hour, the doors were open. I was so relieved I actually ran up the incline and took the steps two at a time. I sat in a pew and looked at the altar. The calm

I had felt in the forest was gone, and I searched for a prayer that would help. It didn't come. Unable to control my shaking and chills, I got up, went over to the Mary altar, lit a candle, cried, and begged for help.

~~~

"Ms. Colorado?" Dr. Sakai asked, lifting a page from my chart a week after I'd had the small lump in my breast biopsied.

"Yes."

"I'm afraid I have some bad news for you. The results came back positive for carcinoma in situ. Oh, I see on the chart it's your birthday. Sorry to give you this news, but we will need to get you into surgery as soon as possible. Depending on what we find, that may be sufficient or you may need additional treatment such as radiation or chemotherapy. The good news is it's a small tumor. You are lucky. We caught it early."

My life as I knew it was over, and it happened in a split second. I was in shock, but had to make critically important decisions quickly, and do so in the ambiguity that is characteristic of approaches for treating catastrophic illness. On the drive home from my appointment with Dr. Sakai, I pulled over to our local beach. I needed to clear my head and compose myself before breaking the news to my family. The golden sand was warm beneath my bare feet. I sat down and looked up.

What should I do, Ancestors, what should I do?

It was early afternoon, the sun directly overhead in a bright blue sky, and yet the lighting was subdued. How odd. A small bank of mottled clouds amassed and covered the sun. All at once, I knew what to do. If needed, I'd take the radiation therapy. When I did, I would be "blanketed," protected. The spirit of the Sun would be kind to me.

Sitting on that beach, I'd felt confident in taking a course of radiation, but not now. The door in front of me looked medieval; small, not even six feet high, but its thickness of nearly eight inches gave me the shivers. It seemed more like a fortification than an entry to a modern treatment room.

Ancestral spirits had grown strangely quiet since diagnosis, almost as if they wanted me to experience the abyss. Perhaps they were telling me I would not make it. Why else wouldn't they give me a sign, a good dream? Anxiety devoured me. I didn't know what was worse, dying of cancer or the treatment for it. And deep in the hidden recesses of my psyche was a belief that fueled my terror and drove any moment of peace from me—I didn't know it at the time, but I believed that I did not deserve to live, a belief forged in the violence of European-American Indian history and the ferocity of its expression in my early childhood.

"Good morning. You're Apela? Please come with us."

A young woman and a man, both dressed in nursing scrubs, escorted me down a carpeted corridor that opened to a two-story, theater-style hall. Off to one side, on an upper level, was a large window that fronted what looked to be a sports broadcast press box. Through the glass, I could see a chair and microphone directly behind a console. The control room overlooked the strange table situated in the middle of the treatment room. A piece of equipment like a metal umbrella was affixed to the table and lay off to one side like a wilted flower. My mouth was dry, and I shook uncontrollably.

"Step behind this screen, remove your clothing, and put this on," the nurse said cheerily, and handed me a paper hospital gown. "When you're ready, come out here. We'll be waiting." She walked over to the treatment table and stood there patiently.

I already felt half-dead from weight loss and overall weakness. Like death itself, the frigid hospital air brushed against my flesh and added to the bizarre sense of disconnection.

"Don't worry, this won't hurt," the nurse said, as she carefully opened my gown. "Let's see. Did you get your little tattoos? Oh yes, here they are. We need these points to line things up."

"What things?" I asked nervously.

"The small red light that directs the radiation. Oh, here it is, see? Yes, OK, just fine."

I looked down at my chest, and as I did, red laser crosshairs appeared on my breast—or what the surgery had left of it.

"OK, we'll be right back," she said chirpily, pivoting and walking quickly from the room. A moment later, the male nurse followed her, looking as if he'd forgotten something.

They left so quickly, I didn't have time to protest.

A soft, deep thud emanated from the direction of the entryway. Panic hit. The door had just been closed. The radiation I was about to get was so bad they needed an eight-inch-thick door to protect themselves from what was going to impact me directly.

A moan escaped me. Maybe I cannot survive this.

An electronic voice crackled through the microphone. "Try to lie completely still. Don't move. This will only take a few seconds."

I turned my head to the left; the nurses were in the control room watching me.

From my right came a whine, like a dentist's drill but higher pitched and quieter. The umbrella lifted from my right shoulder and moved on its arm over my chest to the left side and then back over. Maybe it happened more than once, I don't know. A few moments later, I heard the far-off sound of the door opening. The nurses returned.

"See, it wasn't so bad," they said earnestly. I looked up at their youthful, clean-cut faces, taking in how hard they were trying to encourage me. I wanted to cry.

Surprisingly, for the first few weeks, they were right; it wasn't too bad. However, a 5,400-rad dosage, spread across six weeks, adds a cumulative wallop. By week six, I could barely walk, my skin had broken down, and lymphatic fluid poured down my chest. I didn't think I could survive the remaining three sessions. Seconds into my sixth week of treatment, a strange sensation filled my body. I felt light on the table as if I were levitating off it and simultaneously turning clockwise. My soul was being peeled off from me. The expression "going over the slippery log" made complete sense.

I am dying. I turned my head to look down at the carpeted floor and heard myself say something unexpected. "Mother Earth, I am coming to you. I love you." And at that exact moment, the treatment stopped.

This time, I had to be helped from the table and held in order to stand.

"Are you all right?" the nurse asked.

"I almost died."

"I know." She nodded miserably.

"I don't think I can make it. Can I take a day off?"

"No, you cannot miss any sessions. You must complete all the treatments as scheduled. They have to give you the maximum dose your body can tolerate, so they bring you as close to death as possible. It's the only way. I'm sorry."

The nurse watched me closely as I made my way to the changing area. I was afraid to show any weakness lest she try to keep me in the hospital. I concentrated while getting dressed, using every fiber of energy I had left. Deliberately, trying to look as normal as possible, I walked past the check-in counter and out the door to my nearby car. I knew it was dangerous to drive alone in this state, but I needed to feel my Ancestors' presence. I blasted the air conditioning to keep me alert. The farther I got from the Pacific Cancer Institute, the better I felt. As my mind cleared, questions arose. *What made me think of calling to the Earth?* Something was afoot, and as sick as I was, I suspected the Ancestors were involved. A flicker of hope moved through me.

A half hour later, I staggered from my vehicle to the front door. Fumbling with the key in the lock, I leaned against the doorframe in order to remain upright. Unexpectedly, the door flew open, I slid through, then fell back, against the inside wall. An ocean wind gusted through the house and slammed the door shut behind me. Simultaneously, an old black briefcase, precariously situated between storage boxes I'd been sorting through, dropped to the floor. A single sheet of paper slid out of it. Pushing myself away from the wall, I lurched toward the stairs to the bedroom. The paper lay just beneath the first step. Curious, I held on to the newel post and leaned over to pick it up. It was a 10-year-old agenda from an Indian Studies week at Berkeley. I didn't even know I still had it and couldn't think why I'd have saved it. I turned it over. It was covered with notes I'd taken from Lakota Healer Pete Catches's talk on Sun Dance.

I gasped as I read, "In the old days, the pull of the Earth, the faith of the people, showed itself in what we are."

My heart soared. These old notes were a message from the Ancestors. I had misunderstood what had happened to me. The sensation of my body dropping to the ground wasn't because my spirit was relinquishing my body; it was Mother Earth holding on to me, pulling me back into my body. It was a direct experience of her love and power. I held the paper to my face and wept with joy, but there was more to come.

Slowly, a step at a time, I made it to my bedroom, slid under the top blanket, fully dressed, and drifted off, holding the document on top of my chest. A few minutes later, I awoke. My bandages were sopped and uncomfortable; I was sweating and fighting off nausea. Lying there helpless, unable to rise, the happiness was gone. Even the Earth epiphany wasn't strong enough to lift my suffering. I was too weak to change my dressings, yet my mind raced. I scanned the room for something to think about or easy to do. Nothing. I took a quick look at the side of my bed. A huge draft of a doctoral dissertation lay on the floor, awaiting my corrections so that my student Brian Rice could advance to his doctoral candidacy. I was weeks late and felt awful about it. Weeks ago, I'd placed the report next to the bed, hoping I could get through it while confined. I wanted to; the research was daring and prodigious. Brian Rice, Mohawk (one of the Six Iroquoian Peoples), was making a contemporary English interpretation of the Creation Story. All existing versions were from early ethnographers and so full of academic self-indulgence, jargon, and 19th-century language, they were almost worthless. Unless you were fluent in one of our native languages, which most young people, including myself, were not, there was nothing to rely on but these crude, rudimentary versions of the cosmology and emergence of Iroquois. This fat tome lying on my floor promised to be the best version I'd ever read.

Carefully, turning on my left side, I reached over with my right hand and picked up the two-inch-thick, unbound document. I was too weak to hold it all, and papers slid out of my hand and scattered across the carpet. I cried with frustration. No more than two or three remained in my hand.

Resigned and desperate, I looked at a random page:

> *Otsi:tsia (Sky Woman) began to boil the water until it reached the boiling point. She then cut and grated chestnuts and put them into the boiling water. They began to sputter out of the cooking vessel, and the hot mush began to stick to her body. Even though she was badly burned and her flesh peeled off, she never cried out, remaining steadfast in her duty and remembering what her uncle had told her—"Look at the Tree of Light, my standing tree blossoms are dimming and beginning to die out. You are the only hope of bringing back light to the Tree and this world.... Whenever someone wanted to enter the place of the Tree of Light, they would have their flesh removed and then be remade so that they were spiritually prepared to enter its abode.*[†]*"*

[†] Thank you to Brian Rice for your kind permission to reprint this extract from your dissertation.

Vital life energy flowed through me, and I knew that, live or die, I would be all right. For the first time in my life, mixed-heritage or not, the Sky Woman had reached through the veil and touched me.

I thought I'd feel better after that. But the next night, a new trial visited me. Dreams came—terrifying and lucid—always with the same theme: a flaxen-haired woman running from violence or being murdered, and no one caring. Sometimes the setting was in The Shadows, the redwoods lodge where I'd taught.

In case I still hadn't gotten the message, in the last dream, the woman and I actually met. Head in her hands, she wept inconsolably. The setting was a monastery in Dark Ages Europe. She sat on a marble bench that looked out through a Gothic arch to a traditional indigenous burial mound. Quietly, I approached and stood next to her. I wanted to comfort her, to say something, but found myself unable. She looked up, tears slipping silently down her face. I looked into her green eyes and felt an outpouring of love, an Ancestral balm.

Upon waking, I realized that the Creation Story I needed to find was that of my European Ancestors.

Chapter 13

KUVITO

*"What passes from this world travels back to the Sky
World and becomes recognizable as the star constellations.
Then they help human beings to know when to fulfill
their life duties by their position in the sky."*

IROQUOIS CREATION STORY

Benin, West Africa, 1998

Just a few months out of radiation treatment, I was far from well.
The skin on my legs and arms was hard, like a sheet of plastic;
my stomach and guts hardly worked, and skin on the actual site
of the burn oozed and peeled. I was toxic. Looking at me then,
you'd have seen a tiny, skeletal person with a mind gripped in an
obsessive thought loop.

Will, I live? Is the cancer gone? What if it's not gone? What if it
comes back; what horror, what pain will I face? I'm so scared. I
can't live not knowing. I must live not knowing. Someone, Spirit,
please, help.

I never voiced any of this, even to loved ones. Treatment was complete. Now there was just wait and see. Monthly checkups for the first six months, then, if still alive, I would go to bimonthly, then semiannual, and finally, annual checkups. If I made it eight years, my survival odds would be the same as a person who had not had cancer.

Given my state of health, I wondered why my friends, physicians Erick Gbodossou and Virginia Davis Floyd, had invited me to the PROMETRA conference in Senegal with traditional healing communities from Benin. If they thought I could make the long trip and ceremony, it had to be a good sign. Maybe they thought this was part of my healing? But what if they thought this was a good way to round out my life? I didn't dare ask.

Either way, I fully wanted to be there, to set foot on African soil, the ancient motherland. For years, I had dreamed of it and wondered how it must look and feel. When the chance came, and despite the threat of suffering or dying in a strange, distant place, I immediately said yes.

~~~

In 1500, the estimated population of the African continent was about 700 million. By 1900, the slave trade, European colonialism, and internecine warfare had reduced the total number to 95 million. Nearly 86 percent of the population had been lost within 400 years. By modern times, just a few hundred Traditional Healers survived to practice in West Africa, and many of those were poorly trained or flat-out charlatans. Yet today, most Africans trust and rely upon Traditional Healers (even when Western care is available), and with the advent of HIV/AIDS, the shortage of health care is even more acute.

When Erick Gbodossou completed medical school as an ob-gyn and psychiatrist, he returned home. He was determined to revitalize the ancient health care system and to link it creatively with the sparse Western care facilities that existed in his land. In doing so, he reasoned he could expand the quality and availability of health care services exponentially, and at the same time, renew the culture and life of his People.

He did not know that it would take 11 years to find the small group of authentic Healers. At first, all he found were the quacks. When colonialism tries to wipe out cultural healing practices, what really happens is that only the good practices are suppressed because they are visible, whereas the dark practices of pain, domination, manipulation, extortion, and control flourish because they are not seen.

Then the West says, "It's good we destroyed the traditional culture, because it was all superstition. Look at the darkness."

When I'd asked Erick how he had found the authentic Healers, he told me it was through the children. "When I went to a village, I would go to the children and say I had some ache or pain, and they would take me straight to the best Healer. The children know who the real Healers are."

From this beginning, with children as guides, Erick created PROMETRA, a model and network of linked Traditional Healers and Western practitioners that spans 25 countries and provides critical health care to people who otherwise have none. Thirty years later, despite the stringent initiation requirements (including encountering a lion in the wild and chanting it to sleep), there are nearly 15 thousand practitioners in Senegal alone.

I have written my name next to Dr. Erick Gbodossou, although I do not hold myself equal to him or his accomplishments. I write my name next to his because you can't understand what I am about to say without first knowing that there is a deep loving, brother-sister relationship between the two of us. Outside of that love, I could never have embraced what I was about to experience during my visit to Senegal.

~~~

Thirty hours of flying delivered me to a circle of thousands gathered about a village tree, the axis mundi for the community, where a strange, ritualistic pageant was taking place. Dancers, first one then a second, appeared to emerge from the tree, stepping out onto the pale yellow, warm soil of the dance arena. Each was dressed in exquisitely patterned satins trimmed with wildly iridescent ribbons of gold and silver threads that glimmered and shone in the overhead sun. The head coverings giving three-dimensional form to Mystical Beings were draped over the Cultural Practitioners' heads so that no face or human shape could be seen. The Beings stood, looking at the surrounding body of participants. Suddenly, one broke forward and charged the audience. People screamed and ran in terror. Just as the Being neared the periphery, a man, dressed in three-quarter-length baggy pants and brandishing a long, engraved, supple stick, whipped the air and drove the Being back from the crowd. Again and again this happened. Each time, the crowd reacted with great dispatch; nervous, the audience occasionally laughed at a close call. I wondered dully what was going on, and as much as I wanted to engage with the sheer wonder of what was unfolding, all I could think about was getting back to my hotel and into bed.

On the ride back, I asked Erick—my curiosity restored by the respite of the brief drive—what the stick and the scarily potent Beings represented.

"The stick," he said, "is Kuvito. It is the place of concentrated positive energies that take away bad spirits. In the Mina-Ewe language of Benin and Togo it means, *ku* ("to die") and *vito* ("those who come back to see those in life"). The Kuvito stick is used by the initiated person to guide the spirit Kuvito and to protect the uninitiated."

~~~

Even with 100-degree temperatures, the hot wind felt good on my face. Nearly 60 of us were packed together on an old wreck of a blue, paint-peeling ferryboat headed to Gorée Island. Everyone was in good spirits—glad to get out of the conference rooms and into life. From a distance, the island was picturesque. Small single- or two-story buildings dotted the approaching shoreline. Colorful stucco walls of yellows, creams, and rusts trimmed in large green-and-blue washed wooden shutters created an ambience of a holiday destination. But as the boat chugged up to Gorée, tied up to the dock, and off-loaded, a heavy feeling of dread fell upon me, like the fear that had been riding me for months. I was familiar with the phantom—the Devourer of Spirit—but this felt so much stronger.

A wall of resistance and terror welled up in me, just as our captain pointed to the shoreline and the closest building, the House of the Slaves. My resistance darkened with a sense of revulsion, and as much as I wanted to escape, the crowd surging off the vessel pushed me forward and into the building. On we marched to the small ground-floor room where tickets were sold. Packed shoulder to shoulder with scores of Vodun Healers, I became aware that mine was the only non-black face in the room. No one here knew I was American Indian; in fact, most people had not even heard of American Indians. I realized, in that moment, *I am the white person, the slave master.* My heart raced; my chest felt compressed. I struggled to breathe, to keep from fainting, then looked about, desperate for a place to hide. There was nowhere to go.

How do you approach a place that holds human depravity, a place of torture; a place designed and executed by one's own Ancestors? Even as a strong, healthy being, the outcome of such an encounter is doubtful; but what if we are ill, weak, and in hiding, maybe for generations? What's the ritual for facing this? Or is it so atrocious that no ritual is powerful enough to transform it?

Even now, years later, I've come down with the flu as I write this. Perhaps, more accurately, illness is part of what moves me back into the experience and makes possible the telling of it.

Gorée Island is one of the places where Africans who had been taken into captivity were housed and made ready for deportation to the New World. The stone and concrete, square-cornered building speaks of organization and efficiency. Here's the room for the men, and there's the room for separating the mothers from the children. Here's a room to hold young girls for breeding. Here's a hold—a dank, dark hole in the ground to throw "recalcitrant" slaves into. All the rooms are small, way too small for the thousands who passed through. It worked because the victims were shackled to the walls by their necks. Fear and excrement flowed down their unclothed bodies and covered the floors in a vile, slimy cesspool. There was no hope. The sick were thrown to the sharks. Upstairs, separated from this misery by just one floor, was a lovely residence for the French administrators.

In the front of my mind, I knew that France had colonized this part of Africa. I did not expect that the horror of Gorée would demolish any sense of separation I held between myself and my French ancestry. In that place, in that moment, I was the perpetrator! To make it worse, my Native American consciousness fully grasped the level of colonial atrocities.

Gorée instantly called to mind Wounded Knee, where the US Cavalry gunned down Sioux Elders, women, and children, even as they tried to run away in the deep snow and bitter cold of winter. I lucidly relived standing at the mass gravesite on the hilltop, buffeted by the winds that seem to sing the names of the victims. I recalled Sand Creek with sadness, and relief that finally, the US Park Service had put up a marker, the first of its kind in the nation to acknowledge the Sand Creek massacre. The mutilation and killing of more than 100 friendly Cheyenne and Arapahoe Indians—two-thirds women and children—by 700 US volunteer cavalrymen from Colorado had been ignored until recent times. I had gone to those places as an Indian, only slightly conscious of the hidden bifurcation of my European soul.

My legs trembled. My body shook. I leaned against a stone wall to keep from fainting. The cool wall offered no comfort; instead, it seemed to radiate the screams of the victims. My body lurched forward. I wanted out of this place, now! There was no way out except to lean into the group moving through it. Slowly we shuffled, just a few of us, ahead of the pack, into a tower overlooking the rocky shoals of Atlantic tides. An opening in the turret wall—the Door of No Return—was the threshold where Africans stepped from their homeland into the Middle Passage and slavery. Some slaves, driven mad with pain, chose to jump to death into the shark-infested rocky waters below rather than board the ship.

I'm dying, I thought, as I looked through the doorway. *No! I don't want to die. I want to live.* Fear and nausea seized me with such intensity I dissociated. Distanced slightly from the moment, my rational mind considered the danger. Cancer thrives in the emotion of self-hatred, yet here I was, steeped in it.

I asked myself, If I die, so what? Considering what French people did here, I deserve to die.

Psyche's dark menace moved closer, a velvet-gloved hand squeezing tiny, incremental bits of life force from me. As the grip relaxed for what might have been its final tightening, two hopes filled my heart. The first was for my youngest daughter, who had accompanied me on this journey. Even if I did not survive, Chyna would carry the story forward. Our family would never again be unconscious of the atrocities committed by French people. The second was my life's work in the Indigenous Mind doctoral program begun in the Shadows. The program had been a pathway through the darkness of colonial heritage to the Earth Spirit and wholeness of our tribal Ancestors. This work had given me and others the chance of restitution, to make conscious the cultural shadows and help prevent repeats of such horrors—but it was a sad thought. The recent university termination had extinguished its light, and there were no other similar programs.

It appeared as if the Ancestors agreed to my annihilation. When I prayed for a sign of life, nothing came. Nothing. My life force dimmed. But Gorée is a powerful place, said to be overlit by a female deity, Maam Kastel, a spirit of compassion related to Kumba, or creativity; perhaps it was She that moved me through this encounter.

The crowd, shoulder to shoulder in 100-degree heat, shifted just enough to position Mame Coumba Lamba, a holy man and keeper of the Mysteries of sacred waters, next to me as we approached the exit.

Looking into my eyes and smiling, he said, "My sister, there you are!"

I wept silently as I looked back into his deep black eyes, hazed over in spirit and age. How could he love me? How could he forgive?

In a second, I was outside the door of the Maison des Esclaves, instantly bathed in the warmth and searing light of the tropical sun. Fluorescent pink, purple, and white bougainvillea covered the nearby buildings, directing the view to the bottle-green sea.

Children, fresh-faced and happy, ran up to me, carrying armloads of trinkets to sell or to simply laugh and share a song. Tourists and cameras were everywhere. Breaking through the last of the crowd, I ran to the ocean, desperate to cleanse myself. Kicking off my shoes, tearing off my socks, I sighed and felt the soft, white sand beneath my feet and the cold salt water swirling about my ankles. I came back into myself then, and for a few moments, I wasn't French, I wasn't Indian; I was simply a woman, enjoying a clean, beautiful moment in a distant sea.

~~~

The further into our itinerary, the deeper we went into the traditional practices. This was an annual gathering, a public demonstration, of the most accomplished healing practices and practitioners. Mr. Makua, Hawaiian Kahuna, and I, along with other privileged guests, were seated beneath a covered grandstand. Again, it was close to 100 degrees with nearly equal humidity. For most of the day, the Vodun "police," a sect that protects the people and is a beginning level of practice, treated the crowd of thousands to demonstrations of traditional powers. A voice emanated out of a small stack of dried leaves; the leaves were burned and then re-formed. The entire time the "voice" kept talking, water was changed into wine. Amazingly, dancers dressed in haystack-like dresses, which draped from the neck, disappeared before our eyes, but the costumes kept on dancing! It is not good to penetrate spiritual moments, but stunned, I risked an edgy cultural question, not normally asked of an Elder.

"Mr. Makua, is this magic?"

He was quiet for a moment, his big, dark Polynesian hands moving around the top of his walking staff as he searched for the right words.

"Some of it is," he said softly. "I know what they are doing. These guys are good."

I had seen magic before.

Lakota Medicine Man Leonard High Hawk had put his hand in a fire, pulled out an ember, and held it before us. "You gotta make a believer of the People," he said, with a grin on his young, handsome warrior face.

These Vodun practitioners were going way beyond that. The manifestations of spiritual power, sound, color, and dance merged with our spirits and carried us along with the pulsing, swaying procession moving before us. Whether it was the searing heat, suffocating humidity, or something else, a strange sort of mind-altering languor set in. It seemed to cast the spectacle of sound, sight, and motion into a quiet, slow-motion event. I wasn't even surprised when a distinctly different group appeared and vanished before me, because it felt like I had hours to take them in. The leader wore a red headdress and was barefoot and bare-chested like all the other drum circles that passed by. Unlike any other group, he sported a long cloak patterned in scores of golden equilateral crosses on a field of black. The cloak, elegantly draped from his shoulders, was long, and he carried it with such practice that it appeared to float as it slid silently across the beach sands. An upright red feather staff standing on either shoulder completed the stunning ceremonial attire.

"What is that?" I gasped out loud.

Makua leaned forward in his grandstand seat next to me and rubbed his hands across the top of his staff.

"Deneb guys," he answered. "The Swan constellation is the source of all movement in the universe. Science has discovered what Indigenous Peoples have long known. There are black holes in the *okole* ("butt") of the Swan, and it is from this place that she lays her cosmic eggs. Just one time, I was allowed entry into the heiau, the Hawaiian pyramid temple at Ho'naunau, the ancient sacred refuge site. You know, a family of the right lineage still takes care of the place, and no one is allowed in there without their OK. I went in, and a buzzing began to fill my ears. I knew what it was. I lost all sense of time. A vision came of three gifts, three golden eggs. Then, I came back to myself, left my offering, and retreated from the temple. I've been fulfilling what those gifts promised and the empowerment that came with them for the last few years.

"European people have the gift of fire, of cosmic movement from the Swan, but they have forgotten it. All that's left is the stories they tell their children, the fairy tales—Mother Goose stories."

"But, Mr. Makua, it could be found again, right?"

Yes, he nodded. And my heart sang.

~~~

On the last full day of the conference, when the clusters of leave-takers winnowed down, I slipped out of the lobby and headed down the grassy slope of the hotel grounds to the sunlit ocean, my last chance to experience the Atlantic from Africa.

Water's edge, a mad, rushing, halting, point-and-counterpoint of swirling sand, rocky shoal, and sparkling waves that crash and mingle with the cry of seabirds. Black jagged outcroppings of rock, some jutting above the water, seized, swirled, and draped shimmering sands like gossamer sheets about their pillared bases.

Tidal pools teemed with life and hundreds of discarded clear plastic bags—affordable "bottles" for selling drinking water. Dakar is arid; water is precious. Without a government sanitation system, local people rake up and try to burn the debris with organic rubbish. Vapors of stinking, noxious clouds blanket the city—but what's the choice?

Kicking off my slippers, I set foot in the primal waters of Africa. The water was cold, clear, and refreshing. As I coursed down the beach, something shiny caught my eye. Nearing it, I made out the skeletal remains of a huge fish and a crustacean, enormous by Pacific comparison. Studying the clean, white bones, I gasped. Among the bones, a small, perfect rune lay in the sand; a three-tined *Y* representing the footprint of the swan—Algiz. Three in one, an ancient European tribal greeting of peace. I bent down, reached into the water, and scooped up the "rune." It lay across my palm, trickling seawater onto my hand. Wonderment enfolded me. "Thank you," I whispered as the winds lifted my hair and caressed my face, and cold Atlantic waters swirled about my feet. My French Ancestors had just said, "Hello."

~~~

On the very first morning of our arrival in Senegal, Mr. Makua and I had met at the hotel dining room for breakfast. Although it was late February, New Year's Eve party favors adorned each place setting. "Bonne Année" was boldly painted across the floor-to-ceiling restaurant windows. Silver cardboard tiaras sat on our plates.

Glancing down at his crown, Mr. Makua smiled gently and said, "Remember what we talked about last week? We are coming to Africa to open our crown chakras!"

Lovingly he touched his crown. Taking his cue, I plunked mine on my head, intending to wear it briefly before breakfast. As it turned out, the crown and I had plenty of time to bond; Mr. Makua and I had become initiates into African time. A half hour after our seating, someone brought a menu. Another half hour passed before we could order, and then about 40 minutes more before we saw our meal. When the food finally arrived, we looked at each other and laughed. We had come to the big leagues of indigenous cyclical time! No doubt about it. During the week, we learned a few things about working with this sense of time.

So, when our little delegation—Mr. Makua, my daughter Chyna, two indigenous youth representatives, and I—were seated for our final dinner, we knew it would take one hour to order our meal and another before the food came. What to do? Softly, like the voice of a siren, the mousse au chocolat on the pre-set dessert table began to call.

"Let's begin with dessert!" we said in unison, and instantly attacked the table.

It was a wise choice. The fabulous French-inspired Senegalese chocolate mousse was fluffy, rich, and so smooth it melted on the tongue. Halfway through our second or third dessert, Mr. Makua began to speak about moments of time travel. He was like that, on another wavelength, one that the young people and I loved to hear about. We dropped our spoons on our saucers and listened, enraptured.

"It's as easy as taking off your shirt. Only thing—you have to know how to get back. Time begins with the canoe, the Southern Cross. It comes through that way. Last week, at home, I was in the parking lot of Mauna Loa Summit Trail. A tourist couple had just come down the trail from their hike up the mountain. They looked at me strangely. 'Aloha, good morning,' I said.

"Without answering, the woman walked up to me and said 'We just saw you on the summit; it's not possible you could get here before us. There's only one trail. How did you do it?'

"That's bi-location. There's no way I could have walked there." He chuckled, glancing down at his calves darkened by the scars of flesh lost to Vietnam land mines.

Taking us in with a sweep of his hand, he repeated, "It's easy, anyone can do it."

When the young people left for another trip to the dessert table, Mr. Makua looked at me and said, "A couple weeks ago, I met a young *Ha'ole* ("Western") woman at the Puna restaurant. That night, when I went [astral projecting], I saw her again. The only part of her that made it, in this dimension, was her head. It was sitting, cut off, on a platter-like thing. She didn't know this was her situation. She looked at me in recognition as we passed. I didn't do anything. There was nothing I could do. You have to know who you are."

"I never want to travel like that; I don't want to see things like that!" I said quickly, as if to block any possibility that the story pertained to my life.

Deep down, I knew that Elders never share such things randomly. So I did the only thing possible—I bolted from the table and made for more chocolate mousse.

~~~

The informality of Dakar airport reminded us of the value of a designated waiting room. For our five-hour delay, we sat in brown, polyester, overstuffed couches, drinking cup after cup of tea, savoring our last chance to talk with local Healers who had been allowed in for the occasion. When our flight was called and we stood to leave, Erick came to my side and quietly offered me a good-bye gift—a Kuvito.

"One uses this stick to communicate with the Transcendents, to assist in receiving messages from the Ancestors to us. It is the link to the vertical family—the Ancestors who lived before us and who come after us. It is protection."

The flight back across the Atlantic was a turbulent hell. For eight hours we bounced, slammed, and dropped in the crosscurrents tumbling and slicing their way from the north. I didn't mind. Every time we lurched and fear hit, I reached down, touched the Kuvito, and glanced at my backpack stowed beneath the seat in front of me. The swan rune from the beach was in protective tissue and secured in an empty matchbox. I had direction, and I had spiritual protection. I would find and reclaim my French indigenous ancestry. I was filled with hope, and this was good because the road ahead was not clear. It would take purification, sacrifice, and some gifts.

Chapter 14

MARY MAGDALENE

Aix-en-Provence, France, 2000

Corinne, a friend who'd been raised in France, and I had been cooped up in planes and trains for most of three days, traveling from Maui to France. Nature was what we needed, not sleep, and certainly not the museums or architectural wonders of Paris—we'd done that on a prior trip. The country was enjoying unseasonably warm and inviting weather, so we decided to bypass the city and hopped into our red rental car for the eight-hour drive south to the Mediterranean.

It was the end of May; Europe's summer holidays had not yet begun, so beaches were empty and clean. Standing on the shore facing the morning sun, I made an offering, kicked off my shoes, pulled up my skirts, and waded in. The water was cold and refreshing and lifted the logy feeling of jet lag. Energized, we decided to explore nearby Saintes-Marie-de-la-Mer and find a place for lunch.

Twisting and turning through narrow medieval streets, we made our way to the main part of town. Surprisingly, lots of dark-skinned, indigenous-looking people—colorfully and dramatically attired—passed by. My heart leaped. I never expected to find Native people in France. They noticed me, too, especially the blue-inked Oneida Creation Story tattooed on my ankle. I was about to ask Corinne who they were, when we passed by a parking lot filled with pickup trucks, campers, and old curved-roof wooden wagons decorated in brilliant designs. Adjacent to the lot was an arena draped with a huge advertisement for a performance. "Gypsy Kings! One Night Only." Spray-painted across the surface were the words, "Sold Out."

"Are these Gypsies?" I asked incredulously.

"Yes, but I don't know why there are so many of them," Corrine whispered.

Ambling down the seaside walk, we came upon an outdoor café. Tiny tables covered with primary-colored cloths were appointed with golden-colored pottery decorated with dark-green and purple olive-branch designs. We pulled up a couple of chairs and sat down. Two elderly men wearing battered fedoras, tattered wool vests and trousers were seated at the next table. You could tell by the rhythmic cadence of their language that they were Gypsies. The Elders nodded as we sat down and then returned to their conversation, animated and punctuated with gentle laughter. In a moment, our waiter appeared. With a bit of de rigueur flirtation and teasing, he took our order and slipped back inside.

The tone of the grandpas' repartee rose in the waiter's wake. Gradually, Corinne and I began to catch the humor of their talk and joined in the laughter. They weren't the least surprised or offended; instead, were pleased and struck up a conversation, which gave us a chance to ask what was on our minds.

"Why are all the Gypsies here?"

"It's the Feast of Saint Sara the Egyptian, our patron saint," they responded, somewhat stunned at our ignorance. "It's the biggest Gypsy gathering in the world. Thousands are here because it is also the Feast of the Three Marys: Mary Magdalene, Mary Salome, and Mary Jacoby, disciples of Christ who came here to the South of France following the crucifixion. They were put adrift without oars. Their boat landed here. With them was Black Sarah, their servant and our saint."

Just then, a group of Gypsy musicians spotted the Elders and came up to offer a song. Accordion, guitar, tambourine, and violin filled the air with a slow sorrowful lament that built to a glissade then spun and erupted into a fast, fiery dance of passion. The men tapped their feet and clapped their hands in time. For a moment we did, too, but the waiter returned with *l'addition*—time to pay our bill and continue our journey, people were waiting for our seats. As we stood to leave, one Elder leaned over conspiratorially, hand cupping his ear to block the sound of the music, and advised, "Go to the church and see her." He smiled gently and nodded as if to say, you'll see.

Temporarily blinded by the transition from the searing midday light into the darkened cathedral, we stood waiting for our vision to return. When it did, I received a shock. The entrance to the Saint Sara cave was a small funnel-shaped slit beneath the altar floor in front of us. Moving down the aisle, we ducked our heads and entered. Hundreds of tapers and votive offerings illumed and filled the rocky ingress with radiant warmth. Black-faced, sweet-featured, and adorned in layers of exquisite lace and silk gowns and robes was Saint Sara. Gypsy families lit candles and stood before her for family photos. Men in absolute reverence prayed, then softly slipped a hand underneath the dress to touch her breasts or vulva. I held my breath. This was not a Christianity I had ever known; it was sensual, sacred, and palpable. The only response was silent gratitude.

Back upstairs, I made my way to the side altar. The last time I'd been in a Catholic church was in Marin, years ago. I wanted to be respectful, but even after the rite of reconciliation in the tiny church in Paia, I was still leery of the church. Looking around, I settled on an altar situated beneath an enormous painting of a woman dressed in a blue, Roman-style dress. True to form, she was big-bodied, pale-faced, and carried something in one hand. Her features did not attract me, but equally, did not repulse me, since the painting was devoid of the ubiquitous, bloody, medieval iconography. I knelt, introduced myself, explained my ongoing feelings of estrangement from the church, and asked permission to pray. It seemed OK, so I proceeded with my petition. My dear friend Bill Simon was very ill. I wanted my prayer to be consistent with his devout Catholic beliefs, and I wanted him to heal, but I felt so awkward. The only Catholic prayers I knew, I had memorized in childhood. I finished my prayer and remained kneeling for a few moments in case something, some insight would come. It didn't. I rose to go and found myself making the sign of the cross.

~~~

It was midnight when I turned out the lights. The jet lag had hit, but sleep would not come. Our spotlessly clean, family-run hotel had seen better days; my room was small, with just enough space for a double bed; wallpaper rippled in spots and had faded to a comfortable sepia. But the owners were friendly, and I loved the local touches—a single, small window inexplicably adorned with a costly tab-topped panel of jacquard fabric and a four-inch trim of olive-colored grapevines. A tubular thing, about three inches in diameter, straddled the top of the bed—a southern French pillow that had no case and was wrapped in the bottom sheet. You couldn't bunch it up, or even move it without destroying the bedding. If you rested your head on it, it went flat. But it did give a local ambience, and I was excited to be here in search of my French Ancestral roots, which traced to a tiny hamlet nearby.

Even at this late hour, the room was still uncomfortably warm, but the cooling temperature infused the space with a heavenly scent of lavender and a light earthly aroma of golden sand. My room overlooked the terra-cotta-tiled roof of the kitchen extension one floor below, which made it fairly accessible if someone wanted to enter. But the neighborhood was small and felt relatively safe. I decided to leave the casement-style window open a few inches to catch an errant breeze and to enjoy the intoxicating scents of the land.

I tossed and turned, forever it seemed—the travel and time difference were too much. Maybe reading would help. I'd brought two books. The first was one of my French family's history, compiled by a priest relative; I'd studied it inside out and, besides, it was a reference document, not a relaxing read. The second book was *The Templar Revelation*. The topic appealed to me; an image of a family shield from the 1200s clearly depicted a Templar cross on its surface. This was significant. In medieval times, each guild of artisans and every symbol on a crest had to be approved by the king, in this case Saint Louis. However, the book proved to be drier and more intellectual than my weary brain could absorb. A few minutes into it, I gave up, tossed it on the nightstand, once more turned off the light, and finally fell asleep.

A thin, cool energy moved from the open window, caressing my legs as it crossed my sleeping torso. My spirit was suddenly alert; an Intelligence had just entered the room. Reaching out with my senses, eyes still closed, I scanned my environs. I felt no malevolence, but there was a Power present, and it was watching me. I wanted to wake, to burn cedar, to respect this nocturnal visitor, but my sleep felt like a drug, and I could not rouse myself. The best I could do was to acknowledge the Spirit in my mind. I asked forgiveness for my improper greeting and invited it to stay. In the instant before I fell back asleep, I turned to face the window as if to be sure to notice anyone else entering.

Sometime later, maybe an hour or so, I awoke again. A thin, sharp edge poked against my left hand. With my eyes still closed, I reached my hand around to define the contours of a small rectilinear shape. *Oh, the bookmark.* I sighed. Just I had been about to head out the door for the airport, I'd glanced at my mail, and grabbed a couple of bookmark advertisements for *Angel Magazine*.

In my half sleep, I smiled. *So, that's who you were!* As if an angel dropping by was completely normal. Picking up the bookmark, I turned over, placed it on the nightstand, and fell back into the weird, leaden, jet-lagged sleep.

Time passed.

I am standing in a peculiar rose-gold atmosphere infused with glimmering earthen-colored motes. Dawn already? No, maybe it's dusk. Have I slept all day? Can't be sure which. Am I sleeping? Awake? An intense feeling, a hypervigilance, honed in family violence, grips me. Something nears. A light surge of energy suffuses me, enveloping me in a powerful, sensuous rapture of wisdom, beauty, certitude, and compassion. The Source is a woman, so beyond words, and I am not allowed to look at her. With her left arm around my shoulders, she holds me close. I cannot turn, but glancing to the right, I just make out the drape of a long, flowing blue-gray gown.

Her right arm gestures ahead and to the left. It is her land, as it was in ancient times, her earthly time. A fragrance, sweet, clean, and dry, washes over me. I behold and instantly stand at the edge of a grove of rough-barked olive trees, gnarled with age. I look more deeply; a numinous shimmer emanates from the center of the tress to meet my gaze.

There's something so familiar, so embracing. Life, death, all separations dissolve into a warm shower of bliss that is reunion. The magnificence of the sight and feelings overwhelm me. I never want to leave but will perish if I look even a second longer.

Again I stand beside her in the peach sky of the in-between worlds.

Who are you? I wonder.

Thunder rumbles as the answer springs to my lips, "Mary Magdalene."

Rain whooshed down, a crescendo of bird song rose and met it in ecstatic susurrus. Thunder came so close and loud, the room shook. Rain roared off the tiled kitchen roof below my window and woke me. The clock read 7:30 a.m. Glancing at the nightstand, I picked up the bookmark that had poked me during the night and read, "Angels mark your passage, Apela Colorado."

A sense of rapture coursed through me. I'd been anointed.

Alive with energy and inspiration, I threw back the blankets and jumped to my feet, laughing and singing, a woman on fire!

Hurriedly, I pulled on my dress, washed my face, and ran down the spiral staircase, journal in hand, and made for the breakfast-area.

I must get this down! I must never forget it. Oh, my God, does this mean I'm a Catholic again? I laughed aloud, reflecting what I'd read about Mary Magdalen as the one who unites opposites without obliterating either. I was in a paradox and about to discover the power of standing present to it.

The very next morning, my phone rang. It was my first cell phone, and not knowing about roaming charges, I took the call. It was from Ringing Rocks Foundation, which was awarding me a one-million-dollar grant to restart the Indigenous Mind master's and doctoral program. There was one catch—it was to be housed at the University of Creation Spirituality, a university headed by ex-Catholic priest, author, and theologian Matthew Fox and administered by a team of nuns.

Before the visitation, I could not have accepted the gift. My apprehension and distrust of the church would have prevented it. But in this case, a mere 24-hours later, I eagerly accepted and spun around in a dance in the narrow confines of my hotel room.

In iconography, Magdalen, like the tree, holds the worlds together, and is often depicted holding a jar of balm for healing as well as anointing the dead. A second call came that morning. My beloved friend Bill Simon, who had done so much to help me reconcile myself with Catholicism, had just died. Uncannily, just before my trip to France, he had called to wish me a good trip and urged me to learn about Mary Magdalen. It was our last conversation.

~~~

On my return to Maui, the bliss that I had felt in the halo of the Magdalen visitation was tempered by my increased sensitivity to my physical state. Racing out of Macy's one afternoon, with a sack full of items for an upcoming trip to Japan, I stopped dead on the curb. *My car. Where did I park it?* I looked right, left, ahead—I couldn't see it anywhere. An eerie feeling swept through me. Not only did I not remember where I had left my car, I didn't even know how I had gotten to the parking lot. *I must have driven; I'm looking for a car,* I told myself, but I remembered nothing of the journey. I looked at the Macy's bag in my hand. *Obviously, I came here to buy something. But when? How?*

An icy fear clutched my heart. What else didn't I know? Panic surged through me. Furtively, I glanced about.

How long have I been standing here in front of the store? If it's a long time, people might notice, think I'm crazy; maybe call the police. What's happening? What is wrong with me? Think, Apela, think! Retrace your steps.

I tried and, with mounting horror, discovered there was not even a vestige of memory—nothing of the drive, the time I left, what I had been thinking. Nothing.

Struggling for control, I scolded myself, "This is stupid; breathe, get in the present." I drew a deep breath and slowly released it. It didn't help. Frantically, I surveyed my surroundings. *OK, I'm in a warm tropical climate. In the distance, whitecap waves dance on the ocean. I'm surrounded by verdant green mountains and bright blue sky—what is there to be afraid of?*

I trembled. In this strange state, time was fluid, I couldn't think practically, and I knew it. What to do? How to get home? *Is home even where I think it is? Am I having a mental breakdown?* No, I was aware of my surroundings. How I came to be here was the only thing missing. *That and my car*, I chided myself, hoping that humor would relax me and restore my memory. I needed to sit down, to pull myself together. I spied a perfect spot—a sunlit bench nestled in palm plants that edged the parking lot. Carefully, in deference to my fragile state, I reminded myself, *Look for traffic both ways. OK? Then cross the road.*

As I walked toward the bench, the eerie feeling continued. I didn't know the day, year, or even if I was awake. I had barely sat down, when my handbag emitted a soft ring that hit my overwrought nerves like a fire alarm. Grabbing my cell phone from the outer pocket, I looked at it like an alien artifact. The world remembered me, even if I didn't. Looking at the phone, I observed, *Hmm, five bars—didn't know T-Mobile offered inter-dimensional coverage.*

The voice on the line was familiar and so welcome—Jesse, a traditional Yaqui Healer from Arizona.

"Hello, Auntie, how are you?" he drawled in his warm, Native way.

"Jesse," I blurted out, with a nervous laugh. "Thank God you called! I've lost my car, and I'm afraid I've lost my mind. I'm at Macy's parking lot. I can't find my car or retrace my steps. It's like a blackout. I can't remember anything—how I got here or why, and until this call, I thought I might be caught in a nightmare. It feels too real, yet I can't get home. I'm scared, Jesse, I don't understand what's happening," I said, my voice choking with emotion.

There was a slight delay as something clicked into place, and then we both laughed at the absurdity, impossibility, and awfulness of the moment. The laugh felt like a hug. I wasn't alone anymore.

Taking a leisurely breath, Jesse said, "Yes, I know what you mean."

"You know what, Jesse, I just realized this isn't the first time I've lost myself. It's been happening more and more lately."

The truth was, I was really scared, and desperately sought a mystical explanation to block a growing recognition of what was metastasizing within. Even in this moment, where I might get help, I jumped in with a flood of words. Jesse remained quiet, letting me get it all out.

Instead of saying what was really troubling me, I said, "Maybe it's the obsidian mirror?"

A few months earlier, Juan, an Aztec Medicine Man, had given me an obsidian mirror, a central sacred object from his culture. If I used it right, he said, the mirror would take me to other dimensions where I could receive wisdom and healing to bring back into this life. Maybe I was doing something wrong. But I'd been careful to ask about protections and ways of working with it. Juan advised me, "Stay in your heart, work through love."

"Yes," Jesse responded, "and when you find your car, give me a call."

Sitting on the green wooden bench, surveying the parked cars before me, warm rays of sun caressed my fear-frozen face and shoulders. I closed my eyes, forcing myself to think of beautiful things, things to give me energy. In a moment, I felt something, a pull to the left.

"What have I got to lose?" I muttered, and I opened my eyes.

Standing, I walked zombie-like to the left. There was my car, tucked between two larger vehicles, just four spaces away! I laughed at the absurdity, not simply because I found my car, but also because of how I found it. The car that my memory and analytical mind could not find was right here, where my feelings took me. For once, my overworked Western Mind had surrendered to my heart. I called Jesse back and told him as much. I could feel his happiness. "That's good, Auntie, that's good," he said, and hung up.

For the next few weeks, I practiced my new power—going to my heart when the moments of dislocation occurred. My cat and lovebirds showed me when I'd centered myself. Aloof by nature, they drew close to me the instant I moved into my heart. It was good preparation. I was on my way to Kyoto, Japanese capital of the "Heart-Mind" for a university study tour of Buddhism, a trip that would connect Keola to his mother's homeland and confront me with a gift only a Heart-Mind could perceive.

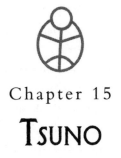

Chapter 15

TSUNO

*"Whenever you see my path divided, it will remind you that
there are two types of minds that have come into the world above
and to the Earth below. The same will occur among the human
beings as well. There will be those who will live among the rest of
the creation, and there will be those who will try and control it."*

THE CREATION STORY

Kyoto, Japan, 2008

Sidewalk, bus, subway, and train took us north from the urban,
Western-influenced life of Kyoto, the ancient capital of Japan, to
the small mountain village of Ohara. The university schedule
had called for a visit early in the week, but heavy rain and
thunderstorms delayed it until the end of the trip. Even now, our
umbrellaed group made frequent stops to shake the weight of
intermittent showers from the fabric canopies. Step by determined
step, up the steep path to Sanzen-in, a Tendai temple, we went.
The path had an unusual quality; it was black, soft, and wet like
the nose of a Labrador retriever. Sweet!

Lush, wild bamboo crowded and pushed over the walkway as if to remind us our path is impermanent. Spiky, lime-green leaves slathered in water shimmered. Bamboo nodes soaked black on golden glowing stalks, appeared as magical measures of loss and gain in each ragged breath and pound of the heart. Abruptly, and in complete symmetry, the bamboo stopped exactly against a curious ablutions fountain. Fashioned from a traditional, raised-handle Japanese bucket and mounted on a wooden frame, icy, pure stream water gurgled and rushed through a spigot of deep yellow bamboo, falling into a smooth, weatherworn container. A biscuit-shaped dipper fabricated from the bottom and sides of a bamboo joint formed the cup. A sliver of stalk formed the handle. Breathing in the clean, cool, pine-scented air, we paused. One by one, we poured water, first on one hand, then on the other. Lastly, we rinsed our mouths before crossing into the realm of the sacred.

Our guide, John, and I fell back, letting the group go ahead. They crossed a footbridge, and the path went silent. As if on cue, John and I prayed. A slight wind whispered through the trees. I looked up. A veil of mist dissolved as it rose, revealing a serried range of mountain peaks. In its rush to the heavens, it seemed to pull our small path, like a tail, along with it. We came to an overlook in a thicket of wet woods. Below us lay terraced fields, fallow in autumnal rest. A large crow, pretending to have commerce with the field, stood stock-still, watching us and perhaps warning of something. Nearby, on a toolshed, sat an enormous golden eagle who eyed us so strongly, we left. Moments later, we regrouped on the main trail and continued our hike in earnest to the mount.

Boreal mist glistened on the black tile roof of the temple. We slowly approached the timbered archway, the biggest we'd seen. It was hugged on either side by stone walls nearly 20 feet high.

The sheer drama of the design drew the eyes upward, but a raised threshold kept us in the present. We stepped across into Sanzen-in. Immediately before us was a *tsukubai*, a stone basin with a metal, dragon-shaped spigot. I cleansed for the second time that day, and acknowledged, as tradition dictated, *we have all we need.*

In unhurried, deliberate motions, I returned the dipper to the two weatherworn branches that were its resting place. Then I turned and faced the reception hall, a single-story, white-walled building with a tiled roof. Exposed wall supports that had not been plastered framed the windows in a dark latticework, a simple functionality that breathed refinement. Looking at the world through the rectangular fretwork parodies our linear, three-dimensional view of life. We were light and matter, separation and oneness. Yet the view, a perfect balance between constraint and focus, illustrated that the sight that separates also unites, and that as we experience separation, we simultaneously experience being held.

But there was no denying a slightly uneasy feeling; the precision of the architectural savvy suggested other, unseen purposes. Once again, the relentless, crushing lethargy that had plagued me in the past came on. I needed solitude. I made my way to the 17th-century reception hall where I was met with racks of multilingual information brochures. Selecting one in English, I read about the background of the temple.

Sanzen-in, constructed in the eighth century, is a special order of temple, one whose chief priest, Dengyo Daishi, or Saicho, was a member of the Imperial family. With the emperor's backing, Saicho could select a superb location and have the time and artists needed to harmonize design elements that embodied and imparted the sect teachings. In this case, it was Tendai, or eclectic

Buddhism, the practice and place that "brought it all together." I thought this was a big claim to make. In all the world-class sacred sites I'd visited, no one ever said, "This is the place where it all comes together." If this were truly where it "all" came together, where was the indigenous spirituality? All week, temple after temple, site after site, I'd seen no evidence of the original, earth-based spirituality of Japan or even awareness of its absence. "Eclectic Buddhism" sounded like a New Age fantasy, or worse yet, a claim made by a conquering religion.

"Prove it," I heard myself say, and instantly regretted it. If this place was real, it was a terrible thing to say; insulting spirits is generally a bad idea, and paradoxically, I'd had no intention of saying what I did. The words just slipped out.

"Damn it," I groaned, thinking how ill-prepared I was to face a spiritual challenge. I mustered my strength and entered the labyrinth of temple rooms. Sliding shoji doors opened, closed, and partially ajar, formed temporary halls and a large meditative area. It was devoid of all furnishings save the warm sheen of tatami mat flooring; ancient, smooth, worn support beams; and carefully placed signs of kanji, the black-brushed Japanese calligraphy. The far wall was open to a light-filled garden of meticulously groomed greenery, precisely situated rocks, and the murmur of small streams.

Looking past the garden, I sighed, realizing the enormity of the temple complex. We would be here a long time, and all I wanted to do was get back to my hotel and rest. Six days with six sects of Buddhism was overwhelming. My body was filled with a strange exhaustion; I longed for home. I thought about the long trip back and wondered if I could make it. I looked around, trying to hide from the group to give myself a bit more down time. The soft glow of light refracting off glass, and the gold of shop shelves caught my eye. What would I do in there? Perhaps I could find a small bell charm for my backpack. Even though it was a bit embarrassing to be heading to a shop rather than an altar, my choice gave me some energy. I walked in and quickly spotted the bells. Selecting one from a glass bin, I walked to the checkout counter.

In temples, even the smallest purchase is treated with regard. The clerk carefully cut cedar-colored paper, wrapped, and then tied my tiny purchase with raffia. Knowing the group was about to catch up and seeing there was no way to hurry her, I anxiously looked about for another place to hide. Just past her shoulder, across the hall, was what looked to be a shop display case. In the center of the display was a small black statue. My heart leaped—it looked like a Black Madonna! Could it be? What would a Western earth goddess be doing here? I may never know the exact reason; perhaps it was the possibility of a feminine, spiritual presence, or an icon that was familiar, but whatever it was, it pulled so strongly, I practically ran over the countertop to reach Her. Even as I did it, I thought my behavior was weird.

Rushing across the aisle, I dropped to my knees before the display—right there in the aisle. The shopkeeper gave me a sideways glance that did not deter me. I was beyond appearances; I was a woman consumed with a quest. My heart sank. The delicately carved, ancient dark image was another holy man, though this one curiously was not Buddha.

It made no sense. This was not an icon of the sacred feminine, nor was it indigenous. I continued kneeling in the busy corridor. Something drew me here, something strong. What? I surveyed the niche. Great sheets of calligraphy draped the entire back wall of the alcove top to bottom. Immediately before me sat a slotted offering box, and on top of that sat a tray holding a multitude of tiny scrolls. I looked up to my left.

There it was! A black ink, wavy-legged, skeletal Being, imprinted on its own document, surrounded by a sea of calligraphy, an image so strong it seemed to be looking right through me, powerful yet familiar. *It's the Medicine Man petroglyph!* I knew this Being. I could not have said why I was overjoyed to find it. It was as if I had found a love I'd sought all my life.

I pulled back a bit to take in the entire altar display. The juxtaposition of indigenous iconography with Japanese Buddhist art spun my mind around. I looked closer; something was different. This Being had horns and an odd sideways smile. Maybe it was because He had me in his power, but I couldn't pull away or make out the message. None of the surrounding symbols were familiar. I needed help.

A Tendai monk materialized from nowhere. Bending at the knee, he skimmed about a half inch above the floor, tucking his robes beneath his calves as he came to Zazen, a meditative kneeling position, next to me. I was seeing in a sacred way—catching the monk's movements in slow motion told me so; the same with his sudden appearance.

I folded my hands and bowed my head in greeting, and the monk did the same.

"Who is this?" I asked, looking at the drawing.

Thinking I meant the statue, he responded, "It's Ganzen Dai Shi, the great teacher who founded this temple. He meditated before a mirror, and Tsuno Daishi, the Horned Great Master, appeared.

Ganzan Dai Shi bonded with him, and after that, he could heal people. Sanzen-in is for healing."

I thought back to Copper Mountain and the day Hanson Ashley discovered the Medicine Man skeletal-appearing petroglyph. Happiness flooded my heart. It was the same here. The indigenous ways of Japan were not dead; to the contrary—in this national temple, an ancient healing spirit enjoyed a place of honor.

Then the monk uttered the words that changed everything. As if from a thousand miles away, I heard him say, "Actually it was an ogre, a demon."

These were the same words I'd heard a thousand times, words used to sanction, incite, and fuel the extermination of indigenous spirituality and the rape of the Earth. The message hit me like a tsunami. Involuntarily, I reared back from the altar, and with the sound of his voice still hanging in the air, I blacked out. I was there kneeling, but there was no *I*.

In a second, or maybe an eternity, I came back to myself. A lifetime of repressed fury and pain had vulcanized into a single point of rage. *Apela*, I admonished myself, *you are in a temple steeped in patriarchy. Anger can be dangerous. Control yourself, breathe, look down, show no emotion.* Shaking with the effort to contain my feelings, I heard a breathless voice, my own, ask, "Is Tsuno a pre-Buddhist icon?"

"Yes, probably. In the old days, most of the people in this area were farmers and worshipped many local kami or spirits. When they got sick, they turned to these nature spirits. Buddhism would have found a way to accommodate (I heard *expropriate*) the old beliefs. After the monk made friends with Tsuno, he could heal people," he reiterated. "That's why this is a healing sect, and why we have a local custom of hanging the picture of Tsuno on the entry of houses."

The monk excused himself for a moment and returned with an informational brochure for me. He bowed and left. Surely, he had felt my anger. I wondered what he thought.

I breathed, lifted my head, and once again faced Tsuno. A wave of residual anger slipped across my consciousness, and in defiance of all the grandeur, wisdom, and ages surrounding me, I declared, "I don't think so. Even if you are a devil, there's a message in this I need, and I am going to find it."

Chapter 16

MIRRORS AND HORNS

Maui, Hawaii, 2008

I returned home and seemed to be dancing in and out of a place of wild energy and profound fatigue. I slept for 14 hours one night, three the next, and had a fever I couldn't shake. I'd wake from a nap still weak but in the grip of post-Tsuno mystic ecstasy. A promise of healing tickled the edge of my consciousness. I had to understand the Tsuno experience.

My only tangible "leads" were the intense anger I'd felt and the Tsuno print I'd purchased at the temple gift shop. John, our Kyoto host, had promised a detailed translation of the informational flyer the monk had given me but could not get to it for at least two months. I couldn't wait that long, so I went to the computer to search for information on the Horned Spirit. Hours on Google passed without success. Restless, I walked to the kitchen sink for a drink. Looking through the window, I raised the glass of water to my lips and beheld the answer—the Hongwanji Mission right across the street! Why hadn't I thought of it? Especially since the

Japanese Buddhist mission had just hired its first woman sensei, Mariko. She seemed approachable and spoke some English.

My mind churned with possibilities. In the moments I knelt before Tsuno, my feeling of exhaustion had briefly disappeared. Was it because I'd connected with a primordial healing spirit or, as the Buddhists would have it, a demon of illness and death? If it were an agent of healing, I would get better, and it would not only be for me but for generations in the past and generations to come. If it were evil, I would be adding to the pain carried by my Ancestors, future generations, and myself. I had to get this straight, and Mariko seemed the best way.

I'll just go over there and talk with her. But what can I say? Talking about a pagan Japanese spirit with an ordained Buddhist minister might be disrespectful, unproductive, and cause collateral issues within our small community.

Considering ways it could go wrong reminded me of conversations with missionized American Indian Elders. Indigenous language and stories invoke Ancestral presence, but Indian Affairs boarding schools had violated and victimized generations to expunge the culture and expropriate the People. Sharing traditional knowledge triggered unhealed trauma and instantly halted intergenerational transmission. I was concerned something like that might happen with Mariko. Surely, the Indigenous People of Japan had not converted to Buddhism without a struggle. Generations after the invasion of the Americas, I still carried unresolved intergeneration trauma. Somehow, kneeling before Tsuno had brought it out in one moment of total fury. Who knew what shadow lay in wait?

Approaching Mariko seemed impossible, and I was about to give up when an idea came. It was simple—images communicate across cultures. I'd take a photo or two to start the conversation. Excitedly, I dug through the pile of stuff from the Japan trip on my desk. At the bottom of the heap was my digital camera. Anxiously, I scrolled through the photos, looking for one that captured both the Tsuno image and surrounding sheets of calligraphy.

Surprisingly, I found what I needed. Even in the emotional volatility of the Sanzen-in moment, I'd taken a photo of the entire altar with the image and all the surrounding sheets of calligraphy. If Mariko could make it out, I might not need to wait for John's translation. Relieved, I gave myself a mental pat on the back, but on closer examination realized the print was too small to be read. I'd have to enlarge it. I looked at my watch; I had just enough time to make it to the photo shop. Grabbing the camera, I threw it in my purse, tore out the door, and jumped on my bike for the three-block trip. Luckily, the manager was free and helped me figure out how to enlarge the calligraphy and retain the whole altar image.

In fewer than 15 minutes, I popped out of the shop with a cardboard enlargement envelope so big it served as a wind foil on my bike. Zipping along with a gentle assist from the trade winds, I sped down Luakini, the street of the Night Marchers, the deadly ghosts of ancient Hawaiian warriors, to the mission.

The closer I got to Hongwanji the more my confidence subsided. I was unfamiliar with the formalities of Japanese spiritual protocols—but no worries, she wasn't home or at her office. I went home, waited a few hours, then returned and knocked at the office door again; still, no response. The third time I tried, the sensei popped out of her garage right next to me. I jumped in my tracks; her approach was just like the monk at Sanzen-in who'd slid up beside me before I'd even noticed his approach.

I introduced myself, briefly explained the purpose of my visit, and asked if she would help me. She nodded in agreement and invited me to sit with her on the temple steps and enjoy the late afternoon sun. I got out my notebook, pen, and enormous photo, and sat down next to her.

Placing the enlargement on her lap, Mariko gave a cursory interpretation of the kanji. "It's about healing. The first column is a chant you say to Ryogen, a monk and founder of Sanzen-in, and this column..." Her voice faded. "Oh, the last line is missing on the photograph."

Damn! I thought I'd been so careful with the enlargement process, but she was right, getting the kanji to a readable size had cut off the last line. Embarrassed and frustrated, I figured the consultation was over. To my surprise, she identified and interpreted other symbols in the photo, confirming what I'd heard in Japan. In prehistory, ailing Ohara villagers had called on Horned Beings, nature spirits of their local sacred mountain, Mount Hiei. The practice was so effective that the area became a renowned center of healing.

I sat riveted as she told me about the changes that happened in the 10th century. Ryogen, a Tendai Buddhist monk with strong Imperial connections, arrived at Ohara. Coincidently, a terrible plague broke out. A main tenet of Tendai is teaching according to the capacity of the listener. Wanting to eradicate the plague and to demonstrate the power of the new cosmology, Ryogen decided on a dramatic course of action. Framing the problem in local cosmology, the monk identified a great Horned Being as the source of the plague and drew on an ancient Kagami mirror ceremony to confront the Spirit directly.

In the dark of the evening, Ryogen lined up three mirrors and knelt before them. He lit candles, meditated, and called to the Spirit. Suddenly the Horned Being appeared; instantaneously, Ryogen projected his spirit into the mirror to merge with the Being. The monk's body began to change, his eyes grew big and round, his mouth extended from ear to ear, his ribs stood out, and horns appeared on his head. The image of Buddha dissolved as Tsuno came forward, and from then on, Ryogen could heal. Ryogen asked one of his monks to draw a picture of him transformed as Tsuno, and ordered that the picture be placed at the entrance of all homes suffering from the epidemic. The plague subsided. Villagers began the shift away from their original beliefs and the emperor funded the building of Sanzen-in Temple on the site.

Hesitantly Mariko stated, "I don't know if I would do that. I am a Buddhist monk, I have compassion, but I don't know if I would have merged with the ogre."

I wondered if her concern was the same as mine. I was suspicious of the "official" story. My early days in the American Indian Movement had shown me how spiritual beliefs can be exploited by social elites and become a weapon of social control. Ryogen shows up and so does the plague. He calls the Horned Spirit a demon, yet from his encounter with a nature spirit, he takes the power to heal. I kept my doubts to myself and didn't push the point. I respected Mariko and the path she had chosen and sincerely appreciated her help. Leaving her with a small gift, I crossed the street and returned home.

I was doing all I could to resolve the healer-or-demon contradiction of the Kyoto experience, but still my health deteriorated.

A week later, I went to a conference held at a local hotel, and rounding a corner, I bumped into Kapi'ioho, a Hawaiian Cultural

Practitioner and friend of many years. We greeted each other in *Ha*, the traditional exchange of breath.

"Do you have a moment to talk with me?" I asked.

He nodded and motioned for me to join him at a nearby table. Quickly, I filled him in about my encounter with the Horned Spirit at the Japanese temple. I withheld telling him about my illness and fear that I may have exacerbated it because of loving Tsuno. Kapi'ioho's dark eyes filled with fuzzy white spirit light.

Adjusting his kihei on his shoulder, he tilted his head slightly and began: "Horns symbolize what sacrifices itself for us. We use the horn to call that Spirit. It is the reminder. The Aumakua, Ancestral spirits, remind us to remember the sacrifice of the animal.

"Some men take the horns and put them on their own head, like a helmet, to show their connection to the animal, but they may forget the sacrifice and say, 'I'm as great as this god or animal. I sacrifice and feed you, so worship me.' Maybe this is what the monk did."

He continued, "Spirituality in its purest form is created in the center of the universe; created between things. In that space between things is the goddess Uli. She is darkness, not the lack of light. The in-between space, Uli, is enormous energy, harmony, and healing.

"Spirituality is based upon the blending between power and harmony. They need each other and must go together. Kahunas go into Uli, become Uli, and then come back out. Religious people can't get close. They are not supposed to. You meet the Aumakua, helping spirits, and things that sacrifice themselves for physical existence and then become that—those horns or symbols of what they represent. We come back and draw the true figures or images.

"I don't go to Uli with a question; maybe I have them in my mind somewhere, but I don't think about them. I go to Uli, and certain things are revealed. Maybe an answer to an issue or something spirits decide I need. I go with an empty cup and fill it with whatever is given. It brings a lot of clarity. That's what is given. When you go there, you don't want to come back, but to stay as long as you can and then come back as soon as you can.

"I've worked to help others go to a deeper place, to help them find peace from within. Bring peace in, and the *hewa*, things that control us, have to get out, but it's a fight because it's gotten comfortable. The body nearly stops. We have to work to get the senses going."

As he spoke, a strange spell came over us. I didn't know it then, but he was taking me to Uli and back, showing me the way.

"Excuse me," said a conference organizer who had just come up to the table. "Kapiʻioho, you're speaking next."

"Sorry," he said as he rose to leave. "We'll have to call this to a close for now."

He gave me a quick hug and left.

~~~

Cultural Practitioners know when they are needed. Eiichi was like that. A few days after I met Kapiʻioho, Eiichi dropped by to hear about my Kyoto trip. Born in Japan, he had been a Hawaiian resident for more than a decade but returned home often to pursue his passion—researching the indigenous spirituality of his people. Our conversations, a rich dynamic of Japanese and American Indian perspectives, quickly raised spiritual questions and revealed insights we would never have come to on our own. Eiichi stepped through our doorway, bowed, and proffered a small bouquet. I bowed in return, accepted the flowers, and gave him a hug, island-style.

We moved into the living room and knelt on the floor around the coffee table littered with Kyoto mementoes. I summarized my Sanzen-in experience and dilemma. He studied the print of Tsuno, looked up at me, and said, "You know, in the old days, *oni* were spirits that had horns, and they were female. You can still see this belief in traditional Japanese weddings today. The bride wears a special white hat." He used his hands to outline a large peaked ceremonial headdress like a pope's miter. "We call it *tsunokakushi* which means, 'hiding your horns.'"

Perusing the kanji about the mirror ceremony, he looked at me and said, "In tribal Japan, mirrors were not made of glass but of copper. The color is associated with blood of birth and menses and is connected to the woman. These mirrors were not for seeing the face and makeup. They were a holy tool, a vessel for the spirits that reflected eternal truths, our true teachings. We have a special mirror, *meikyo*, which is sometimes given to the person who has attained enlightenment. The mirror is round, about six inches across, and slightly concave. The metal back is engraved with a sacred symbol. When the mirror is placed with direct sunlight before it, the image on the back projects onto a flat surface. Magically, it shows the process of enlightenment. We say we polish the mirror of the mind to reflect reality."

"Maybe," he continued, "the anger and the bad feelings you got listening to what the monk said were like the old Zen practice of striking meditating monks sharply with a stick—a sudden violent act to induce enlightenment. The chance to polish your mirror."

He stood and bowed from the waist. "Sorry, I have to get back to work. We can talk about this again if you like."

I walked him to the door and watched as he crossed the road and got into his car.

Eiichi had confirmed that, traditionally, the Horned Being was a feminine healing spirit.

I fervently prayed this would be true for me, but over the next few weeks my symptoms, physical weakness, forgetfulness, and fevers worsened.

~~~

I was stymied, yet I couldn't let go. Understanding the Tsuno experience seemed my only hope for healing. For the hundredth time, I went through my notes from the trip. This time, I noticed a faint message scribbled in the margin "Sun god named Amaterasu, Japanese folk tale..." John must have mentioned it during our temple visit. I typed "Amaterasu" into my computer's search engine and clicked on the first link.

Susanoo, god of the Rumble, earthquake, and thunders, is tormenting his sister, Amaterasu, sun goddess, because she is accorded the highest status. The rivalry goes on and on, becoming so intense and destructive that Susanoo wipes out agriculture and even the weaving hall in the heavenly plane. In despair, Amaterasu flees to a cave and, for good measure, rolls a large rock across the entrance, casting heaven and earth into darkness. Crops fail, people suffer, and demons flourish. Distressed, other creative gods consult with the god of wisdom and come up with a plan. They make a sacred mirror and hang it on a tree in front of the cave. To pique Amaterasu's curiosity, the gods tell bawdy stories and laugh outrageously.

Amaterasu hears the sound of their laughter and wonders what's going on. She decides to take a peek. When the rock rolls back, the mirror reflects her light. She has never seen herself before and comes forward for a closer look. Thus, light and life are restored to the land.

I looked up from the screen. Sun goddess? That couldn't be right. Conception, birth—everything feminine is tied to the moon. But what would it mean, especially to Abrahamic religions, if the sun god were a goddess? The possibilities were staggering. Imagine how different world religions, governments, social institutions, humanity, even I, would be! My mind raced. I had stumbled on paradigmatic dynamite, an intellectual game changer.

I didn't feel the shift of energy—a still closeness of energy, a certain darkness. I was in my head and too busy fact-checking to notice that my spirit had gone off to the shadow of my psyche and returned with the key to my recovery—consciousness of the trauma-fused notion, beaten into my child self, that I deserved pain and suffering because I was bad.

An hour had passed in my internet search, and I'd failed to turn up anything more on Amaterasu. Just to see what would happen, I closed my eyes and tried visualizing the story about Amaterasu by putting myself in the various roles.

I stand in darkness but am able to make out the entry to the cave, the tree standing before it, and the assemblage of gods. I don't join any of them. Instead, I place myself in the cave. The enclosure is claustrophobic, the voices and laughter outside inviting. I am next to Amaterasu. The rock rolls back with an earthshaking roar. Held in an umbra of darkness, I follow her glance toward the tree. She sees herself in the mirror! Brilliant, clear, fire-like light lasers off its surface right through my mind. Through her awakening, I see and feel the beauty of my own soul.

In the same mythic moment, I am shown all that is keeping me from that state, from her. In a vision, I stand in a large warehouse filled with diaphanous white light. Old weatherworn wooden boxes are piled high in a corner. The instant I see them, I understand. Each container represents caustic self-judgments and negative ideas of myself—all of them false and inherited through historical trauma, including the displacement of women, as much as my personal life challenges. This is what separates me from my own creative potential, my own light. The large number of boxes, mute testimony to the magnitude of my error, is heartbreaking. I despair of ever being able to unpack and offload the weight.

But I had underestimated the power of this radiant being and her ceremonial mirror. My life was changing already, and I was about to see how. That night I fell into a deep restive sleep. The next morning, in the way of thanksgiving, I turned to the internet again and discovered an English translation of an old Japanese text. In it Amaterasu speaks: "My child, when thou lookest upon the mirror, let it be as if thou were looking on me; let it be with thee on thy couch and thy hall, and let it be to thee a holy mirror."

I was euphoric and fully confident I was on the road to healing. But as days slipped by, I was forced to admit that the fevers, bodily weakness, and debilitating fatigue were not subsiding; worse yet, I'd begun to reembrace the old trauma, to blame myself for my failure to heal despite the mystical encounter and psychological insight.

~~~

Early one morning, I got a blessing. Kneeling before my Ancestral altar, I looked up at the photo of Auntie Mahi Poepoe. We had met years earlier through my work with Indigenous Elders. Auntie was feisty and defiant and the best friend you could have. If you met her, you'd never guess she was a Healer. Kmart stretch pants pulled tight about her large frame, horn-rimmed glasses hanging on a neck chain, and loud, often earthy humor made her easy to dismiss until you got to know her. Auntie was Aloha, the divine breath, essence of Hawaii.

Looking at her photo, wishing she were still alive, I remembered asking her, "Auntie why are so many Healers passing on right now?"

"Because, we come in a wave, and we go in a wave. *E ma mua e ola mau*, forwarding into the eternal, we leave our essence (back on Earth). We come to the doorway when called. We are travelers between worlds."

A few weeks later, she passed. A light went out on our island and in my life.

I knelt before her now, as much from weakness as reverence, and prayed. "Auntie, I'm in trouble. I'm really sick. I should have asked for help a long time ago. I've had so many blessings, from Magdalen to Amaterasu. I can be in my heart, feel my feelings, and I have seen the psychological blocks that held me back since childhood. But nothing is taking away this sickness. Please, Auntie, can you help me?"

Clear as a bell, I heard her voice, "Don't worry, girl; we got your back."

As if on cue, Jesse, my Yaqui Healer friend, arrived on the island unannounced from his home in Arizona. I bumped into him at the local food court the very day he got here. Delighted, and in acknowledgment of an Ancestral hand in the serendipity, we made plans for a ceremony, a meal, and as it turned out, a doctoring for me the very next day.

Jesse is a licensed masseuse, and a good one; he'd also apprenticed with Auntie. Today, when many of us doubt or fear our traditional healing ways, the popular massage framework relaxes us. It makes us think we know what's going on; besides, who doesn't like a healing touch?

I'd been on the table about five minutes when Jesse said, "Auntie, where have you been?" (I knew by the question—which was not, Where do you hurt? or How are you feeling?—that he had already diagnosed my illness.) "You're not in your body; your spirit is standing about two feet away from you. It's fine, but your body is not. What's going on?"

"Jesse, I've been sick for months." For a second, just as I named it, the ugly, painful grip of dissociative haze lifted. "Ten days ago, the doctor gave me heavy-duty antibiotics. He thinks it's a sinus infection that has spread, but there's no direct evidence." My voice choked. "Ever since I came back from Japan, I've been getting sicker and sicker."

"What happened?" he asked nonchalantly.

It seemed as if he already knew, and before I could answer, he pressed his fingertips into my side. Between alternating moans of pain and sighs of relief, I offered a quick overview of the events around the altar of Tsuno and what I had learned since then.

"Hmmm," Jesse replied, and stepped back from the massage table.

I knew it was serious.

"What I know about those mirrors is that a soul can be trapped in them. The mirrors started out one way, but warriors found they could use them to take control of people or kill them. They could see a soul's movement and know what a person was going to do. Where's the spirituality in that?" Looking directly at me, he said, "You're lucky no one moved in [to your body] while you've been out. Feel this?" he asked as he worked on my feet.

"Yes," I hissed, as a white-hot pain tore through my leg and spine. I caught my breath. "But Jesse, I don't think it was only bad medicine," I said, thinking of the happy face and love I felt for Tsuno. "I've experienced bad medicine before—the confusion, depression, and dragging, progressive loss of vitality and, most importantly, the inability to catch what's going on. That's only part of what's been happening. Something else is lurking behind my illness.

"It's like…" I struggled for words and then heard myself say, "I'm in a house of mirrors."

Jesse completed his treatment. Then, standing at the foot of the table, he looked at me and said, "No, Auntie, the mirror experience you've had, it's not bad. It's like two souls doing the same thing or work. You recognize each other. That monk who joined with Tsuno was waiting there a long time. Can you think how many hundreds of years? When he saw your light, and felt your compassion, he saw a way out— Just a minute," Jesse said, and called for his wife, Trini, who is gifted with the Sight.

Coming to the head of the table, she looked over my torso and the space around me. "Do you see something?" Jesse asked. She looked into his eyes and nodded.

"But," I said, struggling to make sense of the situation, "are you saying that the monk, Ryogen, was caught in the mirror, and something that happened between us freed him? That seems too big for me to believe."

"Well," Jesse replied, stretching the word out while continuing to do pressure-point work on my left arm, "whatever you reflect, reflects back with a multiplier effect. You were in a moment of being in your God-self at that Tsuno altar at Sanzen-in. You were at the place where you're making it happen—the creative state, which is the highest, most intense, spiritual state. The God state is all of you opened up, connecting, vibrating with life. You experience happiness and love.

"Then the monk kneels next to you and pushes the exact buttons— 'You're evil!' It's the missionaries all over again; the Inquisitors torturing the French. From this high state of awareness and openness, all of you felt it—the rage against it and the guilt that feeds on it, fueling cancerous disease. That's when your Spirit left your body.

"You need to forgive. Release all that hurt. Forgive yourself, then release the fear from all that hurt. Let go of it. Breathe it out.

"The Now allows us to be in the grace of the Creator; it allows all our gifts to be brought forward because we are living in the continuous Breath of God. This is where we can do the greatest good for our neighbors and ourselves. Being in this state allows your gifts to be before you continuously…" his voice trailed off.

And then, I did breathe, sweet and long, and expelled a huge sigh of relief. The load was off my shoulders. I felt light, happy, free, clear-headed, and back to myself. I had one misgiving—the severity of my symptoms, the vertigo, fever, and memory loss, and how long they had persisted, suggested that total recovery in one session was unlikely.

"Now sit up and let me give you a blessing," he said.

I did, and he bestowed the blessing. The doctoring was complete. But I wanted to be certain. What authority did Jesse have to speak about the mirrors? Granted, he's a Healer, but if you're going to expound on the essence of a culture—like the mirror to the Japanese—you better have the right to do so. I remembered what Kaulaity had told me years ago about receiving and giving precious, life-sustaining, traditional knowledge. He said, "When I give you something, I give it to you clean. You do the same; don't put no shit on it."

An inkling of an idea flitted through my mind. "Jesse, how come something as sacred to Japan as the mirror is coming through to us? Things like this are culturally sanctioned and require initiation. Do you have Japanese genealogy?" I asked, thinking I was crazy as I did so.

He nodded. "Yes I'm Yaqui, but my great-grandmother was a Sato. The name got changed to Soto. Her family came to work on the railroads in Arizona in the 1800s. When she married my great-grandfather, a Mexican Indian, her family disowned her, and that's why we know nothing of that side."

I was speechless. It was not only that an American Indian Medicine Man had been delivered right to my door without any planning or foreknowledge on my part, but that he had the right genealogy for the job. Amazing. Truly amazing.

That night, I decided to read a bit to help me relax into sleep. Picking up one of the research books stacked on the floor by my bed, I read a Zen description of mirror meditation. Zen says that until we are enlightened, the mind will always create things in the mirror. But in reality, there is no mirror. I shook my head in recognition and laughed out loud. Through all of it, feeling caught in a house of mirrors, the mirror experience at the temple, and again with Amaterasu, I realized I had never seen a mirror.

Welcome to Japan.

Chapter 17

GARAMANTE

Maui, Hawaii, and South Africa, 2008

It was gone!

Through the gap of my loose-necked hospital gown, I traced the line of rugged-looking metal staples running from my breastbone up toward my left shoulder. My breast was gone, but—perched on the side of my bed, legs dangling off the floor and IV needles in each arm—I realized something else. The flu-like symptoms I'd suffered every day of the 13 years since my first bout of breast cancer were gone, simply gone.

A week earlier, I'd noticed a slight itchiness and a tiny—like a fourth of a pencil eraser—discoloration on my nipple. On the lookout for recurrence, I made an appointment the same day. Within 24 hours, the results were in. Stage One cancer, a rare type, different from the first time—and this one was deadly. Surgery was scheduled for the very next week.

Now my life looked as bright and promising as the sparkling blue waves of the Pacific, visible through the hospital window. When

Keola came to get me, I met him at the door, fully dressed and ready to go.

For the next couple of months, I vacillated between an ecstatic optimism and deep insecurity—afraid to trust life, afraid to trust myself. I fought back against post-mastectomy depression. It seemed crass to feel anything but thankful, especially when I considered the synchronicities that saved my life, including the encounter with Tsuno and Jesse showing up at the exact right time. But the struggle with a half-pound, rubber prosthesis slithering up and down my chest in the tropical heat did get me down. That and other indignities, like trying to rig up a swimsuit that would keep the thing in place. To my utter humiliation, the one time I did get in the water, I discovered, in full sight of sunbathers on the beach, the damn thing bobbing along on the waves beside me. Still, I told myself, *You're alive. Be thankful.* And I was—but there is no getting around the grief of debilitating life changes.

And that's the way I felt, trying to be strong, trying to be thankful, and fighting sadness as I headed to South Africa to meet with Credo Mutwa, preeminent Zulu Elder.

Healer, philosopher, and teacher, Baba, or Father Mutwa, was the last High Sanusi, the most advanced level of Zulu wisdom carriers. His knowledge of ancient migrations underpinning human history is renowned. The way he knows things hidden in the mists of time is almost as compelling as the wisdom itself. Oral history weaves the paradox of specificity and universality to shed light on the complexity of our interconnections and negate racialist distortions that occur in our modern day, oversimplistic jumps to universality.

When Baba doesn't know something, he accesses the Great Memory—the ability to recall events in the life of the human species. The source lies in the stars. "It is not easy for us humans to achieve star knowledge on Earth," Baba confides. "It involves much suffering and discipline. But if, as Sanusis, we are able to do so, it is our God-given duty to bring the enlightenment back to Earth for the benefit of all living beings on this planet." The Great Memory belongs to all of us, but surviving Cultural Practitioners can fully activate it through immersion in paranormal states of awareness and by honoring our interspecies bond. Hawaiian Cultural Practitioners, Mr. Makua and Auntie Poepoe, were just such people.

I'd first met Credo Mutwa in 2002, following the United Nations' Earth Summit Meeting in Johannesburg, South Africa. As a part of my Elders Networking Project, I'd arranged for Auntie and Mr. Makua to participate; I came along as their helper.

The summit's work hinged on a nonstop, back-to-back series of UN-style meetings aimed at developing global sustainability policy. By the end of the week, all we knew of the country was air-conditioned, windowless conference rooms. But our forbearance was rewarded with a visit to the Cradle of Humankind, the world's richest hominid site, a 90-minute drive from Johannesburg, and a visit with Credo the following day.

To get to the archaeological site, we had to drive through a wildlife preserve in a Land Rover. It was late winter, and the desolate landscape made it easy to spot animals—rhinos, lions, wildebeests, and warthogs—but I realized with a slight sheen of sweat on my lip, it was also easier for them to spot us, especially when the vehicle slowed for a closer look! Adrenaline surged through my body, and I silently prayed for protection. As if the driver had heard me, the vehicle made a right turn and snarled its laborious way up a large, rock-strewn hill. About two-thirds of the way up, the driver pulled sideways to the incline and parked.

"You'll have to walk the rest of the way up—this is as far as we can go. The dig is at the top. They're expecting you."

A couple of younger colleagues and I clambered out of the vehicle and made for the crest. Elders, including Hale Makua, stayed behind. At the summit, a beautiful, young, Zulu woman, standing before an eight-foot-deep pit, met us. Unprecedented for patriarchal Western science or African tribal ways, she was the first South African tribal woman to head a major dig. But the relaxed attitudes, friendly teasing, and laughter showed that the team had clearly worked things out.

They took us through the complex scientific research process with dispatch. When she finished, she asked if we had questions. I did.

"It's so good to see a tribal woman in charge of a World Heritage site dig. How did you come to be here and why?"

Teasingly she responded, "My granny always said, 'You're too big for your britches,'" and tossed her head back with a beautiful smile.

She looked at me and, in a more serious vein, asserted, "My friends say, 'Come back to the city, have fun. It's cold and dirty out there on the dig.'" I tell them, 'I don't mind; I'm digging for my Ancestors.'"

Her words struck like lightning. "Digging for my Ancestors"— the truth of my life right here in front of me, in concrete terms, at an origin of humanity. A feeling, a spirit moved through me in such a way that I urgently needed to connect with her to feel the reconnection through time. But she was totally focused on making a scientific presentation. It felt a bit awkward, but I asked anyway. "Can we pray?"

"Sure," she said, then yelled and waved her arms, calling the team to circle around the edge of the dig. African prayers, the sound, soft, still, and powerful, seemed to open a trap door beneath my feet and drop me to the center of the Earth. I could have been there, seconds, hours, or lifetimes—no way to tell and no desire to do so.

When we finished, the distance between us was gone; we hugged and smiled like the long-lost relatives we were. Reluctantly, I turned to go back down. A dozen steps removed, and a tempest of emotions hit me. I detoured off the path toward the edge of the hill, vying for privacy and a moment to pull myself together. Instead, when I stopped moving, projectile tears forcefully and uncontrollably moved down my face. I lifted my glasses to wipe my eyes. Returning them to my face, I beheld a dramatically different vista. The cold bleak landscape had become a warm, moist, tropical world. A sea of aquamarine water stretched out before me, the sight of which filled me with reverence and joy.

I remained in this revelatory state for some minutes until I questioned what was happening. Instantly, I was back on the Cradle of Humankind trail overlooking the windswept landscape. I looked again, trying to find that holy place; it was gone, but the feeling was not. If I could get to Mr. Makua still haloed in the numinous, he could tell me what it meant.

Headlong, I plunged down the uneven, rock-strewn wasteland toward the Elders in the vehicle, but was abruptly halted by Audri Scott Williams, a fellow summit participant. "Look, see those white marks?" She pointed to a striated basalt rock in the ground. "It's the Star Beings. It's their sign; they've been here."

I nodded, too spirit-soaked to speak, and hurtled down the hill to the Rover. Makua's bench seat was shoulder-level to me. I ran to that white-haired Elder with all the strength I had. Gently, he leaned over, placed his massive brown hand on the left side of my head, and said, "You remember."

I nodded my head over and over, still weeping. Only later would I question, *What did I remember?*

We visited Baba the next day. Virginia Rathele, Bushman Healer and Baba's wife, greeted us warmly at the door and showed us to a large dining-room table.

Offerings in hand, we waited. A sense of the sacred preceded Baba and grew as he approached. Simultaneously, we lowered our heads and remained this way until a soft murmur of voices told us Baba, swaddled in white, had arrived.

Taking his chair, the High Sanusi drew a breath and sat in silence for a few minutes, then looked up, taking us in one at a time, and said with no preliminaries and never having heard of us before, "We used to have a Great Chief, Mawela or Maui. People say he was a god, but he was a real man. He sailed east from Libya in a great canoe, pulling islands out of the sea as he voyaged. He was a great man, but we do not know what happened to him. Do you?"

An audible collective gasp escaped our delegation. We could scarcely believe that Hawaii and South Africa shared the same oral history of Maui, demigod of initiation, each island pulled from the sea, a new consciousness. But how could Baba identify the essential connection between us and discern it so quickly? His precision bespoke a level of mastery none of us, including the Hawaiian Elders, experts in the *huna*, or mysteries, of their own culture, had ever witnessed.

Taking turns around the table, we introduced ourselves. Mr. Makua, the head of our delegation, acknowledged the shared oral history. Again, silence enveloped the room. Baba turned to his wife, seated next to him, and spoke to her in his Zulu language. She rose, disappeared into the next room, and returned with a wooden box. Baba looked inside, nodded, and withdrew a huge Y-shaped necklace. A chain of copper links bound together fist-size calumet rocks; a copper wheel covered in hieroglyphs joined the parts. Brass leaves topped a round stone lined like a world globe. Five hundred years earlier, Zulu women forged the necklace to encode critical knowledge they feared would be lost in the European invasion.

"Tell me, Honorable Ones, can anyone here read this?" Baba asked as he extended the necklace to our group. "Many wise people from my tribe have tried but were not able. I am the last one."

His invitation was a test. If we were or were not Cultural Practitioners of sufficient depth, he would know it immediately. There are no half measures in such moments. Our hopes were on the Hawaiian Elders. Just as Auntie received the necklace, I saw her hands tremble with spirit, and knew something profound was about to happen. Bead by bead, symbol by symbol, she interpreted the artifact as one might read a page of print. The necklace recorded the destruction of the Zulu Way, the suffering it would cause, and it predicted the conditions for a renaissance, including the reconnecting of Indigenous Peoples. "And that is what these rocks are telling me," Auntie concluded.

Rejoicing, Baba clapped his hands. "I wish, truly wish other Sangoma Healers had been here to see this woman from far off, from Hawaii, read this necklace. And I swear to God it was exactly as I was taught."

"Honorable Ones," Credo repeated, letting us know the conversation had shifted, "ancient knowledge brought humanity out of the dark into the light. The stars are our signal. They are not regarded as lights in the sky but as dwelling places of important Beings. The stars have been our friends for years. They taught our mothers the mysteries of fire.

"The Cradle of Humankind is the place where the first Star Beings came to Earth. They were not able to return home and instead decided to create a civilization based in love here on Earth. They did. You can tell where they lived by the shell middens. You see, they did not eat warm things. They ate raw things from the sea. Their civilization lasted until invader warriors from the north came in and destroyed it."

Shaking with barely concealed excitement, I caught his eye. He nodded assent, and I asked the question burning in my mind. "Baba, why is the sea-green color so important? Since we visited the Cradle of Humankind, it's all I can think of."

"That's the color of the Star Beings' eyes. You can still see their descendants today. We call them beachcombers—no," he said, looking for the correct English term. "Wave Walkers."

~~~

Now, six months after my surgery, I was returning to South Africa with Mary Ann, a friend of the Hawaiian Elders. I'd thought I would have many opportunities to ask Mr. Makua and Auntie about my experiences during that first visit in South Africa, but tragically both died suddenly following our return to the islands. Poignantly, just days before leaving Maui for my second visit, I'd discovered video clips of Auntie and Makua reflecting on their meeting with Baba. The messages were so apt, it was as if they knew they would be gone when Baba received them.

After a long drive to Kuruman, I was once again in Baba's presence. We greeted each other, and then I switched on my computer and showed him the video clips. Tears coursed down his cheeks as the images and sounds wrapped around him. Afterward, we sat in silence for what seemed an eternity.

Then our esteemed Credo asked, "Is it possible for one to have a copy of this?"

Taken aback by his humility, I responded, voice choked with emotion, 'Yes, yes, Baba. This is for you. That is why I came all this way, to bring these messages to you."

Virginia stepped forward to receive the DVD. "This is good," she said. "We can share it with other Sangoma, so they can see our connection with Indigenous Healers around the world."

Again, the room fell silent. When it felt OK to speak, I brought up my forthcoming Wisdom University trip to the painted caves of the South of France. I asked Baba how I might prepare. He took a drink of the Coke sitting on the table before him. Leaning forward, he put his hands together as if in prayer.

"It's already deep inside you. When you are there, it will come out of you—ancient truths will emerge from you. Remember, all the great cave paintings show animals, many of whom are pregnant. This shows that these paintings were prayers of our most remote Ancestors of Ancestors. These prayers were made to ask the Earth to preserve life, to keep the animals in existence. They were not just shamanic dream images.

"In Lascaux there is one remarkable painting that is extremely important to Africans. It is a pregnant animal with a strange head and two straight horns, like needles facing upward. This is an animal that exists in Namibia today—a large deer. In Afrikaans it is called gemsbok. Whoever drew this animal must have been in Africa!

"Where you are going is the most amazing part of the world! When the paintings were made, people were traveling all over the world. This is a birthplace of humanity, a place of prayer, a place where ancient peoples expressed their earthly concerns of all sorts.

"May the winds of light carry you to the cradle of human awareness and artistry. Let the spirits come out of you—the gods do this. In this way, feel them. The Earth itself will make ideas and prayers from many thousands of years ago come out."

Our audience was at an end. We presented our offerings, thanked him, and rose to leave; however, the conversation had invigorated Credo. He not only made it out the door and down the steps of the house, but also showed us around his healing compound: an adobe roundhouse, or rondavel, for HIV/Aids patients, including a special hammock he had designed to mitigate pressure on surface wounds; a second rondavel for orphans; and a third for the preparation of traditional, herbal medicines and ceremony.

As we made our way to the car, Baba pointed out landscape features, a garden for traditional healing plants, and a ring of large standing stones. "It's very good for a woman who has suffered abuse to sit in the center of this circle. It will heal them." Lovely little clumps of purple flowers grew at the base of the rocks. The flowers were not planted nor watered—they took root and flourished because of the power of the rocks themselves. "More magic was done with rocks than anything. Many don't understand today," he noted.

Continuing a few steps down the road brought us to a chain link fence circumscribing an enormous 10-foot-high image of a woman. Signage in front of her read, "Mary Magdalene"! I could scarcely believe my eyes and turned to him for an explanation.

Baba was happy to explain the origin of the statue. An artist and welder, he'd created the Magdalen himself.

"But why?" I asked.

"People must never forget the roots from which they came. We come from a time when the female was considered sacred. Somewhere along the line, we went off track, but slowly the sacredness of women is coming back. Never before have people been so aware of the preciousness of life. Never before have humans risked their lives to save whales, trees, dolphins—preservation of life as was done in the days of Antu, the oldest goddess ever worshipped by people in Africa and Europe. Antu was the first named Great Mother, and the one animal sacred to Her was the honeybee. Out of the honey was made a beer-like wine, which was intended to arouse in the human soul the deepest feeling for the Earth. It is still made today, to be drunk by initiates so that the Spirit of Old can come out of the person.

"In Her times, there was no war; people did not fight; they were Garamante, followers of Antu. They removed their left breast, not to shoot bows and arrows but to show they were perfect in Her eyes! Mary Magdalene was a Garamante, a daughter of Antu. *Garamante* means climber, traveler, one who mounts lions or lionesses to ride them. These were the first African people to ride in two-wheel chariots all the way from the Holy Land of Sudan. *Garamante* also means, 'Sudan or Darfar, country of the children of the Mother.'"

For the first time since my surgery, I looked down at the flat space on the left side of my chest and smiled.

Chapter 18

THE CAVES

Dordogne, France, 2005

They were just glossy pictures in a National Geographic article about the painted caves of the Dordogne, but the 35,000-year-old visual communication pulled me in as if I were right there—and I knew I had to visit them. The deep prehistory artists were Indigenous People of France, untainted by Roman and Mongol invasions, the Crusades, the Inquisition, and the derivative and projected colonial barbarity that blanketed our history in shame and spilled over into my childhood through alcoholism and violence. Connecting with the paintings promised a release, a redemption; but, as the Wisdom University trip I was leading to the South of France drew nearer, so did a growing sense of apprehension. I thought often of Credo's words and drew strength from them: "It's already deep inside you. When you are there, it will come out of you—ancient truths will emerge from you."

~~~

Kathy, one of the participants, and I were 10 minutes into our 15-minute walk up the hill, and we paused to look out across the tree-clad valley and breathe in the faint fragrance of dry, golden soil and pine resin. Waves of heat shimmered above the tree line, a buzz of cicadas echoed off limestone cliff faces and wrapped around us like a mother's arms. The 100—degree, late fall day lulled us into a dream state that intensified our struggle to place foot after foot.

The Dordogne is famous for its wine, caves, bucolic green meadows, meandering rivers, picturesque medieval villages, and a rich Mary Magdalene mystical tradition. My visitation experience a couple of years earlier had filled me with a burning desire to know Her.

When Wisdom University invited me to organize a Magdalene study trip, I'd jumped at the chance. As an afterthought, we added an optional visit to Font de Gaume—the only painted cave still open to the public. Because of the damage caused by uncontrolled tourism, more famous caves such as Chauvet and Lascaux were closed permanently except to scientists.

I took a close look at Kathy. Rivulets of sweat slid down her beet-red face. "Are you OK?"

"Oh, sure. I'm OK. It's not the heat. I'm a sweater. Always have been. I was just thinking about my claustrophobia. Had it for years—got so bad I finally went for treatment."

Like a firebrand her words seared through the layers of my subconscious.

My God, I'm claustrophobic too! I can't go into this cave! But it's my Ancestral land, I want to go in. What happens if I get in and can't handle it? Can I get out? Sweat lodge panic attacks and the dread I'd felt entering the room where I received radiation flashed through my mind. Nothing had lifted it, neither Indigenous nor Western therapies.

I can't do it. I'll have to ask someone else from the university to take over. This is completely unprofessional. I may lose my job. Ancestors, help me, please.

Anxiety built with each step. Part of the fear was pragmatic. Caves are dangerous places with tight passages, holes, and darkness; if the light goes out, you cannot find the way out. Glancing toward the cave entrance, I stopped beneath the shade of an oak. The cicadas stopped too.

"Kathy, what did you do?" I asked desperately.

"Well," she said confidently, "I found when I was having a claustrophobic attack what I was doing was projecting myself out, looking for danger, trying to protect myself. The more I looked out, the worse it got. The answer was to come into my heart. Look inside. When I did, I was OK and still am."

Before, if someone had said, "Go into your heart," I would have dismissed it as sentimental claptrap. But after my visit to Japan, the words sounded profound. I could feel what she meant by *heart*.

"So, how do you do it?" I asked.

"I just remind myself. That's all. And I'm OK."

Her simple advice made sense, but something else did not. Why, in all of the pre-trip planning, had I never once considered my claustrophobia? This critical memory lapse had the markings of a visit to Uli, the sacred place of turnabout. How could I doubt it? Kathy was here with the right information at the exact time I needed it. Time to grow.

I can do this, I resolved, until I faced the twin mouths of the cave— two black openings like eye sockets in a skull.

The words of my psychologist friend Daniel came to mind: "It elicits the most fear, actually, terror. Going into the cave is going to the root of fear. Doing so puts life in balance. When you enter a cave, you're entering different dimensions. What one experiences is in response to one's preparedness for it—like in a dream, or the spiritual world, and actually in the social world as well. People come toward you if you want something to emerge. There's a reciprocity. Something is there, waiting. Our willingness to go into it dictates the volume of our experience."

I was more than willing. I wanted to see Font de Gaume and really wanted to rid myself of the fear of closed places. Taking a couple deep breaths and offering a prayer of supplication, I stepped into the dark mouth of the cave. To my surprise and relief, the cave featured subdued track lighting. I relaxed—but only for a moment.

Thump! The big entry door closed behind us with the screech of a key turning in the lock, echoing through the cavern. Trapped! Adrenaline rushed through my veins. The urge to flee possessed me.

Breathe, get into the heart, and breathe. I have to get out. No, stay, breathe; get out of the mind, into the heart! I'm in my heart. OK, better. The 52-degree temperature helped. Maybe I could do this. Even the sharp downward drop of the path helped me stay present. Looking down to watch my step calmed me. When anxiety started to rise, I picked up my pace and trotted as if I were casually confident. Abruptly, the ceiling dropped and walls closed in. I was scared; breath ragged. Just a bit over five feet, I still had to duck, but despite the increasing severity of the incline and decrease of aperture, I held my own until I rounded the next turn. Immediately before me was a passage so low and narrow, I doubted I could get through without turning sideways. I'd reached my limit. I had to get out, but couldn't go backward.

People were following behind, and there was no room for people to pass. I had to proceed. The situation reminded me of an Oneida understanding: A shell that protects our spirit surrounds our body. When we are dissociated, the right circumstances, a sacred site like this, might bring the body and spirit back together.

It took all my will power, but I pushed through and popped out into an enormous high slit of a gallery. The atmosphere shifted immediately, an uncanny sense of being watched took over. I looked up directly into the dark, mischievous eye of a gigantic polychromatic bison. The art was astonishing. Ancient artists or shamans used earth pigments of blood-red, pale yellow, black, and even a purplish color, and integrated cave contours to emphasize anatomical features. The heads of animals turned to observe the viewer—a twisted torso effect unknown in art until modern times. Picasso, who was not known for his humility, came out of the caves and announced, "We have learned nothing in 12,000 years."

The entire wall of the gallery was covered with paintings of horses, aurochs, and mastodons; but it was the reindeer, reminding me of my childhood encounter with the deer, that arrested. More than 200 caves have been discovered with thousands of etchings, figurines, bas-reliefs and other man-made features, yet this is the only narrative painting. Two reindeer face each other. One, a male, stands to the left, nose lowered, nearly touching the head of a female lying prone. She is giving birth.

As I stood transfixed before this image, a single drop of water, one that had taken thousands of years to permeate the earth and limestone, dropped from the ceiling directly on the top of my scalp. The coolness spread across my head and down throughout my body. When I exited the cave, I was free of claustrophobia for good.

～～

One year after the visit to Font de Gaume, I organized and led a university study tour devoted solely to the caves. Impressed with the healing that happened to me the year before, I wanted to go in a respectful way with a local expert as our guide. A university board member from France recommended Pascal Raux.

Pascal was a busy man. When not leading cave tours, researching, writing, or lecturing, you could find him at Roc de Gazelle prehistory park, demonstrating fire making, flint knapping, and other Stone Age skills. On our first meeting, he admitted that he didn't have much use for Americans, "Crazy New Age people."

"I am Paleolithic man," he said, brushing broomstick-straight gray hair from his eyes and taking another puff on his odorous Panther cigarette. "I am forever in the cave. It is my world. It is difficult for newcomers to be in the cave. You become tired, but afterward, when you come out, you feel alive, energized. We go into the caves because we have lost the principal meaning and *raison*, reason of life. We go into the cave to try and restore this. Today man thinks he is superior—that all life is only about man, and nature is nothing. But nature without man will survive. Man without nature will not. This is a lesson of the cave. We are small. Nature is large. We are a little piece of the whole.

"The caves can function today as they did in Paleolithic times, but if you come as a tourist and pay money to get in, it's meaningless. The caves are a place of initiation."

Following this rather stern admonishment came a thrilling surprise. Pascal would take us to two caves, starting with Cougnac, the crystal cave, where we would be permitted to pray and chant. Two days later, we would complete our trip at Chauvet 2, the most ancient cave of all, the one with the most paintings of fierce animals and the famous *Venus and the Sorcerer*.

We gathered outside Cougnac the following morning. With Pascal's OK, we formed a circle to smudge ourselves before descending. My daughter Chyna, who speaks French, held the abalone shell so I could light the sprig of cedar that rested on the edge of it. The evergreen burst into crackling flame, then died down, releasing billows of minty clean-smelling smoke. She took the smudge to the participants, who blessed themselves with the smoke, then called out their family name and stated their intentions. When it came to me, I did the same, then turned to face the mouth of the cave and asked permission to enter.

Stepping through the medieval-looking security door, we descended a short flight of stairs, walked briefly on a damp, hard-packed clay surface, then took a long, severely inclined set of steps to an even more downward-sloping path. The cave ceiling dropped as we progressed; the air grew cold and the atmosphere intense. Stalagmites appeared, scattered at first, then clustered like a dense forest. Pascal stopped and pointed out a series of flat-topped, graduated, calcite cones.

"Xylophones," he noted offhandedly, and pointed to striations on the cones. "Scientists found pencil-like bones lying next to these. They had matching marks, so we know they played these stalagmites like an instrument." With that, he produced a thin striker from his cracked, worn leather vest, and struck a pinnacle. A sound—sweet, pure, and light—rang out and soared through the dark cavern. He struck a few more stalactites—a musical scale. Satisfied, he popped the striker back into his vest, pivoted, and strode off in his typical run-walk.

We thought we were already in the cave. Actually, it was an entry. A few twists and turns later, we came into the chamber that gives the cave its name. Crystal icicles ranging in color from pale white to gold and a light rust radiated out in concentric rings from the center of the cave ceiling to the outermost edges. Like a gigantic chandelier, the stalactites hung directly down from the heart and flared out to the extremities. Stalagmites ranging from a few inches in diameter to massive tree-trunk-size stretched and reached as if longing for their overhead counterparts. Alabaster pillars, fused stalactites and stalagmites, gleamed in the radiance of their union.

Reluctant to leave the beauty, but curious, we moved into a second, circular-shaped cavern. Quietly, Pascal pulled me aside and pointed downward to a shallow, ovoid earthen pit about five feet wide. He looked at me expectantly.

"*Ourse*," he said. "*Ourse*."

"Bears? Bears?" I said in shock and disbelief. "A bear slept here?"

He nodded excitedly. "Yes, cave bears more than 12 feet high slept here for thousands of years."

Looking over his shoulder to be certain the group was OK, he turned on his flashlight and gestured for me to follow.

"Come."

Nearly jogging across the uneven floor, we made our way to a far wall where he used his flashlight to illuminate a large area.

"See?"

I did. Deep scratches scored the surface from the ceiling downward. Claw marks of bears digging the mineral-rich soil for nutrients. I thought of their North American descendant, the black bear that watched my gramma and me as we hoed the earth so many years ago. Maybe that bear thought we were on to something nutritious.

Rejoining the group, we made our way toward a smooth, translucent wall in the back. Pascal stopped to open a metal box mounted on a post. A click of a switch zapped us out of a dimly lit, dreamlike state to show a brilliantly illuminated cave wall saturated with black, yellow, and red-ocher paintings—horned sheep, reindeer with flowing antlers, and the torso of a shaman, head disappearing into a vulva-like entry.

"Do you see it?" Pascal asked quietly. I didn't until I let my vision go soft. Etched behind, and incorporating the polychromes in the foreground, was an enormous feline looking right at us! In the terrifying moment of realization, Pascal doused the lights. A shiver of fear rippled through the group.

"Chant. Now you can chant," Pascal urged.

We did, with all our might, then stopped suddenly, in unison, as if under the aegis of a choral director. Silence so profound that drops of water pierced the darkness of the cavern and our minds. Huddled together, we stood waiting in the blackness. Something was coming; you could feel it. Pascal said nothing. One second, two seconds, three; a low-pitched rumble like distant thunder, emanated behind us, raced around the periphery, and built into a full-on roar just before it terminated, exactly in front of us.

Speechless. We could not say a single word, none of us.

Click! On came the lights. "We go," said Pascal, stepping aside to watch us exit. Chyna, known for her indigenous reserve, stepped over to him, looked him straight on, and said in French, "You knew that would happen, didn't you?"

He shrugged. "I knew it was possible."

Stepping out of the cave, we looked up at the starlit sky. Ursa Major, the Great Bear twinkled overhead. "You're still here. You're still here," I whispered.

～～～

The 10-hour drive from the Dordogne to Chauvet Cave in the Ardèche region of France gave me lots of time to think. A single drop of water in Font du Gaume had removed a psychological barrier and empowered me to enter the caves of my Ancestral Creation Story; the roar of a leopard had confirmed the ceremonial power of the caves was still intact and had wondrously and terrifyingly manifested for us. But receiving a message through time from Paleolithic Ancestors compelled a response. I wasn't sure what it was.

Chauvet 2 is a to-scale exact replica, created by the French government, of the real cave. For purposes of preservation, the actual cave will never be open to the public, but I still wanted to see the replica for the variety and number of paintings, an artistry that can never be duplicated, and the near perfect condition of the images. But what called to me was its reputation as a sacred, ceremonial cave, notably a bear cult altar featured in *National Geographic* pictures. In the original cave, perched on a triangular slab of rock, is a massive bear skull; bear skulls ring the base of the rock. Scientists, experts with strong ethics and appreciation of aesthetics, have left the altar in situ. No one has touched it since the Paleolithic people—including a child whose footprints were found in the hardened cave floor—gathered around it. I longed to experience the deep sacredness of my "Whiteness."

It didn't seem likely. The smart young tour guide who met us operated off a government-approved timetable and script. In short order, she'd formed a group of our visitor gaggle, given us headsets, and imposed "cave rules" of behavior. I questioned why I'd come.

I didn't have to wait long for an answer.

Within minutes, we were standing behind a pipe railing looking on the altar. Falling behind the group, with awareness of an approaching group coming up behind us, I dropped to my knees in gratitude and offered a prayer for the health and survival of modern-day bears, the Indigenous People who still maintain the bear ceremonies, and: *Please, please help us modern-day descendants remember our indigenous minds, spirituality, and connection to the Earth.*

I caught up with my group just in time to hear our guide say, "This year we completed DNA research on some of the fossils, and were surprised to learn that some of the bones on the floor here"—she casually cast her flashlight on a general spot—"were not of a cave lion but a snow leopard." She cast her light on a finger of limestone hanging from the ceiling. "We used to say," she continued, "that this ocher painting of a long-tailed, spotted feline was a lion, but now we believe it's a snow leopard."

My mouth dropped open. For the past few months, following the start-up of my Cultural Practitioners networking project in Kyrgyzstan, lucid dreams of the snow leopard, sacred animal to Kyrgyz Healers, had been coming to me. Now, visiting the ancient home of my French Paleolithic Ancestors, I'd come to the cave that held the memory and power of the snow leopard. Something was trying to come through, but what?

There was no time to reflect as the guide hurried us toward the last and deepest chamber. We rounded a bend and landed at the edge of a Paleolithic stampede. Rhinoceros, bison, mammoth depicted facing left and serried, moved away from sixteen lions, depicted mostly as heads and on a different, larger scale, watching from the right. The dark-edged, polished, ferrous-oxide-washed limestone screen glimmered golden like the eye of the cave lion dispassionately sizing us up. We froze in our tracks.

The guide's shrill voice sliced through our Paleo-time bubble and landed us solidly on our collective chronological feet. "And this"—she gestured toward a limestone cone suspended from the ceiling—"is one of the most important features, *Venus and the Sorcerer.*"

A black charcoal-drawn pubic triangle inscribed with a white vulva split hangs eye level at the pointed end of a stalactite. Her ample thighs and proportions and choice of anatomical imagery are completely classical and in keeping with the Venuses found in central and eastern Europe. But Chauvet Venus is also unique. Her right leg is the left leg of a lioness, situated immediately above her lower torso. Her left leg serves as the left leg of a bison-headed male, a shaman, and faces the pubis, back to us, coitus just a breath away. The sensuality of the scene is deepened by the cave darkness framing the limestone. To Her right are two more felines looking at Her and a lioness looking at a cub.

I had entered the Sanctum Sanctorum, the Holy of Holies, the unmediated by words or history, Creation Story of my Ancestors. Hanson Ashley's words returned to me, *When you're out of balance, you need to go back to the Creation Story of your people. At that place of Creation Emergence, you put yourself in balance and, from that place of Creation, tell your story in a new balanced way.*

I was ready.

Chapter 19

THE WHITE BLESSING

Bishkek, Kyrgyzstan 2008

Bolot was a good driver. He needed to be. We left the capital, Bishkek, early for our six-hour drive to Talas, which passed directly through the Roof of the World, some of the highest mountain peaks in Central Asia. We overnighted en route to the sacred site of Arashan.

The Soviets who built the highways and ruled the Kyrgyz for 90 years had invested little in the country. The roads showed it. One look, and your life flashed before your eyes. People barreled along these arteries barely a lane-and-a-half wide at rates of speed nearly as high as the mountain altitudes. Adding to the adrenaline rush was the lack of any lane demarcation and the constant honking of horns. Cars wanting to pass headed straight into oncoming traffic. But all of it was kid's play compared to the Kolbaev tunnel.

Plunging out of the diamond light of the pinnacle highway, we shot straight into a narrow tube of total darkness. Angled along the side of the mountain, the road was scarcely more than exposed sheets of jagged, layered shale. The grade was worse: straight up for 15 or 20 minutes, then 20 more straight down. A haze of noxious gas, visible in oncoming headlights, burned the eyes and stung the throat. On top of that, I had a wicked, high-altitude headache and nausea and was so drowsy I could barely keep my eyes open.

The road had been difficult on many levels. Nearly a month in Central Asia, with just two days before my departure, I still had not accomplished what I'd traveled halfway around the world to do. I was there to meet Indigenous Healers and invite them to be a part of a global network of Healers. I'd worked years to raise the funds and had waited for the right doors to open, and I finally got the chance. What I found was discouraging. Even in a remote land, czars and the USSR had suppressed indigenous Kyrgyz spirituality and culture just as badly as world powers had with indigenous cultures worldwide. Islamic religion had also played a role in the displacement of traditional ways. However, the culture was beginning to rebound since the country obtained independence in 1991.

One of the challenges to the cultural renaissance was a post-9/11 influx of radical mullahs from the Middle East. Up until then, a relaxed Islam and tribal spirituality got on. Now, just as the country struggled to forge a national identity, fractious divides grew and deepened. Meetings disintegrated into finger pointing and shouting, "This is against the law of the Prophet." At an especially rancorous gathering, an Elder introduced himself to me as a member of the Eagle Clan. That alone triggered a five-minute tirade against Tengerism, Central Asian traditional spirituality, on the part of an indigenous Elder woman. It hurt to see Native people in such a state. As we walked away from the meeting and found a moment of privacy, I asked if this had ever happened to him before. He stopped, looked me in the eye, and said, "It happens every time."

"There they are." Bolot pointed to a small cream-colored Lada parked on the side of the gravel road—our contacts, Elders Zhaparkul and Gengish.

We rolled up behind and got out to greet them. Despite the late morning hour, the sun had just cleared the summit of the massive mountain range before us. Shadows spilled down the west face, silhouetting the two men. It was only as we drew close that I could make out their traditional Kyrgyz attire—knee-high riding boots and long velvet jackets. *Kuchor*—stylized, twisting lines of beadwork symbolizing the curved ram horn, dreams, and imagination—adorned their lapels. Most compelling were their *ak kalpaks*, white wool pyramidal hats. Like the snowcapped mountains behind them, the hats signified consciousness dissolving into light, *Nurga Ailanat*. The Healers were sacred mountains in human form.

The sight left me speechless. This was real.

We greeted each other, holding hands for a moment, then hopped back into our SUV and followed the Lada. The road ended in a greige mountain, wrinkled and creased with shadowy lines, like an old face. This was the sacred site of Arashan. On our left, a rushing glacial river cut through an exposed hillside. A single, one-room building stood to our right, the ceremonial house. Between the two was a silver-gray pebble path that led past the house, twisted, turned, and then disappeared in the brush at the base of the mountain.

As I got out of the vehicle, Zhaparkul opened the back door of the Lada to pull out a large wool blanket. To my shock, a forked walking stick poked out of the folds and struck the ground. The "blanket" opened. A tiny form materialized—Sonumbubu, 83-year-old grandmother, Healer, and Sufi mystic had arrived.

I kicked off my shoes and adjusted the scarf on my head before stepping into the ceremonial house. It was just one room, but it was dazzling. Feltwork and embroidered tapestries in vivid, contrasting shades of red, hot-pink, orange, deep blues, greens, and blacks draped the walls. Cushions in traditional *shyrdak'* interlocking, mosaic-type patchwork patterns circumscribed the floor. In the center was a tablecloth covered with fry bread, cookies, crackers, and candies.

We sat, I with my young interpreters, Zemfira and Guljan, across from Sonumbubu, and Zhaparkul and Genghis immediately to her left and my right. Sonumbubu began to chant. Her voice cracked with age and did not falter, but her atonal prayer had the strange effect of disrupting my normal thought patterns and quieting my mind.

I don't know how long it took or how it happened. One moment I sat cross-legged in the ceremony house, the next I was out of my body. I looked down on the slopes of the Tien Shan mountains and saw myself standing there as a young woman. It was the 1978 American Indian trip to China. We were in Xinjiang. Lakota Medicine Man Collins Horse Looking, face wind-burned and happy, returned to the group. He came up to me, shaking with controlled excitement, and nodded his head. "Yes, I found the place and offered the Pipe. I prayed for the Earth, for our cultures, and that, we, Indigenous People would remember who we are and how we are related."

A foamy white line began to move from me as a young woman over the mountains to me in the here and now closed the points in an ellipsis of swirling whiteness, counterclockwise with a clockwise peripheral spin.

Throughout this visit, whenever I asked about the mountain range, I had been given the Kyrgyz name. It was not until this vision that I realized I was at the Tien Shan range—but on the opposite side!

Sitting in that ceremonial house, I saw pattern and direction in my life. Chance alone could not explain the coincidence of arriving 30 years later at the same remote place, the place we had offered the Pipe so long ago. As an Elder, this mattered greatly. So much of the ensuing time had been filled with hardship and failure. I had questioned whether my life and work with Healers had any meaning at all, and I was asking the questions at a time in life when it was too late to do anything differently. Arriving at my starting point showed me I had done what I was here to do. I had come full circle.

The chanting stopped; a sense of peace filled the room.

Zhaparkul spoke, quietly and urgently. "We see your *Kasiet*, your light. We know who you are and why you are here. This is what we will do. We will light our Sacred Fire, the *Uluu Ot*, and we will light it in five places throughout our country, including at the top of our sacred mountain, Suleiman. We want to invite the Elders of your global network to join us, to light their own Sacred Fire at the exact same time.

"In ancient times Kyrgyz lit fires on sacred mountain tops—visible from great distances—to call people together on matters of utmost urgency and bring them together in a way that unifies vision, creates the desire, and gives the power to fulfill it.

"This has been suppressed first by the czars, then the Soviets, and now through orthodox religion, but we will do it anyhow.

"Let the other Healers around the world know. Be certain they know how to make a sacred fire. The last time we did this, we were one people with one language and one fire. After that, we went our separate ways and became Kyrgyz, Siberian, Japanese, American Indians, and European tribal peoples.

"That final ancient fire was done in such a way that we would remember to reignite it when the time is right. When we do, we will wake up and remember we are related—one family—and this will bring healing to the Earth and humanity."

I could scarcely believe what I'd heard. For 30 years, I'd searched for an oral history that united people, especially one that included the indigenous tribes of Europe. I'd come up empty-handed—either no one knew or wanted to remember. Zhaparkul said that Kyrgyzstan was a central location where all races and cultures were one people. How did he know? Thousands of years had passed since the great continental migrations.

The length of time was impressive but did not surprise me. Indigenous Healers think in the whole mind, which enables them to retrieve events from the big cycles of time. When Dr. Gbodossou of West Africa had met Hawaiian Hale Makua, they shared no common language, but both knew the archaic ceremonial languages of their people. Sitting on chairs next to each other, they began speaking in their own native tongue. I wondered what they were up to. In a matter of minutes, they simultaneously slapped their thighs and laughed. They'd gone back in time, tracing archaic origin stories, and stopped when the languages became one.

What did surprise me is that the Kyrgyz oral history not only remembered when northern hemispheric people were one, but also provided a way for the rest of us to remember. We were to network Healers globally and reignite the Sacred Fire. This thrilled me. I wondered where this could lead—when we knew who we were and how to relate to the Earth.

The weight of Zhaparkul's words began to settle on my shoulders, and the initial euphoria subsided. The fire ceremony must happen; I needed to do my part, but how? The remote locations of Healers, the vast geography involved, and funds needed to bring people together—how could I possibly do this, particularly in only four months?

As if reading my mind, Gengish Ata looked up; he'd been texting. "Yes, and you can use your computer to do it."

And use it we did. I returned to Maui, and for the next four months, host organization Aigine Cultural Research Center, located in Bishkek, and I worked nonstop on our computers.

~~~

When March arrived, the ceremony was ready. I flew back to Kyrgyzstan. While in preparation for Uluu Ot, I met Chynara Seiydahmatova at the Aigine office. With a business background and degree in economics from the atheistic former Soviet educational system, she had become an outspoken advocate for women's rights. In recent years, she'd begun to assume her role as a Deer Clan Healer. It was not an easy transition.

"Like my father, I am a captive of logic. I am very rational and analytical. Growing up near Issyk-Kul, I did not see any sense in our Kyrgyz traditions and had a rigid and intolerant reaction to all the 'old wives' tales.' My Soviet education and urban experience intensified these views."

When Kyrgyzstan struggled to gain its independence, she became a part of the movement, and although she had not broken any laws, she was arrested and jailed for 40 days. It was a spiritual wake-up call.

Over tea and cookies, Chynara and I reflected on the meaning of Uluu Ot.

From an indigenous point of view, information, knowledge, and wisdom exist all around us. When we seek help or look for a solution to a problem, Healers use special words to make these sacred things move around and to "catch" the correct answer.

As we talked about the Sacred Fire and what it implied for global healing, Chynara shared a family story about women and spiritual power. "Supernatural phenomena are difficult to explain. They have been rejected, and there are many taboos in the Holy Scriptures that prohibit clairvoyance and prophecies. For this reason, women who had prophetic gifts—it appears that women have these kinds of gifts more often than men do—were burned in fires by the leaders of all religions, at all times, and everywhere. Religions forbid these phenomena to this day.

"I had to go to Mazars [sacred sites] a lot before I experienced a vision in Manjyly Ata (the site of Uluu Ot). There, I saw the same deer that I had been seeing in my dreams, only this time she was female. I recognized the doe by her penetrating gaze, but now she was real, and beckoned to me just as she did in my dream. At the Mazars, all kinds of wonderful things happen that are hard to believe. I still cannot explain this extraordinary seeing, but I have learned to accept phenomena that are hard to explain.

"In 2003, I took a business trip to Ysyk-Köl. Just as the lake came into view, I felt a sudden, very strong physical jolt. Looking at the water, my heart hurt. I was frightened of the pain and sad that I live so far from my father's home and don't come to visit very often. I felt as if I had lived here in other lifetimes.

"My father and mother are both Kyrgyz from the Bugu tribe, a fact that I learned only four years ago. Only now, I understood what this means.

"When I turned 18, my grandmother started a serious conversation with me. She warned me not to laugh and instructed me to believe all she would tell me. It was a story about her great-grandmother who had little horns on her head, which were three to four centimeters long. My grandmother herself touched those horns.

"She was six years old and was helping her old great-grandmother wash her head. Having horns was a family secret of which it was inappropriate to talk aloud. No grown-up relative was ever shown the horns. The honorary right to serve the horned grandmother was given to the eldest granddaughter or great-granddaughter. The presence of horned grandmothers in the family means that women in the family are gifted with a special talent, abilities, and wisdom. People from this line should serve their people and, in return for the service, receive a continuation of the blessed talent.

"'*Kasietin kötörup, kyzmat kylysh kerek*—you must express and care for your gift. Work for others, or the abundance of energy will crush you.' She also said that if any of my daughters or granddaughters or great-granddaughters would have horns, I should not be afraid.

"The reason my grandmother trusted me with the family secret is because I am the eldest daughter in my generation. I had to learn to serve my people; to do that I had to reconcile myself with my destiny.

"At the time, I did not laugh, only because I loved my *taiene* and respected her deep faith in her own tales. Until recently, this only remained a fairy tale to me. But I began to think about the ancient rock carvings that depict humans with horns on their heads. Perhaps this is what women looked like long ago in the Feminine Beginning.' Maybe this explains why the *elechek*, the traditional domed headwear of married women, is important—it hides the sacred secret of a woman.

"It is time to rethink our categories of male and female. For a short time, our task will be to prioritize feminine energy in order to create balance with the masculine and to bring harmony."

Chynara and I had just finished talking when Gulnara, the head of Aigene Cultural Research Center, rushed in. "Apela *eje*, the shamans want to meet with you right now!"

Kyrgyz shamans, 30 or 40 of them had insisted that I meet for a traditional meal of tea, fry bread, and celebration. It was a command performance, one that excited and scared me, for I knew it was a cultural test.

"They want us to come with them," she said breathlessly. "I tell you, what they have said is unbelievable. I have looked for such people for years. There exists a traditional spiritual group, free of extra-cultural religious influence, that has been underground for many years. This group is waiting for us now. We must go."

~~~

My door was still closing as the van lurched forward in a spray of pea gravel. A scroll metal ornament mounted on the dashboard before me became my focal point. I concentrated on it to steady myself through the sway, forward momentum, and braking of our mad rush through town. As we careened about corners and swerved to miss potholes, Victory Peak, Bishkek's highest mountain, spun around the windows of the SUV like directions on a liquid compass.

The decorative object on the dashboard intrigued me. It appeared to be a combination of astrological symbols, but the design went beyond that. Overall, it took the shape of a human being, but the slight aura hinted at something more.

"Can you ask what the meaning of this is?" I yelled over the sound of the engine and the blaring popular music radio station.

The interpreter, buckled up in the seat behind me, leaned forward against his constraints and responded, "It's Tengir, our sky god."

Slowly our SUV rolled up a side street. With a quick left, we claimed a coveted parking spot facing into traffic. We'd reached our destination—an inauspicious, high-walled compound with large, closed wooden doors. A cold sun shone through the leafless trees lining the road. Thin crusts of ice, winter's detritus, clung stubbornly to north-facing gutters.

We knocked.

One of the doors opened just a crack, and Kubanychbek, a Cultural Practitioner, presented himself. The door opened further, but just enough for us to pass through, one at a time. I was glad I was with Gulnara. The atmosphere was charged, but in an indeterminate way; it made me anxious.

Even if someone had told me, nothing would have prepared me for what happened next. We passed through the gates into a surge of oncoming Silk Road–attired Healers. For a second, I could not be certain of what place or time I was in.

A memory like a soft wind moved through me—the caravan, the Xinjiang desert, and Joe. Ah, yes.

Thirty to 40 or more shamans, more than I'd ever seen in one place, all traditionally attired, met me at the gate of a courtyard that surrounded a massive yurt. With prayers, we gathered around a hastily assembled plywood table.

I raised my little bowl of tea, about the tenth I'd had that day, and glanced up as I took a sip. In the background, between the shoulders of two women seated across from me, I spied a child-size yurt. It was brand new, snowy-white with vibrant red trim, and it radiated good energy. I'm small, and I calculated I could probably get through the tiny, open door. I wondered if it was culturally appropriate to do so and asked an interpreter. Apparently, the message got confused. The interpreter left and then returned with a tall, regal-looking woman. She wore a white, satin *elechek*—a cap crown with an attached scarf that tied beneath the chin—as well as a traditional embroidered green coat and long, straight skirt. She was obviously a person to be reckoned with.

The interpreter spoke, "She wants to know why you want to go in."

"No, no," I protested. "It's OK; I don't need to go in. I was only asking if a person *can* go in." Embarrassed, I waited for the translation.

"She says people don't normally go inside. It is a special yurt to help the plants and life grow on Earth, but you are a guest, so it's OK if you go in but only for a few moments."

I was mortified by my breach of cultural protocol. Now, I had to do it. We walked over, and I knelt down to look in the small, round house. The "floor" was mud with sprouting grass seeds, and the entry smaller than I had estimated. I doubted I could get my shoulders through. A quick glance at my hostess's stern face gave me all the impetus I needed. With a little corkscrew action, I plopped in and sat down cross-legged on the wet earth. A light, holy energy filled the interior. Prayer ribbons of various colors hung from the opening in the roof. I was on sacred ground and knew it. I bowed my head and prayed to be worthy. A few minutes went by while I worried that I shouldn't be in this tiny temple.

"It's time to come out now," said the interpreter.

Getting out was harder than getting in. If I pushed too hard, I might damage the structure. Clumsily, I wriggled and writhed out on all fours, finally struggling to my feet directly in front of the matriarch.

Arms crossed, head tilted back with the weight of the elechek, the Elder appraised me. Seconds seemed like hours. I could feel the weight of all the other Healers discretely listening.

"So, she wants to know—what did you see in there?"

All I had seen in my mind's eye were two white spiral things, but I couldn't trust that. I'd had only a couple of minutes, and I was too anxious to get into a receptive state of mind. What to do?

An old TV jingle flashed through my mind. "Ajax cleans like a white tornado." I couldn't say the "white tornado thing." I felt anguished, but I couldn't make something up either.

"I saw two white spirals moving counterclockwise, like a hurricane."

He interpreted, and she responded in calm, sure tones, "Good, good. I only saw one."

The matriarch led me to the end of the table for a traditional ceremony. Two Elders came forward and dressed me in the traditional coat, hat, ring, and earrings of a Kyrgyz woman. When complete, they stepped back, gave me a blessing, and asked me to take my seat before Elmira Murataliev, clairvoyant.

Elmira looked at me for what seemed a long time and then smiled. "You are not a woman; you are a man in a woman's body. This is what is needed for your duty."

Regaining her serious composure, she continued, "In ancient times, there were two clans—Deer and Snow Leopard. You are from the Snow Leopard clan. This is the power to unify."

The clairvoyant studied the symbols and notes she had written on a paper before her. She lifted her head, and in front of all assembled, pronounced her prophetic words.

Your Duty.

Your mission is to unite the people who are children of the Earth.

Becoming one world is a creation of the universe, and it is the way of purification and reunion.

The Mother has given you a duty that is important for building the Golden Epoch.

It is to halt the breakdown of the natural systems of life.

Have you now witnessed the Kyrgyz Kasiet, spiritual power and gift?

You will define, clarify, and justify this Kasiet.

This will help save the world and humanity from destruction.

If you do not fulfill the responsibility given to you,

Stones will rain from the sky.

The earth will open, and tongues of fire emanate, and you will be cursed by your Ancestors.

Do not disappoint the spirits.

They believe in you.

You are capable of doing this, and you will be able to accomplish this mission.

Nearly 80 local people and a dozen international shamans and guests met in Kyrgyzstan the following evening for a late-night spring equinox fire. We were joined by communities around the world, as more than 50 Indigenous Healers went to their own sacred sites to synchronize the lighting of fires. Global prayer groups and hundreds of people added their good thoughts from remote locales.

We didn't need flashlights to find our way over the foothills to the site of the fire.

The snowy Tien Shan peaks reflected the full moon so powerfully it cast a blue-white light over the land. The north wind scraped the clouds from the star-studded heavens and whipped through our clothing. Getting here had been a rough trip.

In addition to time constraints, limited manpower, and lack of previous experience with the Sacred Fire, the most intense challenge came from the Muftiat, the top administrative level of the Muslim system. The Muftiat saw the Uluu Ot as a "return to the darkness" of pre-Islamic spirituality. Two days before the event, the director of Aigine Cultural Research Center received a letter warning her not to conduct the fire; the guardian of the Uluu Ot site was visited and pressured to neither make nor allow the fire on the site; and the government agent in charge of sacred sites was pressured into rescinding our permit.

The resolution of the issue was simple; move the fire about 50 yards from the original site, but the confusion meant that the fire was hastily assembled. Our wood was actually brush—sticks and tumbleweed—and most of it was damp. The entire lot would burn in less than an hour.

Even housing arrangements fell apart. We had arrived by bus from Bishkek late the night before. On the same day, and unbeknownst to us, the director of the Issyk-Kul Sanatorium, our venue, was fired without notice. When we arrived, we were told we had no reservations! It was late, and there was no other place to go. For over an hour, heated arguments ensued; at last, the director of Aigine Cultural Research Center won. Reluctantly, the groundskeeper admitted us to a conference center with no heat, no warm water, and no food. We slept that long night with all our clothing, including jackets, hats, and boots still on.

All that dropped away the moment we formed our circle around the fire pit. An Elder stepped forward to open the ceremony in prayer. Then silence, cold winds, and more silence. No one came forward to light the fire. I looked to the Elder men; no reaction. Gulnara tugged at my sleeve, "You can light it now, Apela eje."

"No, I can't. It's not right. This is not my culture. One of your Elders should light this fire." I glanced at the traditional men.

"Yes, you must. In our culture, the fire is a woman, *Ot Ene*, Mother Fire. Women must light the Uluu Ot—you and two others, one Kyrgyz and another international participant. You are our guest. In Kyrgyzstan we say, 'First God, then the guest.'"

Hastily, I searched my backpack and produced a flint from France and a striker from home. Then I kneeled with the other women in front of the fire pit. *Knick, knick, knick. Knick, knick, knick.* Our strikers hit their stones. Each time a spark landed on the brush, a gust of wind blew it out. On and on it went for about 10 minutes. The Healers waited in silence. Beads of perspiration formed on my forehead while the wind spun its icy cloak about us. At last, a spark caught. The circle erupted in chants and song, urging the flames higher. Prayers and affirmations poured forth.

"From one spark comes a big fire! We will light the fire of our people, and we will light the hearts of our people so that we become one strong voice—that our traditional way of life will become strong and our voice will be heard all over the world."

"The embrace of pure spirit—like fire around the Earth—is going to continue. Embrace those who are different. Hold the space of heart."

"Fire melts and tempers; let the fire of love do the same with you."

"The time for grieving is over."

"The time for renewal is here."

"The fire is the woman."

"The true story about humanity can come out of this fire."

"People are getting to be strong."

"That Sacred Fire will be felt around the world."

"My heart is white. I wish you ak."

The fire died down. Amidst sparks and crackling came the passionate throb of a *komuz*, a fretless three-string instrument— the essence of Central Asia. With a flourish, the musician burned through his set, taking us on a journey that seamlessly merged in the haunting, evocative lament of "Manas," the world's longest epic poem.

Half-frozen yet ecstatic, the Elders made the closing prayer. Uluu Ot, a gateway, was calling forth Altyn Dor, the Golden Age, the Age of Fire. Prayerfully, Zhaparkul proclaimed, "People will begin to make prayers of the heart, not of prophets, etc. Through fire, people's spirits are cleansed. Nature is clean. People connect with the Creator through the heart. People forgot how to pray with the heart. In the coming age, the Creator will be found through the heart. Nature will change, and people's hearts will begin to open. This is the destiny of the rebirth of the Uluu Ot. We can consider ourselves the ones who opened the door to the coming age, from the Age of the Mind. All people say the same thing: the only ones that will survive the change of the age will be the People of the Fire. The gods made it happen. It's destiny. People will see, people will hear."

We turned homeward and walked down the hill, beneath the hazy white light of the Milky Way.

The next morning, we retraced our steps past the sacred springs. We walked single file up and down the dips and rises of the hardpan path to the summit and the rubble of an ancient temple of Umai, Earth Mother. Snowcapped peaks behind us, bright blue sky overhead, we turned to face the sun rising over Lake Issyk-Kul. In the shimmer of high-mountain light, a swan skimmed across the water's surface into the golden radiance of the new sun.

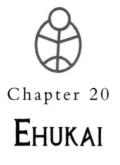

Chapter 20

EHUKAI

Maui, Hawaii, August 2011

Years had passed since the Navajo ceremony; I'd traveled the world trying to be responsible to that vision or even to clearly understand it. My journey had brought me in touch with the Divine Feminine everywhere except for the one I was looking for. Alice Kaʻehukai Shaw was the key. Of that much I was sure, and yet, even her memory remained elusive.

Every few years, I'd walk over to the cemetery where I assumed Alice had been interred to look for her gravesite. Today we visit gravesites to remember and feel close to those we have loved and lost. It's the same for Indigenous People, but with a critical distinction. The *iwi*, or bones, of the Ancestors are conveners that optimize communications between the worlds. With the pond filled and Alice gone, I desperately needed this access to the spirit world and the knowledge it could impart—the most intimate sacred moment of life—conception and an Origin Story that placed women equal to men. Up and down the rows I went, even moving debris from deteriorated monuments—still, I could not find her. Strangely, each failed effort made me more determined. I turned to government documents. One day, I spent three hours in the state's voicemail labyrinth before reaching an actual person. She told me in no uncertain terms that the information, if they had it at all, was confidential for 75 years! "The woman's dead!" I lamented. What possible difference could it make to reveal the date of her death and burial site?

A rage at the injustice done to Alice, the site, an origin point of life, and the suppression of the history about this, burned within me. I needed counsel; I needed to find Noni again, Alice's niece. Digging through old contacts, I found a number, and by luck it worked. Even though Noni worked night shift at the hospital, she promised to come by the very next day.

~~~

Morning sun shimmered through the mango trees and dappled the curvilinear pathway to our house in fractals of light, the tail of the Mo'o. I looked at my watch for the umpteenth time. Nine ten. A sense of excitement and anticipation stirred in me.

In the old days, people chanted their Mo'olelo, their genealogy, as they approached another. Today we simply stand before a home and call out a name.

So it was then that I heard Noni Shaw's voice before I saw her. "Auntie," she called.

I went to the door, opened it, and fell into an embrace so warm it erased 20 years of hit-and-miss encounters.

Rather too quickly, we moved past the sacred Hawaiian images and artifacts that fill the house and made for the kitchen. We pulled out our chairs, she at the head and me at her left, and sat down at the oval table. The koa wood surface cast a soft golden glow about us in the morning light. There was no obvious reason for it, but we began as if someone was looking over our shoulder. Time was of the essence.

"Maybe we could start with me reading what I've written," I offered. "It's about my life, and I'm at the part where I come here and encounter the old pond and the oral history of the Moʻo, lizard goddess. The writing stops here because I'm so infuriatingly blocked."

She nodded in agreement and looked off. I did too, and for a split second, thought I saw over her shoulder something moving, a glimmer of spirit.

"You know, Auntie," she said in the soft, breathy way of Hawaiian language, "I've never forgotten what you told me when we first met, about your encounter with the Moʻo."

It had been years since I'd shared the story of the Navajo ceremony with Noni and told her of encountering and being devoured by the great lizard, and how that vision had led me to pack up myself and my family, leave Canada, my tenured university position, and come here without friends, family, or employment. When I met Keola and found the pond, I thought things would be revealed, that I would understand what the vision was, and what I needed to do to fulfill it.

I brought her up to date, telling her about the canoe project, how Keola and I had joined forces with other friends of the site to form a nonprofit organization dedicated to restoring the area, and how strange and fortunate that we did not have to fight with business people or have existing structures removed. Despite the gross overdevelopment of the Hawaiian Islands, no one had ever built on the filled pond area. In fact, the periphery was guarded by Buddhist, Congregational, Baptist, Salvation Army, Episcopal and even Alcoholics Anonymous organizations.

I explained that, in another stroke of luck, our organization had proved the existence of burials in the area, thus federal law superseded local and state laws (more susceptible to vested interests), the playing fields were moved, fences taken down, and the door opened for renewal. We then erected a large standing stone monument, an altar on the old island. The stone and its pedestal of traditional, dry mortar stones now provided a focal point for ceremony and prayer and served as our commitment to restore the waters.

"Twenty years have passed, Noni," I grieved, "with only a pile of studies to show for it. The pond is still filled, and I can't even find your tutu's grave. I need your help."

Noni took a breath, straightened herself in the chair, and looked down at the table. "You know, I don't like to talk about this to many people. My grandmother's Hawaiian name, Ka'ehukai, referred to a zephyr, the gentle wind that blows mist from the wave, like the *Akua*, Ancestors, are with you, like a whisper. The water is like that where she was born and where she lived next to the pond. When her parents passed, she became the sacred site guardian of Mokuhinia and the lands around it.

"Her brother was my grandfather. He married a commoner, and they had two children, a girl and a boy. Their mom died, so my grandfather asked Alice to raise the children, which she did. But it wasn't all good. My dad had a hard life. The kids were not allowed to live in Gramma Shaw's nice house. They lived in a shack on the small island in the pond.

"Daddy said that sometimes, depending on the Moon, Kaʻehukai would come onto the islet and go to the water's edge. First, she'd put a black cloth on the window of the shack, the one that looked over the pond, and would warn them. 'Don't look out this window no matter what you hear.' They were scared of her, so they never looked."

My heart skipped a beat. To be raised on that sacred island, even in a shack, would have been a powerful mystical initiation, probably terrifying to children and doubly so in a time of great cultural repression. Also, research had just revealed how harshly even the children of the monarchy, including Alice, were treated by missionary teachers. Alice may have been raising them as future leaders.

"Tutu, Auntie Alice treated them more like servants, but my dad never said anything bad about her. He was grateful to have a home. When he grew up, as soon as he could, he left Maui, got married, and had us kids. Deep inside, I think he was hurting.

"Before Tutu died, she called for my father to come see her. Mom went with him, which is why I know this story. When they got to her house, Tutu greeted them and invited them inside. In a few moments, she said to my mom, 'Maybe you would like to go enjoy the garden.' It was obvious she wanted to be alone with my dad. The garden was in back of the house, so Mom had to walk completely through the house to get there. Big oil paintings of each of the Kamehameha monarchs hung on the walls, and the living room was filled with beautiful koa furniture. Mom continued on through the bedroom to the back door, and as she did, she noticed six black Hawaiian dresses hanging in a closet."

This confirmed my research. An Elder who knew Alice had described her as always wearing black. And I knew from cultural

Hawaiians that black is a sacred color, its intensity filters out evil. Research also suggested that Alice had served as lady-in-waiting to Hawaii's last queen, but I had no proof. Here it was. Black dress was required for the queen's ladies and was an implicit expression of traditional spirituality.

Noni continued. "Mom waited in the garden for about 15 minutes, when she heard a cry. You know," Noni said, wiping tears from her eyes, "the kind of cry that is anguish and makes you cry when you hear it. My father rushed out the back door and said, 'Let's go.' He never went back and refused to discuss what had been said. But eventually my mother knew. Alice had asked him to become the next sacred site guardian of the pond, and he had refused."

The air hung heavy about us, deepening the sense of loss, powerlessness, and injustice. "I think," Noni choked, "Daddy was trying to protect us. He knew how hard it would be to continue the spiritual ways of Aloha, of the Moʻo—the danger from religious, political, and plantation interests."

With that, our visit ended. We sat in silence, each of us lost in our own feelings for what the end of this sacred way, the essence of life, meant.

Drained and empty, I went on the internet that night, as was my habit since beginning the Alice research, to check a historical fact about her time. On a lark, I entered her married name, Alice Kaʻae, and hit "Return." To my utter amazement, the Find A Grave website popped up. I clicked. Up came Alice's birth and death dates and confirmation of her inhumation at Waiola cemetery, a half block from my house. The familiar energy and drive to know surged back into me.

Early the next morning, I woke and watched the clock, waiting for the church office to open. At 9 a.m. I called—no answer. I ran full speed over to the office, only to find a locked door. Exasperated, I returned home but kept calling and going back over there for three days. Closed. Not a sign, not a voicemail message, nothing.

The fourth day, I woke with a strong feeling—go at once! It was too hot to walk even the short distance, so I jumped on my bike and pedaled down the road, up over the manicured lawn, past the church, and right up to the office door. To my delight, the office door was open—and so were the possibilities.

Grayle Chong, born and raised Lahaina girl, looked up from her desk. "The office is not open. I just came back from vacation and am trying to organize things for Monday," she said.

Undaunted and perhaps ill-mannered, I answered, "I know, but this is not official business. I'm just looking for a grave." Then, to establish rapport, I introduced myself. She smiled, recognizing my husband as her sister's classmate. In a small town like Lahaina with a recent history of colonial repression, no conversation begins without establishing relationship.

"Who are you looking for?"

"Alice Shaw Ka'ae," I answered. "We've searched but can't find the gravesite."

"Well," Grayle said, quietly, "we had a fire and lost all our records, and we have a lot of unmarked graves. We're trying to make up for it, to fill in. I've sat out there in the sun for days, waiting to catch families visiting these graves. Every once in a while we identify one, still, so much is lost."

I protested, "This is recent. Alice only died in 1956, and she was so important to our community."

"Yes," Grayle, responded sadly, "but the fire happened in 1978. For whatever reason, the minister had all the records in his house when it burned, and there were no copies."

Overcome by discouragement, I slumped down on the chair in front of her desk. "This is tragic," I said, unable to accept the news.

Her compassion, a slight nod of the head, triggered strong emotion in me. I didn't understand. Finding Alice's grave wouldn't bring her back to life, but it mattered—greatly. As Noni had put it, for Indigenous Peoples the iwi, bones, hold the mana, sacred power. In old times, some families would choose a bone of a loved one to keep. The mana would guide, guard, and love you as the person had in life. The practice was a continuance of *ohana*, family, and of mana. The highest respect we can give to loved ones is to see their iwi are protected.

The touch, the instant of relation is a critical part of indigenous spirituality, and even though vision had brought me here, I needed Ancestral blessing to proceed. To get that, I had to connect. This pond, this place-time where soul takes on matter is the quintessence of life. Alice was the Kahu, caretaker of this Way. I had to ask to connect and be willing to accept the response, yes or no.

Filling the empty space between us, Grayle spoke. "It's too bad Mrs. Moon is not alive; she'd know. Mrs. Silva might know…"

Her voice trailed off as a pleasant-looking, white-haired Hawaiian Elder entered the room.

A simple wooden cross about his neck contrasted dramatically against his crisp, white shirt, and highlighted his dark Hawaiian complexion. Everything about him was peaceful. Instinctively, I knew this must be Reverend Kukahiko. My husband Keola had suggested I seek him out. Here he was; I didn't even have to look.

The minister and Grayle spoke for a few moments. Realizing Grayle might not recall my name, I stood and introduced myself. Grayle joined in, summarizing and grounding the purpose of my research. The minister sat down.

"Yes," he said, "I remember Mrs. Kaʻae. She lived in a house on the side of the old pond opposite this church. When we were little, my father drove us over here, to Lahaina. Sometimes we'd stop at her house. All of us kids were scared of her! I don't know why—she never did anything unkind. She was a nice-looking Hawaiian lady of the time. Wore her hair up in a bun on the top of her head."

"Oh!" Grayle laughed. "We were scared of her too. My gramma would make me take food or special things to her. Why me, I wondered, but I would never ask. That's how we were raised, to respect our Elders. My grandmother always respected her. I think she had something to do with the Hawaiian monarchy. I wondered how come none of the other kids had to do this."

"I nevah like." She chuckled, dropping into local pidgin. "Mrs. Kaʻae had long white hair. Sometimes it was down, almost to her waist; sometimes she put it up. I remember she had a rocking chair she always sat in. It was on her porch overlooking the pond, and she always wore black."

"Oh, *puu ewa*, chicken skin!" Kukahiko laughed, nodding his head in agreement. "I was plenty scared. I'd run up to the house, put the food on the porch, and run away. She was never mean, and I don't remember her saying anything, but you could feel something."

"You know," I said to both of them, "Keola told me to look for both of you, but the office has been closed for weeks. I came over here now because that little voice inside urged me to. So, here I am, and not only is the office open, but you, Reverend Kukahiko, happen to come by. There must be something to it."

They both nodded. The air about me stilled.

"Would you please say a prayer for me?" I asked the reverend. "I've been looking so hard." I heard my voice break and felt tears fill my eyes. "It's just dead end after dead end."

Leaning forward, Kukahiko took my hand. Grayle came around the desk, joined hands, and closed the circle. In a soft, gentle, part English–part Hawaiian local way, he prayed that I could do the work the Ancestors of old were asking me to do. My heart opened. *How is it*, I wondered, *given the horrific way outsiders have treated Hawaiians, that this man could sanction his Ancestors having a purpose for me?* Overwhelmed by his compassion, and with a feeling of empowerment, I uttered an amen, shook both of their hands, and made for the door.

As I left, Grayle called out behind me, "The Shaw family graves are over there in the far corner, past Keola's grandmother's grave. In fact, Mrs. Shaw gave that piece of land to the church."

"I looked there a bunch of times," I said," but I'll go look again."

It was nearly noon as I stepped out of the cool office building. Lahaina, meaning "the cruel sun," was proving the truth of its name. The sun was burning hot with lots of humidity and temperatures in the upper nineties. I considered going home and returning later in the day, but it felt important to act on the prayer immediately. Walking the length of the building, I quickly made for the shade of the enormous, old monkey pod tree overlooking the stone wall and gateway of the cemetery. It was easily five degrees cooler beneath it. Breathing deeply, I savored the musty, dry fragrance and relief from the heat. As I looked up at the thick old branches, I found myself considering the self-similar properties of fractal geometry, anything to avoid facing another disappointment.

Three gravesites past the entry, I spied a woman with long blond hair. Standing in the sparse shade of a flowering bush, she held a GPS in one hand and a sheaf of documents in the other.

"Apela," she called out.

She looked familiar. Turning off the path, I joined her by the bush. It wasn't really any cooler. Rivulets of perspiration rolled down our faces as we tried to establish rapport as quickly as possible.

"We met at the archaeology presentation about the pond. I'm part Choctaw and Chiricahua Apache," she urged, trying to jog my memory.

"Yes, I remember. My dad had Choctaw ancestry and my grown children are half Chiricahua." Relationship established, we smiled at the absurdity of two Native Americans meeting in a Hawaiian cemetery in hellishly hot weather. With a nod of recognition, Janet shared that mapping the gravesites was part of her work.

"This cemetery on the periphery of the pond is such an important historical site. We're using technology to identify proper boundaries and find names whenever we can. It's a gift to the church and community. What brings you here?" she asked.

"Well," I responded, wiping sweat from my lip and pushing a scratchy branch away from my head, "this meeting is perfectly timed. I'm researching for a book; part of it involves this site, and I have searched for years for the grave of Mrs. Alice Shaw Ka'ae but never found it."

"You might want to take a look at this," she said, extending her fistful of documents. "It's notes and a sketched map of what we've located so far."

I glanced at the map but didn't see anything. I wasn't surprised or even disappointed. I didn't expect anything. Turning to the documents, I quickly scanned down the first page or two, nothing. On the third page, I spotted the name Shaw. It was the wrong one. Then I saw another and another; my heart nearly stopped. There it was, Alice K.S. Ka'ae. For a second, I stopped breathing.

"Here it is, here it is," I exclaimed. "The name I've been looking for!"

"Well," Janet said, "don't get your hopes up. Unless there are numbers there, it doesn't mean we've identified the site."

"But," I said excitedly, "there are numbers here. Look. What does this mean? Does it tell me where to look?"

Janet glanced down. "It means you're really lucky. We just completed this document; it's only a draft. I just printed it off this morning before I came here. But I'd say you have found what you're looking for. It should be right over there in the corner."

She pointed the way.

"Will you come with me?" I asked.

I knew I was imposing. It was so hot, and Janet was pressed for time, but the moment was so fraught with meaning I didn't trust myself or maybe think I was worthy enough to find it.

She hesitated a moment, glanced at her watch, and said, "Sure, OK, but I've got to hurry."

The lawn, pockmarked and dry from feral chickens digging for insects, kicked up powdery dust that stuck to our sweaty legs as we made our way to the far corner. I'd been over this way countless times and found nothing, but today something felt different. The fragrance of hot-pink Plumeria blossoms wafted in the air and pulled me toward a tree that marked the far corner of the site. In my 20-year search, the Plumeria had always stood amidst waist-high dry grass and dense thorny bushes—there would be no way to see an underlying gravesite.

Today, the area beneath the tree was clear. I whispered a silent prayer, really a supplication, walked over to the tree, and looked down. Written on a bronze plaque was the name, "Alice K.S. Ka'ae, August 31, 1868–April 16, 1956." I could scarcely believe it. I had found her! I looked again and again and still again. As the reality sank in, I became infused with elation and energy, and began blurting out parts of Alice's story.

Janet listened sympathetically, but when I took a breath, she said, "I've got to get back to work."

We shared a sweaty hug, and she left.

Looking down at the grave, I asked Alice, *Why here, why this spot in the cemetery?*

I looked about. The answer came in a flash. Alice was not a member of Waiola Church, but giving the land to Waiola had secured her final resting place where it needed to be—exactly on the edge of the pond. The waters where the Mo'o, life, surfaced. Ancient Hawaiian leaders, many related to Alice, chose to be buried here because it was a place where they could connect to us and love us from afar. A knowing like a gentle but powerful feeling swept through me—the ceremonies and spiritual connections did not die but were right here, waiting. Alice had made sure.

A movement off to the side caught my eye. Mrs. Makekau, Hawaiian Elder, and her 12-year-old granddaughter, Ocean, were cleaning gravesites. She was a bit unhappy; so few people took care of this place anymore.

She motioned to where I stood. "We just finished cleaning that today. It was covered with grass, bushes, and a Kou tree. With only me and her, it took a long time to get that tree out of here. We just got the last of the trunk out this afternoon."

"No wonder, I couldn't find this before. Thank you, thank you! I'd never have found it otherwise."

She nodded.

"Lots of people ask me where to find a family grave. I try to help, but I don't even work here. We just come to *malama*, to cherish and care."

"What days do you come? I'll come by to help."

She told me, then returned to her work. I stood there for moment, alone in the searing heat, giving and feeling thanks over and over again. On my way out, I popped into the church office. Reverend Kukahiko looked up; Grayle leaned forward over her desk.

"You found her!" He laughed.

"Yes!" I exclaimed. "That prayer worked fast."

Then we all laughed together.

Taking the stairs two at a time, I ran into the bathroom to splash cool water on my face and arms. It was then I noticed a twig of something caught in my hair. Carefully pulling it free, I glanced down at my hand. It was ohai, a dried flower with red-orange, mossy-looking tendrils. *Ehukai*, I thought absentmindedly. It looks like sea spray. A warm surge of recognition flowed through me. Ehukai—Alice's Hawaiian name. She is back.

ACKNOWLEDGMENTS

To my ancestral mentors: Chief Daanawáa<u>k</u>, Tlingit; Manfred Kaulaity, Kiowa; Mary Jones, Louisiana Choctaw; Auntie Mahilani Poepoe, Hawaiian; Hale Makua, Hawaiian; Esther Silva, Lake Miwok; Roger Marty, Occitan; Vusamazulu Credo Mutwa, Zulu High Sanusi; Joseph Colorado, Apache; Hanson Ashley, Navajo.

Thank you Ileen Maisel and Michelle Pilley, your vision inspired this book. Andrew Harvey and Caroline Myss, thank you for building the fire beneath me!

I celebrate and thank the following individuals who shared their cultures and lifted hands, hearts, and prayers to create this book:

Virginia Davis Floyd, Kenneth Wilson, Gary Schwartz, Mary Ann Burris, Leslie Danziger, Steven Donovan.

Alaska: Richard and Julia Folta, Clarence Jackson, Adelheid Herrmann, Karen Evanoff.

Hawaii: Keoni Smith, Kapi'ioho Naone, Lei-ohu Ryder, Noni Shaw, Maile Shaw, Florence Yoshima, Addy Silva, and Tad James for the Daddy Bray chant interpretation.

Africa: Dr. Erick Gbodossou.

Japan: Eiichi Maiwa, John Hanagan, Sensei Hara.

France: Pascal Raux, Jean Paul Amanieu, Dominique and Christine Pauvert, Marie Girard.

Alberta: Betty Bastien, Leroy Little Bear, Amethyst First Ryder, Narcisse Blood.

Oneida Wisconsin: Dorothy Ninhan, Buddy Powless.

Arizona: Flora Ashley.

Kyrgyzstan: Gulnara Aitpaeva, Zhaparkul Raimbekov, Ergeshbai Ata, Gengish Ata, Chynara Seidahmatova, Elmira Muratalieva, Nargiza Ryskulova and Bubu Mariam who opened the door.

Altai Republic, Chagat Almashev.

Ubiquity University: Jim Garrison and Claire Ryle Garrison.

The Production Team: Kim Kiser, Beth Duncan, Lisa Fugard.

Photo editor: Veronica Coetzer.

Graphic Arts: Mairamkul Asanaliev, Chyna Colorado.

Mother Earth, Nyaweh, thank you with all my heart.

Personal Corner: Jessie Soto, Ernesto Olmos Hernandez, Illarion Merculieff, Daniel Deslauriers, Jurgen Kremer, Kim Johnson, Kelly Harnack, Indigenous Mind Graduates and my family Keola, Danielle, Cherie, Chyna and Tracey.

In appreciation of the Tides Foundation's Indigenous People's Fund, The Christensen Fund and Kalliopeia Foundation, whose support gave me time to write and the opportunity to work with Indigenous Healers worldwide.

ABOUT THE AUTHOR

Apela Colorado is Oneida-Gaul and a traditional cultural practitioner and indigenous scientist. She is dedicated to bridging dialogue between Western thought and indigenous worldview.

She founded the Worldwide Indigenous Science Network (WISN) in 1989 to foster the revitalization, growth, and worldwide exchange of traditional knowledge and to safeguard the lives and work of the world's endangered traditional practitioners. In 1997, Dr. Colorado was one of twelve women chosen from 52 countries by the State of the World Forum to be honored for her role as a woman leader.

She created the first doctoral program in traditional knowledge at the California Institute of Integral Studies. For twenty years she directed the Indigenous Mind Program, which led students into ways of exploring their ancestral and earth-based, holistic consciousness within a Western academic framework. She continues this work offering workshops in the ancestral remembrance process.

www.wisn.org

Listen. Learn. Transform.

Listen to the audio version
of this book for FREE!

Live more consciously, strengthen your relationship with the Divine, and cultivate inner peace with world-renowned authors and teachers—all in the palm of your hand. With the *Hay House Unlimited* Audio app, you can learn and grow in a way that fits your lifestyle . . . and your daily schedule.

With your membership, you can:

- Embrace the power of your mind and heart, dive deep into your soul, rise above fear, and draw closer to Spirit.

- Explore thousands of audiobooks, meditations, immersive learning programs, podcasts, and more.

- Access exclusive audios you won't find anywhere else.

- Experience completely unlimited listening. No credits. No limits. No kidding.

Woman Between the Worlds
Apela Colorado, Ph.D.

Try for FREE!

HAY HOUSE

Look within

Join the conversation about latest products,
events, exclusive offers and more.

 Hay House

 @HayHouseUK

 @hayhouseuk

We'd love to hear from you!